D1613058

Enactivist Interventions

Enactivist Interventions

Rethinking the Mind

Shaun Gallagher

OXFORD
UNIVERSITY PRESS

OXFORD

UNIVERSITY PRESS

Great Clarendon Street, Oxford, OX2 6DP,
United Kingdom

Oxford University Press is a department of the University of Oxford.
It furthers the University's objective of excellence in research, scholarship,
and education by publishing worldwide. Oxford is a registered trade mark of
Oxford University Press in the UK and in certain other countries

First Edition published in 2017
Impression: 2

Published in the United States of America by Oxford University Press
198 Madison Avenue, New York, NY 10016, United States of America

British Library Cataloguing in Publication Data
Data available

Library of Congress Control Number: 2017935859

ISBN 978-0-19-879432-5

Printed in Great Britain by
CPI Group (UK) Ltd, Croydon CR0 4YY

To Elaine

Contents

Acknowledgments

A number of the following chapters are significantly revised versions of papers that first appeared as stand-alone articles or chapters in edited volumes, or were presented at various conferences.

Parts of Chapter 1 draw on a discussion paper prepared for the Ernst Strüngmann Forum on *The Pragmatic Turn in Cognitive Science* in Frankfurt (October 2014).

Chapter 2 is a significantly revised version of a paper entitled 'Interpretations of embodied cognition', published in W. Tschacher and C. Bergomi (eds.), *The Implications of Embodiment: Cognition and Communication* (59–71). Exeter: Imprint Academic.

Chapter 3 is a revised version of an article published as 'Pragmatic interventions into enactive and extended conceptions of cognition', in *Nous—Philosophical Issues* 24: 110–26.

Chapter 4 is based on a paper I co-authored with Katsunori Miyahara, 'Neo-pragmatism and enactive intentionality', in J. Schulkin (ed.), *Action, Perception and the Brain* (117–46), Basingstoke, UK: Palgrave Macmillan, with permission of Palgrave Macmillan.

Chapter 5 is derived in part from an article published as 'Are minimal representations still representations?' *International Journal of Philosophical Studies* 16 (3): 351–69, copyright Taylor & Francis, with permission.

Chapter 7 is an updated revised version of 'Where's the action? Epiphenomenalism and the problem of free will', published in W. Banks, S. Pockett, and S. Gallagher (eds.), *Does Consciousness Cause Behavior? An Investigation of the Nature of Volition* (109–24). Cambridge, MA: MIT Press, with permission.

Chapter 8 is a revised version of a paper co-authored with Matt Bower, 'Making enactivism even more embodied' *AVANT/Trends in Interdisciplinary Studies* (Poland) 5 (2): 232–47.

Sections 9.4–9.6 are drawn from the essay 'Enactive hands', originally published in Z. Radman (ed.), *The Hand: An Organ of the Mind* (209–25). Cambridge, MA: MIT Press, with permission.

Section 10.3 is based on my lecture 'Reflective skills: Between Dreyfus and McDowell', presented at the Eidgenössische Technische Hochschule (ETH), University of Zurich (October 15, 2013).

Section 10.4 is a revised version of a journal article, 'Doing the math: Calculating the role of evolution and enculturation in the origins of mathematical reasoning', *Progress in Biophysics and Molecular Biology* 119: 341–6.

My collaborations with Katsunori Miyahara and Matt Bower have been extremely fruitful, and I want to thank them first. I also thank an anonymous reviewer for helpful comments on an earlier draft of this book submitted to OUP, and Peter Momtchiloff at OUP for his editorial advice. I've also benefited from discussion with many colleagues at various meetings where some of these chapters or parts of chapters were presented in earlier form. They include Kenneth Aizawa, Micah Allen, Jelle Bruineberg, Anthony Chemero, Andy Clark, Jonathan Cole, Katja Crone, the late Pleshette DeArmitt, Hanne De Jaegher, Ezequiel Di Paolo, Chris Frith, Vittorio Gallese, Cecilia Heyes, Daniel Hutto, Michael Kirchoff, Patrick McGivern, Lambros Malafouris, Richard Menary, Albert Newen, Karenleigh Overmann, Zdravko Radman, Matthew Ratcliffe, Erik Rietveld, Mark Rowlands, Rob Rupert, Susanna Siegel, Evan Thompson, Deborah Tollefsen, Dylan Trigg, Somogy Varga, Stefano Vincini, Michael Wheeler, and Dan Zahavi. I also thank my past and current students at the University of Memphis for continuing inspiration: Benjamin Aguda, Nicolle Brancazio (now at Wollongong), Michael Butler, Tailer Ransom, Kevin Ryan, and Christina Warne-Friedlaender.

Across all of these pursuits my wife Elaine continues to be my *sine qua non*.

Finally, I express my appreciation to the Humboldt Foundation's Anneliese Maier Research Award which has supported my research since 2012; to Keble College, Oxford University, which afforded me the opportunity to finish the final draft as an invited Senior Research Visitor there during Trinity term, 2016; and to research support provided by the Lillian and Morrie Moss Chair of Excellence at the University of Memphis. I've also benefited from support as Professorial Fellow at the University of Wollongong, and as Research Fellow at the Center for Mind, Brain and Cognitive Evolution at the Ruhr Universität, Bochum.

List of Figures and Table

Figures

Table

1

Introduction

Is cognition *in the head* or *in the world*, or in some mix of brainy and worldly processes? Continuing research on embodied cognition in philosophy of mind and the cognitive sciences has motivated numerous debates about questions such as this. There's a strong tradition in both philosophy of mind and cognitive science that takes cognition to be a fully in-the-head event. In this introductory chapter I'll discuss a few of the more recent versions of this view. I'll then begin to sketch the contrasting view of enactivism, an embodied cognition approach that has roots in phenomenology and pragmatism.

Enactivist approaches to cognition suggest that, at least in basic (perception- and action-related) cases, cognitive processes are not just in the head, but involve bodily and environmental factors. This view clearly poses a challenge to what has been the standard science of cognition, especially to cognitive neuroscience, and to any science that claims to provide full and exclusive explanations in terms of one factor, e.g., neural processing. If cognition is not reducible to brain processes, or to any other single factor, and if indeed it does involve many other aspects of embodiment and environment, then how precisely should a scientific study of the mind proceed? Can there be an enactivist science of mind? In sketching out an answer to this question, a number of issues, involving intentionality, representation, affect, agency, and so on, come into focus and I address these issues more fully in subsequent chapters.

1.1 Cognition-in-the-Head: Some Recent Approaches

Even if we define cognitive processes broadly to include not just beliefs and desires, but also states that refer to bodily action and to interactions with other people, we still find that mainstream cognitive science offers narrow accounts that place all the action required for full explanation in mental states that correspond strictly to brain processes. The term 'narrow' is a technical one in philosophy of mind, referring to internal mental representational processing or content. Standard explanations in cognitive science define cognition as constituted by mental or neural representations. I explore the complex question of what counts as a representation in *Chapter 5* (section 5.2 and following). For introductory purposes, a few examples will provide a good sense of this approach.

The first example concerns action—specifically aspects of action that involve planning and intention formation. The processes involved can be characterized at subpersonal and personal levels of explanation, but all of them remain narrowly within the traditional boundary of the mind-brain. Consider the well-known Libet experiments. Libet and colleagues (1983; also see Soon et al. 2008) asked about neural dynamics involved in the readiness potential (*Bereitschaftspotential*)—a brain signal that begins approximately 800 milliseconds prior to any particular bodily movement—and its relation to our immediate sense of deciding to act. The experiments are not only well known but also controversial. Here I won't go into details about the experiments (see section 7.3 for more details) or about controversies that pertain to methodology, but I will summarize briefly the basic idea and say something about the philosophical controversy.

The question Libet tried to answer is whether consciousness plays a role in the initiation of action, and he interpreted this to be a question about free will. Libet's results indicated that on average, 350 milliseconds before the subject is conscious of deciding (or of having an urge) to move, the subject's brain is already working on the motor processes that will result in the movement. That is, the readiness potential is already underway, and the brain is preparing to move before the subject makes the decision to move. The conclusion is that voluntary acts are 'initiated by unconscious cerebral processes before conscious intention appears' (Libet 1985, 529).

There are different interpretations of what these results mean. Most of them focus on the question of free will. Libet himself finds room for free will in the approximately 150 milliseconds of brain activity remaining after we become conscious of our decision, and before we move. He suggests that we have time to consciously veto the movement. Others, however, think that the brain decides and then enacts its decisions; consciousness is epiphenomenal in this regard. The brain inventively tricks us into thinking that we consciously decide to act and that our actions are controlled at a personal level. On this view, free will is nothing more than a false sense or illusion.

For purposes of this introduction I will simply point to a central assumption made about the kind of cognitive processes that are supposed to be involved in free will. The assumption is nicely expressed by Haggard and Libet (2001), who frame the question, and refer to it as the traditional question of free will: 'how can a mental state (my conscious intention) initiate the neural events in the motor areas of the brain that lead to my body movement?' (47). They are right that this is the traditional way to ask the question: it's precisely the way that Descartes, and many thinkers in the modern philosophical tradition, would frame the question. It's the question of mental causation, which places the cognitive processes of free will in the head where brain and mind meet up.

To assume that this is the right way to ask the question overlooks the possibility that free will is not something that can be explained simply by looking where Libet experiments look. For example, one can argue that these experiments have nothing to do with free will. The latter interpretation challenges the assumption that free will can be characterized in terms of the short timescale of 150 milliseconds. This type of response can go one of two ways, however. The first way simply leads us back into the head, into discussions of intention formation where cognitive deliberations generate prior intentions that have a later effect on intentions-in-action. Because the Libet experiments address only motor intentions or, at best, intentions-in-action, they miss the mark since free will is more about deliberation and prior intention formation. Such explanations are worked out in representational terms of beliefs and desires in processes that are best characterized in terms of a space of reasons, but still very much in the head. The second way leads outwards into the world, and to the idea that free will is not a property of one individual brain, mind, or organism, but is relational, so that social and environmental factors contribute to or detract from our ability to act freely.

To say that something like social relations are involved in free will, however, does not necessarily lead beyond traditional concepts of the mind. This is clear when we turn to look at ongoing debates about social cognition or 'theory of mind' (ToM). These debates are framed in terms of methodological individualism, i.e., the idea that ToM can be explained by a causal mechanism (a ToM module or a mirror system) located within the individual. Today the growing consensus is that there are two networks in the brain responsible for our ability to understand others: (1) a ToM network that includes the temporo-parietal junction, medial parietal cortex, and medial prefrontal cortex (e.g., Saxe et al. 2009), and allows for some form of theoretical-inferential mindreading concerning the other person's mental states; and (2) mirror areas in premotor and parietal cortexes, supporting a mental simulation of the other's actions, intentions and emotions. Taken together, the neuroscientific findings may justify a hybrid style of mindreading, or suggest a two-system approach of online perspective taking and offline social reasoning (Apperly and Butterfill 2009).

Complicating such views, however, mainstream theories of social cognition have started to take note of objections coming from embodied cognition (EC) and action-oriented approaches. This and more general concerns about the claims made by EC theorists have motivated a way of thinking about the role of the body that retains a standard representationalism—so-called 'weak' (Alsmith and Vignemont 2012) or minimal EC (see section 2.1). For example, Alvin Goldman and Frederique de Vignemont (2009) suggest that none of the many things that EC theorists usually count as important contributors to cognitive processes—anatomy and body activity (movements and postures), autonomic and peripheral systems, relations with the environment—really do count. Rather, the only 'bodily' things relevant to an account of cognition in general, or social cognition in particular, are body-formatted (or B-formatted) representations in the brain. As they put it, B-formatted representations offer a 'sanitized' way of talking about the body, and 'the most promising' way to promote EC (2009, 155).

B-formatted representations are not propositional or conceptual in format; their contents may include the body or body parts, but also action goals, represented in terms of how to achieve such goals by means of bodily action. Somatosensory, affective, and interoceptive representations may also be B-formatted, 'associated with the physiological conditions of the body, such as pain, temperature, itch, muscular and visceral sensations, vasomotor activity, hunger and thirst' (156).

Social cognition, on this weak EC view, is embodied only to the extent that B-formatted representations involved in perceptual mirroring are used to represent the actions or mental states of others. Similar strategies aiming to 'sanitize' embodied cognition more generally can be found in accounts of broader aspects of cognition. As one example, several theorists point to body-related simulations (representations) as important for language and concept processing (e.g., Glenberg 2010; Meteyard et al. 2012; Pezzulo et al. 2011; Pulvermüller 2005). Goldman (2012; 2014) argues that one can develop an overall EC approach simply by generalizing the use of B-formatted representations. All of this is consistent with the standard representationalist 'mentalistic enterprise' of reconstructing the world (Jackendoff 2002), of 'pushing the world inside the mind' (Meteyard et al. 2012), and a very narrow-minded conception of embodiment.

1.2 Cognition-in-the-World: Phenomenologically Inspired Enactivist Approaches

Enactivist approaches to cognition are inspired and informed by phenomenological philosophy. Varela, Thompson, and Rosch (1991), who first defined the enactivist approach, found significant resources in the phenomenological tradition for rethinking the mind. For example, Husserl's concept of the 'I can' (the idea that I perceive things in my environment in terms of what *I can* do with them); Heidegger's concept of the pragmatic ready-to-hand (*Zuhanden*) attitude (we experience the world primarily in terms of pre-reflective pragmatic, action-oriented use, rather than in reflective intellectual contemplation or scientific observation); and especially Merleau-Ponty's focus on embodied practice, which so influenced both Gibson's notion of affordances and Dreyfus's critique of classic cognitivism (also see Di Paolo 2005; Gallagher 2005a; Noë 2004; Thompson 2007). Less noted are relevant resources in the American pragmatist tradition; many of the ideas of Peirce, Dewey, and Mead can be considered forerunners of enactivism (see *Chapter 3*).

Enactivist versions of EC emphasize the idea that perception is *for action*, and that action-orientation shapes most cognitive processes. Most enactivists call for a radical change in the way we think about the mind and brain, with implications for methodology and for rethinking how we do cognitive science. Enactivist approaches can be characterized by the following background assumptions, explored in subsequent chapters of this book:[1]

1. Cognition is not simply a brain event. It emerges from processes distributed across brain–body–environment. The mind is embodied (see *Chapter 2*); from a first-person perspective embodiment is equivalent to the phenomenological concept of the lived body. From a third-person perspective the organism–environment is taken as the explanatory unit (*Chapters 3* and *9*).
2. The world (meaning, intentionality) is not pre-given or predefined, but is structured by cognition and action (*Chapter 4*).
3. Cognitive processes acquire meaning in part by their role in the context of action, rather than through a representational mapping or replicated internal model of the world (*Chapter 5*).
4. Enactivist approaches have strong links to dynamical systems theory, emphasizing the relevance of dynamical coupling and coordination across brain–body–environment (*Chapters 5* and *6*).
5. In contrast to classic cognitive science, which is often characterized by methodological individualism with a focus on internal mechanisms, enactivist approaches emphasize the extended, intersubjective, and socially situated nature of cognitive systems (see *Chapter 7* for how this relates to the problem of free will).
6. Enactivism aims to ground higher and more complex cognitive functions not only in sensorimotor coordination, but also in affective and autonomic aspects of the full body (*Chapters 8* and *9*).
7. Higher-order cognitive functions, such as reflective thinking or deliberation, are exercises of skillful know-how and are usually coupled with situated and embodied actions (*Chapter 10*).

Enactivist approaches are similar to the ideas of extended mind and distributed cognition insofar as all of these approaches argue that cognition is not entirely 'in the head', but rather is distributed across brain, body, and environment (e.g., Clark and Chalmers 1998). However, in contrast to the extended mind hypothesis, which embraces functionalism and finds a role for minimal representations, enactivists reject functionalism and claim that

---

[1] These assumptions are drawn from the following sources: Clark (1999); Di Paolo, Rohde, and De Jaegher (2010); Dominey et al. (2016); Engel (2010); Engel et al. (2013); Thompson and Varela (2001); Varela, Thompson, and Rosch (1991).

the material specifics of bodily processes shape and contribute to the constitution of consciousness and cognition in a way that is irreducible to representations, even B-formatted representations (see section 2.1). In contrast to Clark (2008a), for example, who argues that specific differences in body type or shape can be transduced and neutralized via the right mix of representational processing in order to deliver similar experiences or similar cognitive results, enactivists insist that biological aspects of bodily life, including organismic and emotion regulation of the entire body, have a permeating effect on cognition, as do processes of sensorimotor coupling between organism and environment. In regard to the latter processes, for example, Noë (2004; also see O'Regan and Noë 2001; Hurley 1998) developed a detailed account of enactive perception where sensory–motor contingencies and environmental affordances take over the work that had been attributed to neural computations and mental representations.

1.3 Causality, Constitution, and Diachronicity

One clear objection to both enactivist and extended mind proposals involves the relation between causality and constitution. Both theories are said to confuse causality with constitution (Adams and Aizawa 2008). It's an important objection because it points to a clear difference between these theories and the standard cognitivist approaches.

Adams and Aizawa (2008; Aizawa 2010) argue that the extended mind hypothesis, as well as enactivist approaches (see Aizawa 2014), make an unjustifiable inference from *causal* dependence (where bodily and environmental factors play a causal role in support of cognitive processes) to *constitutive* dependence (where the claim is that such factors actually are part of the cognitive processes). This is the causal-constitution (C-C) fallacy. For example, the use of a notebook or a smartphone to support memory should be understood as causally supporting or enabling a cognitive process, but not as being a cognitive process itself, as the extended mind hypothesis claims. The strict distinction between causality and constitution is closely tied to the idea that there is a 'mark of the mental' (a way to determine what processes count as cognitive and what processes do not). Adams and Aizawa, among others, argue that non-derived internal (brain-based) representational content is what constitutes the mark of the mental. Outside of that nothing counts as cognitive.

The standard cognitivist approach adopts a classic metaphysical view that causation and constitution are independent relations—facts about causal relations do not tell us anything about constitution (Bennett 2011; 2004). On this view, for example, it is possible that emotions are causally influenced by bodily or environmental factors, but what constitutes an emotion is just the mental event that is instantiated in the brain. Michael Kirchhoff (2015) argues that this view understands constitution to mean material or compositional constitution: a *synchronic* one–one, or many–one (where one thing is constituted by an aggregate of things) relation between spatially and materially coincident objects of different kinds. The classic example is that the statue of David is constituted by (but not caused by) the piece of marble that it is. The relation between the statue and the marble is what it is at any moment, and does not change (Gibbard 1975). If x constitutes (or composes) y, then x and y exist at the same place at the same time and they share the same material parts. This classic notion, however, does not account for processes and a theory of the mental has to account for processes.

To account for processes, enactivists appeal to the ideas of a dynamical system and diachronic constitution (Kirchhoff 2015). Brain, body, and environment are said to be dynamically coupled in a way that forms a system, and the coupling is not equivalent to identity of material parts; rather it involves physical relational processes. Significant changes in one part of the system will cause changes or adjustments in the other parts. For the enactivist just these dynamical causal relations constitute the system.

Because these processes occur on several timescales, it will be helpful to introduce a threefold distinction in temporal and dynamical registers. The following differentiation, based on neurobiology and phenomenology (see Varela 1999), can clarify the C-C issue, but will also have relevance to a number of the analyses developed in later chapters. Varela argued that cognition involves processes on the following three timescales, which I'll call the elementary, the integrative, and the narrative timescales.

1. The *elementary* scale (varying between 10 and 100 milliseconds)
2. The *integrative* scale (varying from 0.5 to 3 seconds)
3. The *narrative* scale involving memory (above 3 seconds)

The elementary scale is the basic timescale of neurophysiology. It corresponds to the intrinsic cellular rhythms of neuronal discharges roughly within the range of 10 milliseconds (the rhythms of bursting interneurons) to 100 milliseconds (the duration of an excitatory/inhibitory sequence of postsynaptic potential in a cortical pyramidal neuron). Neuronal processes on this scale are integrated in the second scale, which, at the neurophysiological level, involves the integration of cell assemblies. Phenomenologically, the integrative scale corresponds to the experienced living present, the level of a fully constituted cognitive operation; motorically, it corresponds to a basic action, e.g., reaching, grasping. On a dynamical systems interpretation, neuronal-level events on the elementary scale synchronize (by phase-locking) and form aggregates that manifest themselves as incompressible but complete acts on the integrative scale.[2] The narrative scale is meant to capture longer time periods that scale to complex actions and cognitive processes that may involve recollection, planning, intention formation, and so on. Further distinctions could be made (one could think of developmental and evolutionary timescales, for example), and other more rhythmic time patterns could be explicated, but for our purposes the threefold distinction should be sufficient.

On the standard notion of synchronic constitution, subpersonal, elementary-scale neuronal processes constitute contentful, representational mental processes that in some way scale up to conscious mental states. One might think of this as a form of identity theory. Identity theories usually posit mental state = brain state identities—a central-state materialism. All other factors—bodily, environmental, social, etc.—are causal but not constitutive. On some accounts they are, at best, derived or epiphenomenal relative to non-derived mentality. On the enactivist view, however, one requires a more nuanced distributed-state materialism. In their dynamical relations, neural and non-neural, including embodied, environmental, social, etc., may be causal in a way that they are also constitutive.

In contrast to standard synchronic views of constitution, then, enactivists propose a notion of diachronic constitution, where causality and constitution are not independent. Embodied mental processes (i.e., processes of the embodied-enactive mind), distributed across different factors/levels (neural, behavioral, environmental), and across different

---

[2] This currently has the status of a working hypothesis in neuroscience. See Thompson (2007, 332).

timescales, are constituted in a temporally integrated dynamical system. The constituent elements may very well be in complex, reciprocal causal relations with each other, but just these reciprocal causal relations make the mental process what it is. Thus, an intervention that changes the causal relations in a dynamical system will also change the system as a whole. In a gestalt (what Maurice Merleau-Ponty [1964] called a 'form' or 'structure') the whole is said to add up to more than the sum of its parts. In a dynamical gestalt composed of processes that unfold over time, and characterized by recursive reciprocal causality relations, changes in any processual part (above a certain threshold) will lead to changes in the whole, and changes in the whole will imply changes in the processual parts. In contrast to a synchronic, compositional notion of constitution, these kinds of causal relations are diachronically constitutive of the phenomenon. As Kirchhoff (2015) argues, the notion of a C-C fallacy, where constitution is defined synchronically, does not apply to the type of diachronic processes described in dynamical patterns.

This notion of constitution might be taken in either a strong existential sense or a weaker sense. In the strong sense the claim would be that if one significantly changes, destroys, or removes the causal coupling, the system ceases to exist as such. Coma or death may be good examples of this. If there is a living organism, however, there is always an environment and some kind of causal coupling. In the weaker sense of constitution the claim is simply that cognition is *what* it is because of the nature of the coupling. A change in the way the brain, body, and environment are related will change cognition. The nature of cognition depends on the instantiation of certain dynamical couplings such that a specific kind of cognition would not arise were it not for causal interactions that define the system. The claim here is not, for example, that the environment determines representational contents. One can be in a particular environment and be dreaming or hallucinating—that will depend on the state of the body (e.g., if one is sleeping) or the brain (e.g., if there is an imbalance of neurotransmitters), and that will change one's relation to the environment. One can change the causal interactions with the environment, for example, by putting the organism in a sensory deprivation chamber; that clearly will result in cognition that is different.[3]

---

[3] If one is in a sensory deprivation chamber, one may be hallucinating (and not perceiving something in a physical environment) precisely because the specifics of the

To be clear, enactivists don't deny the importance of the brain, but they understand the brain to be an integrated part of a larger dynamical system that includes body and (physical, social, and cultural) environments. The explanatory unit of cognition (perception, action, etc.) is not just the brain, or even two (or more) brains in the case of social cognition, but dynamic relations between organism and environment, or between two or more organisms, which include brains, but also include their own structural features that enable specific perception-action loops, which in turn effect statistical regularities that shape the structure and function of the nervous system (Gallagher 2005a; Thompson 2007).

If I reach out to grasp something (or someone), my hand is involved, as is my arm, my shoulder and back muscles, my peripheral nervous system as well as my vestibular system, no less than my brain, which in all of its complexity is making its own dynamical adjustments on the elementary timescale as part of this process of reaching out to grasp. A full account of the kinematics of this movement doesn't add up to an explanation of the action; nor does a full account of the neural activity involved. Likewise, if I reach a decision about how to act, the neural components of this activity are a necessary part, but also my location, and who I'm with, and my past practices, current physical skills, and health status, not to mention my mood, will to some degree play contributory roles in the decision formation. Some of these elements enter into the process on a narrative timescale and are not under my current control. In this respect, my body is not just a sensory–motor mechanism. Affect plays an important role—things like hunger, fatigue, physical discomfort or pain, as well as emotion and mood (see *Chapter 8*). Such things are not well behaved in terms of timescale—they involve all three scales. With respect to discussions of agency and free will, for example, whatever agentive action is, it is both constrained and enabled by all of these different factors. As Clark and Chalmers (1998, 9) suggest, if one of the extra-neural components is taken away, 'the system's behavioural competence will drop, just as it would if we removed part of its brain'. At the very least a removal (or an

organism–environment coupling are different. This should not be an argument for the irrelevance of the environment or of the specifics of dynamical coupling (cf. Prinz 2009).

addition) of any component will entail compensatory adjustments across the system.

Evan Thompson (2014) provides a nice analogy. Saying that cognition is just in the brain is like saying that flight is inside the wings of a bird. Just as flight doesn't exist if there is only a wing, without the rest of the bird, and without an atmosphere to support the process, and without the precise mode of organism–environment coupling to make it possible (indeed, who would disagree with this?), so cognition doesn't exist if there is just a brain without bodily and worldly factors. 'The mind is relational. It's a way of being in relation to the world' (Thompson 2014, 1). For some, these claims may seem obvious or even trivial, and yet we often find ourselves doing science as if the only things that counted as explanatory were neural representations.

Processes of social interaction are also not reducible to neuronal processes (or B-formatted representations) within the individual, since they include physical engagement with another person, who is not just a representation in my mind, but someone who can push back in a way that a mere representation cannot. Social interactions also include physical engagement in a socially defined environment, and processes of 'primary intersubjectivity', including affective processes where distinct forms of sensory–motor couplings are generated by one's perception and response to facial expression, posture, movement, gestures, etc. in rich pragmatic and social contexts (Gallagher 2005a). This is demonstrated in the kind of rich analyses one finds in conversational analysis (e.g., Goodwin 2000). Again, this is not to say that all the essential processes of social cognition are extra-neural. Mirror neurons may indeed make a contribution, not by simulating actions of others, repeating a small version of them inside one's head, but by being part of larger sensory–motor processes that respond to different interaction affordances. On the enactivist view, social cognition is an attunement process that allows me to perceive the other as someone to whom I can respond or with whom I can interact. In the intersubjective context, perception is often *for interaction* with others. In some cases, a relational understanding is accomplished in the social interaction between two people where some novel shared meaning (or some decision or even some misunderstanding) is instituted in a way that could not be instituted within the single brain of either one of them alone (De Jaegher, Di Paolo, and Gallagher 2010).

1.4 How to be an Embodied Theorist without Losing your Head

Take any example of cognition and one can run two different explanations—the standard representationalist one *versus* the enactivist one. Sometimes it seems to be simply a vocabulary substitution; sometimes the enactivist description seems to work better, especially if we think of examples that involve problem solving rather than belief; and other times the representationalist description seems to have the upper hand. Even when the representations involved are action-oriented, minimal, or B-formatted, there are clear differences in explanation.

Consider the well-known example of fielding (trying to catch) a ball (McBeath, Shaffer, and Kaiser 1995). We can run the account in both ways, where running it in one case means representing various aspects of speed and trajectory, and in the other case it means literally running rather than representing.

In the classic representational account the problem is first solved in the fielder's head. Speed and trajectory of the ball are calculated and reconstructed by the brain, which solves the problem offline and then simply sends instructive signals to the limbs to move in the most efficient way to catch the ball. As Michael Anderson (2014, 164) points out, this representation-rich view treats cognition as 'post-perceptual'—something added to perception to make sense of it. It's not likely that anyone still believes this story, and there's evidence against it since outfielders who are standing still are unable to reliably predict where the ball will land. Moreover, the account doesn't predict the actual pattern of movement that the fielder makes to catch the ball.

In a weak EC, *action-oriented representation* (AOR) account, calculations are made online as we move, but part of the process involves quick (on the elemental timescale) offline AORs formed in forward models that contribute to motor control. Sensory feedback is too slow to update the system in a timely fashion; the forward model generates a simulation or representation that anticipates sensory feedback from intended body positions on the run and allows for a fine-tuning of motor control. The AOR stands in, briefly, for a future state of some extra-neural aspect of the movement—a body position (or proprioceptive feedback connected with a body position), which is just about to be accomplished in the action of catching the ball. Since the model represents a state of the system that does not yet exist—a predicted motor state—it is said to be offline, or decoupled from the ongoing action (Clark and Grush 1999), and to occur in the self-contained brain. After catching the ball, such representations can then be simulated and taken further offline, reused, e.g., in memory systems, scaling up to enable additional cognitive states. The brain can run such offline models to accompany states in which no running and catching is involved at all—when, for example, I imagine or remember catching a ball. No need for the body itself or for 'a constant physical linkage' (Clark and Grush 1999, 7; Clark 1999).

On the enactivist account, in contrast, the fielder solves the problem without representations, by vision and movement. She runs on a curved line so as to keep the ball's trajectory through the visual field at a constant speed, i.e., visually stationary on the retina. This reliably gets the fielder to the catching spot (McBeath, Shaffer, and Kaiser 1995; Fink, Foo, and Warren 2009). There is no need to compute in-the-head mental representations—of the ball, its speed, its trajectory, and so on. Rather, the cognitive component of this action just is seeing the ball that is 'out there' in the world, and directly acting in the world. The processes involved are dynamical sensory–motor processes that are fully online. These processes do involve ongoing anticipation, but it's not clear in what sense such anticipatory processes, which Clark and Grush equate with AORs, can be described as 'off-line' or decoupled. The forward anticipatory aspect of neural processing is a constitutive part of the action itself, understood in diachronic, dynamical terms, rather than something decoupled from it. The anticipation of a future state or position (of the ball, or of the body grabbing the ball in the next second) requires ongoing reference or 'constant physical linkage' to one's current bodily state or position. To think of such processes as representational is to think that such anticipations are in some way detached or detachable from perceptual and proprioceptive input, which they clearly are not. Such processes may be one step ahead of real-world proprioceptive feedback—but they are also at the same time one step behind the previous moment of feedback, integrated with ongoing movement and perception (see section 5.3). Moreover, they necessarily and quickly dissipate as the agent continues to move. They are not stored as representations for later reuse, although if you catch enough balls your system becomes more proficiently attuned for further performance as well as for re-enacting the process *via* memory or imagination.

On some views, higher-order cognition is 'representation hungry' (Clark and Toribio 1994). On the enactivist account, however, to scale up to cognitive states such as imagining or remembering, the brain doesn't decouple or recreate a process that was representational to begin with; rather, the system (using the same motor control or forward control mechanism) enacts (or re-enacts) a process that is now coupled to a new cognitive action. In remembering, for example, there may be reactivation of perceptual neural processes that had been activated during the original experience. It has also been shown, using electromyography (EMG) that other non-neural bodily processes, e.g., subliminal tensing of muscles and facial expressions, may be (re)activated in cases of remembering, imagining, reflecting, etc. (e.g., Bakker, Boschker, and Chung 1996; Livesay and Samras 1998; Schmidt and Lee 1999).

Here, however, the line between accounts of AORs and the idea of enactive cognition gets blurred, and some may suspect that the difference is merely one of preferred vocabulary (see *Chapter 5*). Thus, defenders of AORs, like Michael Wheeler, give up the criterion of decoupleability as part of the concept of an AOR (2005, 219); and both Wheeler and Mark Rowlands suggest that AORs involve aspects of a system that includes brain, body, and environment. 'The vehicles of representation do not stop at the skin; they extend all the way out into the world' (Rowlands 2006, 224). When the concept of representation is weakened to this extent, however, one might suspect that what proponents of weak embodiment call AORs can be replaced with what enactivists call affordances. Affordances, however, in whatever way they are conceived, are not meant to be representation substitutes, as if they are standing in and doing the job that representations are said to do in more standard accounts. The notion of affordance is dynamically relational in a way that representations cannot be.

1.5 Beyond Predictive Coding

Since enactivist accounts reject standard computational and representationalist explanations they need to provide a different understanding of how the brain works. In this respect it will be productive to contrast enactivist conceptions to the recently advanced, and comprehensive alternative theory of brain function cast in terms of predictive coding (PC) or predictive processing (Clark 2016a; Hohwy 2013). PC has been an important trend in neuroscience that explains brain function in terms of Baysian inference (Friston 2005). According to Andy Clark (2013a, 181) it 'offers the best clue yet to the shape of a unified science of mind and action'. One might think that PC has already settled on the representationalist side since much of the PC literature assumes or adopts the representationalist vocabulary, along with the terminology of 'inference' and 'hypothesis' formation (e.g., Hohwy 2013). An alternative interpretation, however, emphasizing PC's recent focus on 'active inference', pushes some of the basic concepts of PC more towards the enactivist account (see e.g., Bruineberg, Kiverstein, and Rietveld 2016; Gallagher and Allen 2016).

On one reading of the PC approach the brain is pictured as having no direct access to the outside world; accordingly, it needs to represent that world by some internal model that it constructs by decoding sensory input (Hohwy 2013). The brain attempts to make sense out of sensory data 'within a cascade of cortical processing events in which higher-level systems attempt to predict the inputs to lower level ones on the basis of their own emerging models of the causal structure of the world (i.e. the signal source)' (Clark 2013a, 181). On this view, the brain makes probabilistic inferences (forms 'hypotheses') about the world and corrects those inferences to minimize prediction errors. This involves synaptic inhibitory processes based on empirical priors: that is, based on prior experience or on prior states of the system. Predictions are matched against ongoing sensory input. Mismatches generate prediction errors that are sent back up the line and the system adjusts dynamically back and forth until there is a relatively good fit. This is an efficient process since the only data that need to be sent up the line are the discrepancies (the surprises) from the predicted signal, and in the process of revising the prediction, the brain updates its model of the world and revises its priors (Rao and Ballard 1999).

Within this scheme an agent has two means by which to maintain its structural and functional integrity; either through the accurate internal prediction of hidden (external) causes, or by acting on the environment in ways that minimize sensory surprise. The latter, with the ensuing changes in action and perception, is known as active inference. On the one hand, emphasizing only the first type of operation, prediction-error minimization, PC remains strictly internalistic, and active inference only serves the central processes that do the real work. Accordingly, Hohwy

(2016) argues that PC understood in this narrow way is not consistent with EC approaches.

PEM [prediction-error minimization] should make us resist conceptions of [a mind-world] relation on which the mind is in some fundamental way open or porous to the world, or on which it is in some strong sense embodied, extended or enactive. Instead, PEM reveals the mind to be inferentially secluded from the world, it seems to be more neurocentrically skull-bound than embodied or extended, and action itself is more an inferential process on sensory input than an enactive coupling with the environment. (Hohwy 2016, 259)

On the other hand, an emphasis on active inference leads to a recognition of the importance of embodiment and interaction, reflected in recent dynamical variants of predictive coding (Friston, Mattout, and Kilner 2011; Friston and Frith 2015; also see Kilner, Friston, and Frith 2007; Wolpert, Doya, and Kawato 2003). Thus, Clark, who sees PEM processes as closely tied to movement and action, argues that PC offers support for a more embodied and enactive theory of cognition (Clark 2013a; 2015; 2016b).

This suggests that we do not have to think that the outcome of the PC process is the creation of a representation in the brain—'a kind of internal model of the source of the signals: the world hidden behind the veil of perception' (Clark 2013a, 184).

This means that 'inference', as it functions in the [PC] story, is not compelled to deliver internal states that bear richly reconstructive contents. It is not there to construct an inner realm able to stand in for the full richness of the external world. Instead, it may deliver efficient, low-cost strategies whose unfolding and success depend delicately and continuously upon the structure and ongoing contributions of the external realm itself as exploited by various forms of action and intervention. (Clark 2016a, 191)

Clark takes the problem of fielding a ball (mentioned in the previous section) as an example of active inference (2016a, 190, 247, 256ff.). On a PC account, he argues, it may be possible to move away from the vocabulary of representations, even AORs, in the same way that he wants to move away from the idea that PC depends on forming a 'hypothesis'. We can rather think of the brain as engaged in finding the distributed neural states 'that best *accommodate* (as I will now put it) the current sensory barrage' (192). In active inference, the brain does this, not by sitting back and formulating hypotheses, but *via* 'world-engaging action' (192), like running to catch a fly ball. Clark makes room for extra-neural, bodily factors (basic morphology, biomechanical dynamics, kinematics, environmental regularities), citing Gibson's ecological psychology and rejecting the classic 're-constructive' view (246–7). Even on Clark's PC account, however, there remains an ambiguity: on the one hand, active inference (as PC accounts have it) is in the service of generating information that is sent back to the brain for central processing. He cites Lungarella and Sporns (2005, 25) to indicate that the world-engaging action acts as a 'complement to neural information-processing'. This is also how Hohwy (2013) conceives it. On the other hand, Clark pushes towards a more enactive story: the problem solving is distributed across brain–body–environment, and this 'allows the productively lazy brain to do as little as possible while still solving (or rather, while the whole embodied, environmentally located system) solves the problem' (2016a, 248). The enactivist story is in parentheses.

Removing those parentheses, why should we not rather think of this process as a kind of ongoing dynamical adjustment in which the brain, *as part of and along with the larger organism*, settles into the right kind of attunement with the environment—an environment that is physical but also social and cultural (Gallagher et al. 2013)? Neural accommodation occurs in this larger system. Notions of adjustment and attunement can be cashed out in terms of physical states, or more precisely, physical dynamical processes that involve brain and body, autonomic and peripheral nervous systems, as well as affective and motoric changes.

This notion of enactive attunement is seemingly reflected in PC terms that emphasize two 'directions of fit'. The first involves updating predictions or adjusting priors on the basis of ongoing perceptual experience—the world-to-brain direction. The second involves acting on the world to directly shape or resample it in such a way as to test our prior expectations (active inference). In this respect, for PC models, perception may be conceived as an active process whereby I engage in the types of behaviors that are likely to produce sensory experiences that confirm or test my expectations; where, for example, active ballistic saccades do not merely passively orient to features but actively sample the bits of the world that fit my expectations or resolve uncertainty (Friston et al. 2012). Pushing PC towards more embodied, enactive, ecological accounts, Clark suggests that active inference takes the lead in the metaphorical 'circular causal dance'; one might even suggest, more radically, that in contrast to the 'subtly misleading' explanations of PC that makes the world-to-brain direction primary, all inference is really active inference (see, e.g., Clark 2016a, 250–1).[4] In contrast, however, on the enactivist model the dynamic adjustment/attunement process that encompasses the whole of the system is not a *testing* that serves better neural prediction; active inference is not 'inference' at all, it's a *doing*, an enactive adjustment, a worldly engagement (Bruineberg, Kiverstein, and Rietveld 2016; Gallagher and Allen 2016). The fielder is trying to catch the baseball; she is not performing tests or sampling the environment. The brain is not located in the center, conducting tests along the radiuses; it's on the circumference, one station amongst other stations involved in the loop that also navigates through the body and environment and forms the whole.

For example, we know that one's beliefs and values, as well as one's affective states and cultural perspectives (phenomena defined for the most part on the narrative scale), operating as priors, can shape the way that one quite literally sees the world (see section 6.4). How such cognitive and affective states and perspectives enter into (elementary scale) subpersonal processes can be explained in terms of PC models. With respect to affect, for example, Barrett and Bar's *affective prediction hypothesis* 'implies that responses signaling an object's salience, relevance or value do not occur as a separate step after the object is identified. Instead, affective responses support vision from the very moment that visual stimulation begins' (Barrett and Bar 2009, 1325). Along with the earliest visual processing, the medial orbital frontal cortex is activated, initiating a train of muscular and hormonal changes throughout the body, and generating 'interoceptive sensations' from organs, muscles, and joints associated with prior experience, which integrates with current exteroceptive sensory information. This is the organism's response which contributes to shaping subsequent actions. Accordingly, as part of the perception of the environment, we undergo certain bodily affective changes that accompany this integrated processing. In other words, before we fully recognize an object or other person, for what it or he or

---

[4] As we see in Clark (2016a, 251), however, this simply leads back to the notion of pragmatic representations, serving 'epistemic functions, sampling the world in ways designed to test our hypotheses and to yield better information for the control of action itself'.

she is, our bodies are already configured into overall peripheral and autonomic patterns shaped by prior associations. In terms of the PC model used by Barrett and Bar, priors that include affect are not just in the brain but involve whole body adjustments—what Freund et al. (2016, 1860) call 'anatomically informed priors'.

On the enactivist view, brains play an important part in the ongoing dynamical attunement of organism to environment. Social interaction, for example, involves the integration of brain processes into a complex mix of transactions that involve moving, gesturing, and engaging with the expressive bodies of others—bodies that incorporate artifacts, tools, and technologies that are situated in various physical environments, and defined by diverse social roles and institutional practices. Brains participate in a system, along with all these other factors, and it would work differently, because the priors and surprises in the system would be different, if these other factors were different. If, as Clark (2013a, 189) suggests, 'humans act as rational Bayesian estimators, in perception and in action, across a wide variety of domains', which means that they take into account the uncertainty in their own sensory and motor signals, this is due to the fact that brains evolve to function the way they do because they evolve with the body they are part of, and in environments that are coupled in specific ways to those bodies.

Perception, on the enactivist view, involves transactions in the complete (neural plus extra-neural) system. Enactivists emphasize sensory-motor contingencies (e.g., Noë 2004), bodily affect (see section 8.1), as well as the role that intersubjective interaction plays in shaping perception (section 8.2). Perception thus, rather than the result of narrow inferential or simulative processes, involves complex, dynamical processes at a subpersonal, sensory–motor level (in the elementary timescale)—but these processes are part of an enactive, dynamical engagement or response of the whole organism (in the integrative and narrative timescales), living in and materially engaging with structured environments. As Clark suggests, taking into consideration more embodied and embedded practices, we can use 'a variety of tricks, tools, notations, practices, and media [to] structure our physical and social worlds so as to make them friendlier for brains like ours'—thereby stacking the deck (designing our surrounding environments) to minimize prediction errors (2013a, 195). Such redesigns, however, reflect a *metaplasticity* that goes both ways— changing not only the brain, but also physical, social, and cultural environments (Malafouris 2013). We can intervene at any point on the self-organizing circle of brain–body–environment; that intervention will incur (sometimes friendly, sometimes not so friendly) adjustments to the whole.

Changes or adjustments to neural processing will accompany any changes in these other worldly factors, not because the brain represents such changes and responds to them in central command mode, but because the brain is part of the larger embodied system that is coping with its changing environment. Just as the hand adjusts to the shape of the object to be grasped, so the brain adjusts to the circumstances of organism–environment. And just as it is not clear that we gain anything by saying that the shape of the grasp represents the object to be grasped (cf. Rowlands 2006), it's not clear that we gain anything in saying that brain activations represent the world.

With respect to PC models, enactivist views that emphasize a more holistic system of brain–body–environment would clearly favor a move away from internalist and intellectualist vocabularies (and conceptions) of 'hypothesis', 'inference', and 'representation' in favor of more embodied terms like 'adjustment', 'attunement', and 'affordance'. Such terms are not simply substitutes for the PC terms; they change the way that we think of the brain's engagement.

1.6 Enactivism as a Philosophy of Nature

Enactivist EC approaches present a challenge for science. Enactivists, by focusing on not just the brain, not just the environment, not just behavior, but on the rich dynamics of brain–body–environment, offer a holistic conception of cognition. To put it succinctly, however, it is difficult to operationalize holism. Neither experimental control nor the division of labor in science allows for all factors to be taken into consideration at once. Nor is it clear that there could be one single critical experiment that might decide the issue between the representationalist and the enactivist. On the one hand, enactivism makes empirical claims, for example, about the work of sensorimotor contingencies, and in this respect it resembles a research program that can suggest new experiments and new ways of interpreting data. On the other hand, its emphasis on holism presents problems for empirical investigations. To be clear, nothing prevents science from doing its experiments, controlling for variables, and building up explanations one experiment at a time. Yet, each science tends to develop its theories based on its own particular assumptions, in its own vocabulary, and often in isolation from the insights of other sciences. Triangulation doesn't always work just because of conflicting assumptions, vocabularies, and interpretations. One can encounter what I've elsewhere called the 'clunky robot' problem (Gallagher et al. 2015, 74). That is, just as one can design a robot by assigning teams to construct different modules, which turn out to work well as individual modules, it may happen that when the modules are brought together, they don't play well together. No one has considered the relational aspects of how one module will dynamically connect with another in a complex system, and the result is a clunky machine-like behavior. The same problem can be found in theory construction. Scientific experiments, designed within the framework of their own particular paradigm, often study the pieces of a system but don't always consider how the dynamical relations among those pieces work, and don't always have the vocabulary to address those relations. Even working in an interdisciplinary way we often find ourselves building a clunky theory where insights from different disciplines don't integrate well.

This motivates serious consideration of the idea, first suggested by Cecilia Heyes[5] (drawing on a distinction proposed by Godfrey-Smith [2001]), that enactivism may be better thought as a philosophy of nature than a scientific research agenda. Godfrey-Smith, discussing developmental systems theory, distinguishes between a 'scientific research programme' and a 'philosophy of nature'. As he makes clear, a philosophy of nature is a different kind of intellectual project from science, and although science may be its critical object, the two enterprises do not have to share the same vocabulary. A philosophy of nature 'can use its own categories and concepts, concepts developed for the task of describing the world as accurately as possible when a range of scientific descriptions are to be taken into account, and when a philosophical concern with the underlying structure of theories is appropriate' (Godfrey-Smith 2001, 284). A philosophy of nature takes seriously the results of science, and its claims remain consistent with them, but it can reframe those results to integrate them with results from many sciences. An exclusive

---

[5] Here I'm pursuing a suggestion made by Cecilia Heyes, commenting on a paper I presented at the Ernst Strüngmann Forum, Frankfurt, in October 2014.

focus on cognitive neuroscience as *the* science of cognition, for example, would be entirely unjustified on this view. Moreover, the requirements of such a reframing may indeed call for a vocabulary that is different from one that serves the needs of any particular science. Although to work out a philosophy of nature is not to do science, it can still offer clarifications relevant to doing science, and it can inform empirical investigations. In this sense, a philosophy of nature is neither natural philosophy (in the traditional sense) nor the kind of naturalistic philosophy that is necessarily continuous with science. It offers critical distance and practical suggestions at the same time. In some cases it may make doing science more difficult.

That enactivism is a philosophy of nature can be seen in the fact that from the very start enactivism involved not only a rethinking of the nature of mind and brain, but also a rethinking of the concept of nature itself (see Di Paolo 2005; Thompson 2007, 78ff.). If enactivism is a form of naturalism, it does not endorse the mechanistic definition of nature often presupposed by science, but contends that nature cannot be understood apart from the cognitive capacity that we have to investigate it. As Cecilia Heyes suggested in her comments, in the context of a philosophy of nature meant to offer an encompassing view, holism is a strength rather than a practical complication.

Enactivism, as 'a non-reductionist yet scientifically engaged philosophy of nature' (Di Paolo, Buhrmann, and Barandiaran 2017, 253), may still motivate experimental science in very specific ways. Even if in some cases it is difficult to apply a holistic view to a given question, in many cases there may not be any special complication in designing experiments that can test enactivist ideas. For example, one can set all factors to work and then test the system to see what happens when we intervene to knock out one of those factors. Moreover, one need not include absolutely everything in every case when dealing with a particular concrete question, although in the end it may be easier to include than to ignore a factor that is crucial. For example, including embodied interactions in explanations of social cognition might actually be more parsimonious if keeping them out of the picture requires the elaboration of more convoluted explanations in terms of theory or simulation mechanisms (De Jaegher, Di Paolo, and Gallagher 2010). Although in this, and other cases, much will depend on circumstances like the availability of the right lab technology, the whole may sometimes lead to simpler explanations. In short, even if enactivism were to be considered a philosophy of nature, it wouldn't be right to conclude that it cannot offer concrete hypotheses or raise novel scientific questions.

The following chapters are meant to be contributions towards formulating an enactivist philosophy of mind, as part of a larger philosophy of nature. *Chapters 2* and *3* provide a broad background and situate enactivism in contemporary and historical contexts. *Chapter 2* reviews a number of contemporary approaches to embodied cognition in order to clearly distinguish the enactivist version. *Chapter 3* explores a largely ignored background to enactivism in the American pragmatist tradition.

Chapter 4 outlines a theory of enactive intentionality that capitalizes on both the phenomenological and the pragmatist roots of enactivism. Looking at debates about intentionality in neo-behaviorist and neo-pragmatist approaches, I argue that if we frame the notion of intentionality correctly, then the opposition between enactivism and extended mind approaches can be resolved. Specfically, the enactivist approach can borrow from neo-pragmatism and develop an embodied and extended mind account of non-derived intentionality that is immune to objections from the standard internalist theories. On this view, however, intentionality is not equivalent to representation. This leads, then, to an enactivist critique of representationalism in *Chapter 5*. I argue that on standard definitions of representation in philosophy of mind, perception–action processes are non-representational—in contrast to various versions of action-oriented representations defended by Clark, Wheeler, Rowlands, and others.

This motivates the question explored in *Chapters 5* and *6*: How does the brain work if it is not forming internal mental representations of the world? Here I come back to some of the issues that I touched on above. In contrast to the standard conception of the brain making inferences (as found in classic computational accounts and the more internalist predictive processing accounts) the enactivist view is that the brain, as part of the body–environment system (not only regulating body, but regulated by the body and its affective processes) is, as Jesse Prinz puts it, 'set up to be set off' (2004, 55) by prior experience and plastic changes. The brain works as an integral part of the organism which, as a whole, responds dynamically to environmental changes. It's not clear that this is equivalent to the notion of 'active inference' in predictive processing accounts, but from the enactivist perspective, it may be the best way to think of how the brain works.

Chapter 7 argues that the attempt to locate free will within elementary timescales or in neurophysiological processes just prior to action is wrong-headed. I outline an enactivist response to recent debates around the notion that free will is an illusion. I argue that Libet experiments, which show how neural activations in the elementary timescale of milliseconds prior to action anticipate a voluntary movement, even before the agent decides to move, are about motor control processes (where motor intentions are formed)—not about free will, which is best understood on a narrative timescale and which involves larger processes of distal intentions and action in social contexts.

Chapter 8 argues that an enactivist conception of embodied cognition involves more than sensory–motor contingencies, and more than a critique of representationalism. Here the importance of both affect and intersubjectivity is emphasized. *Chapter 9* continues on this theme by returning to an essay by Erwin Straus (1966), written within the tradition of phenomenological anthropology and focused on the human upright posture. I extend and update this analysis as a way to flesh out a fuller conception of embodiment and its relation to rationality. Finally, in Chapter 10, I address what is variously known as the problem of 'scaling up' or the question of 'higher-order' cognition (although I reject these labels). Can an enactivist approach explain cognitive processes involved in reflective thought, deliberation, memory, imagination, and so forth? To gain some traction on this issue I frame my answer in terms of a recent debate between Dreyfus and McDowell concerning the nature of the mind. The enactivist approach can split the difference and establish a space somewhere between the positions of Dreyfus (who emphasizes embodied skills and coping) and McDowell (who focuses on concepts and the space of reasons). I argue that reflection and conceptually rich cognitive operations (e.g., imagining and doing mathematics) involve a specialized affordance space but are continuous with embodied coping, and share the same structure.

2
Variations on Embodied Cognition

The concept of embodied cognition (EC) is not a settled one. A variety of approaches to the study of cognition have been closely associated with the notion of embodiment—including enactivist, embedded, and extended or distributed cognition approaches. The alternatives range from conservative models that remain close to cognitivist conceptions of the mind, to more moderate and radical camps that argue that we need to rethink our basic assumptions about the way the brain and the mind work. Given these different perspectives there is no strong consensus on what weight to give the concept of embodiment. Moreover, contrary to what some may think, not all EC approaches share a common opposition to the classic computational model of cognition.

Given this situation Larry Shapiro (2014a) worries that, unlike chemists and biologists, researchers in the area of embodied cognition may be unable to reach consensus about what their scientific domain of investigation is, what the central concepts in that domain are, and why embodied cognition is an improvement over older paradigms. I suggest, however, that this should not be a worry because embodied cognition is not a science like chemistry or biology, even if it is something like cognitive science, which is Shapiro's third example. At best, it is a research program *within* the cognitive sciences; and in some respects it is more like a philosophical framework for research in those sciences. Although Shapiro suggests that cognitive science does have good answers to the questions he poses, I'm not sure that's true. First, his answers to the question of which concepts are necessary for doing cognitive science, namely 'information, representations and algorithms' (74), are precisely some of the concepts that are under current debate, in part because of challenges from embodied cognition. And second, to the extent that it runs with the cognitive sciences, embodied cognition is interdisciplinary in a way that chemistry and biology (as Shapiro portrays them) are not. If you ask such questions of someone working in artificial intelligence, you will not necessarily get the same answers as when you ask a cognitive neuroscientist, a philosopher of mind or a cognitive anthropologist. Any of these researchers may also be working on embodied cognition. In fact the kinds of disparate topics that Shapiro lists under the heading of embodied cognition—e.g., motor behaviour, robot navigation, action–sentence compatibility, the role of metaphor in concept acquisition, and various question about perception—are in fact topics that are addressed in cognitive science. Indeed, the cognitive sciences and the field of embodied cognition include a bit of chemistry (since hormones and neurotransmitters have some effect on cognition) and more than a bit of (neuro- and even extra-neural) biology. Given that they also include philosophy, one should expect that there will be ongoing debates and dissensus in every corner.

In this chapter I want to map out some of these debates and some of the landscape defined by various senses of EC, starting with a minimal or weak conception of EC that equates embodiment with the representation of the body in the brain, and ending with a conception of radical embodiment found in enactivist approaches. Let me make two prefatory notes. First, the landscape I'll be concerned with is large. By this I mean that the claims made about the various approaches to EC are not focused on a particular problem or particular type of problem in cognitive science. Rather, the claims being made by the various theorists that I'll consider are generally overarching claims about the right way to approach any problem having to do with cognition. It may be that given the current state of science, and a particular problem to solve, one of the approaches may have a better account on offer than any of the others. Each of the theories to be considered may have distinctive explanatory value for solving specialized problems. I acknowledge that in trying to solve a particular problem, a theorist is not attempting to solve all problems or to give the entire story of cognition. For the most part, however, I'll be concerned with the larger claims about the best way to conceive of the overall system.

Second, I acknowledge that there have been other essays that have drawn similar maps to define the notion of embodiment in EC (e.g., Kiverstein 2012; Shapiro 2007; Wilson 2002; Ziemke 2001). A variety of authors have written from different perspectives and with different interests, sometimes endorsing various approaches, and other times criticizing the entire movement. One sees in some of these classifications the outlines of what has become known as the '4Es' (embodied, embedded, enactive, extended cognition)—which has sometimes included more 'Es' (ecological, empathic) and sometimes an A (4E&A, where A stands for affective).[1] One thing that seems clear from such reviews and summaries and transformations in labels, is that the field has shifted and perhaps continues to shift, redefining or redistributing itself in different ways. The following, then, is not meant to be definitive or final.

2.1   Weak EC and B-formats

I'll start with what Alsmith and Vignemont (2012) call 'weak', in contrast to 'strong' embodied cognition. Strong EC endorses a significant explanatory role for the (non-neural) body itself in cognition; weak EC gives the significant explanatory role to what are variously called body or body-formatted (neural) representations (e.g., Gallese and Sinigaglia 2011; Glenberg 2010; Goldman 2012; 2014; Goldman and Vignemont 2009).

The weak embodiment approach places strict constraints on how we are to understand embodiment. So much so that most EC theorists would likely not acknowledge that such constraints describe EC, and would likely take it more as a dismissal of the importance of the body. Goldman and Vignemont (2009) are perhaps the first to explicitly formulate this approach as an instance of EC. Their starting point assumes that almost everything of importance for human cognition happens in the brain, 'the seat of most, if not all, mental events' (2009, 154). Accordingly, the notion of embodied cognition seems all the more problematic if one defines the body as not including the brain, which is what they do:

Embodiment theorists want to elevate the importance of the body in explaining cognitive activities. What is meant by 'body' here? It ought to mean: the whole

---

[1] The origin of the '4E' label has been attributed to me (see Rowlands 2010, 3). I accept only partial credit (or blame). In 2007 I organized a conference on 4E cognition at the University of Central Florida, and used that term. But the label itself emerged from a workshop on the *Embodied Mind* at Cardiff University, in July 2006, which included the following participants: myself, Richard Gray, Kathleen Lennon, Richard Menary, Søren Overgaard, Matthew Ratcliffe, Mark Rowlands, and Alessandra Tanesini.

physical body minus the brain. Letting the brain qualify as part of the body would trivialize the claim that the body is crucial to mental life.   (154)

In addition to removing the brain from the body, Goldman and Vignemont propose to remove the body from the environment: they want to understand the contribution of 'the body (understood literally), not [as it is related] to the situation or environment in which the body is embedded' (154). This clearly contrasts with a core claim found in other versions of EC, however, namely that the body *cannot be uncoupled from its environment.*[2]

Goldman and Vignemont go further, however, ruling out the role of anatomy and body activity (actions and postures), which they consider trivial rather than important or constitutive contributors to cognitive processes. They are thus left with, as they put it, 'sanitized' body representations. They regard the concept of body-formatted representations ('B-formats') as 'the most promising' concept for promoting an EC approach (155). Still, they note that there is no consensus about what B-formats are, and that their role in cognition is still under debate. Such representations, however, are not propositional or conceptual in format; their content may include the body or body parts, but also they may include action goals, represented in terms of how to achieve them by means of bodily action. They specifically 'represent states of the subject's own body, indeed, represent them from an internal perspective' (Goldman 2012, 73). Jesse Prinz (2009, 419) refers to the same kinds of representations. 'Such representations and processes come in two forms: there are representations and processes that represent or respond to the body, such as a perception of bodily movement, and there are representations and processes that affect the body, such as motor commands'. Somatosensory, affective, and interoceptive representations may also be B-formatted, 'associated with the physiological conditions of the body, such as pain, temperature, itch, muscular and visceral sensations, vasomotor activity, hunger and thirst' (Goldman and Vignemont 2009, 156).

The processes involving B-formatted neural representations are purely internal to the brain, and as Shapiro (2014a) suggests, could just as well

---

[2] E.g., 'Given that bodies and nervous systems co-evolve with their environments, and only the behavior of complete animals is subjected to selection, the need for . . . a tightly coupled perspective should not be surprising' (Beer, 2000). Also see Brooks (1991); Chemero (2009); Chiel and Beer (1997).

be thought to occupy a well-equipped vat.[3] Goldman (2014) introduces one qualification to this sort of claim, namely that the contents of such representations require the brain to be embodied since it is 'possible (indeed, likely)' that the contents will depend on what the representations 'causally interact with ... [E]nvatted brain states would not have the same contents as brain states of ordinary embodied brains' (2014, 104). The body is thus somewhat better than a vat for delivering the right kind of information to the brain in its own peculiar way.

According to Goldman (2012), one gets a productive concept of embodied cognition simply by generalizing the use of B-formatted representations. 'Now suppose it turns out that B-formats are also redeployed or co-opted for representing things other than one's own bodily parts or states. These additional representations would also qualify as embodied cognitions' (Goldman 2012, 74). If B-formatted representations 'are used for secondary, or derived, purposes, then ... they would still be classified as embodied cognitions, just like B-formatted cognitions when used in their primary, fundamental role' (74).

B-formatted representations may *originally* have an interoceptive or motor task such that the content of the representation in some way references the body, involving proprioceptive and kinaesthetic information about one's own muscles, joints, and limb positions, for example. Thus, *primarily*, B-formatted representations are interoceptive or motoric representations 'of one's own bodily states and activities' (Goldman 2012, 71). Importantly, however, Goldman considers such information, which may originate peripherally, to be B-formatted only when represented centrally, 'for example, codes associated with activations in somatosensory cortex and motor cortex' (2012, 74), but also the 'interoceptive cortex' (Craig 2002) registering 'pain, tickle, temperature, itch, muscular and visceral sensations, sensual touch, and other feelings from (and about) the body' (2012, 74). Exteroceptive information about one's body, however, comes by way of vision, touch, and so forth, and these modalities involve their own, non-B-formatted representations.

The terms 'originally' and 'primarily' play an important role in these explanations since the notion of B-formatting is only the first part of a

---

[3] Barsalou's notion of grounded cognition also suggests that cognition operates on reactivation of motor areas but 'can indeed proceed independently of the specific body that encoded the sensorimotor experience' (2008, 619; see Pezzulo et al. 2011).

two-part theory. To expand the scope of application, Goldman adopts Michael Anderson's (2010) 'massive redeployment hypothesis', i.e., the idea that neural circuits originally established for one use can be reused or redeployed for other purposes while still maintaining their original function. So, for example, mirror neurons start out as motor neurons involved in motor control; but they get exapted in the course of evolution for purposes of social cognition and now are also activated when one agent sees another agent act. Any cognitive task that employs a B-formatted representation in either its original function or its exapted/ derived function is, on this definition, a form of embodied cognition.

Goldman proposes that another example of this reuse principle can be found in linguistics. Pulvermüller's (2005) language-grounding hypothesis shows that language comprehension involves the activation of action-related cortical areas. For example, when a subject hears the word *lick*, one finds activation in a sensorimotor area that involves the tongue; action words like *pick* and *kick* activate cortical areas that involve hand and foot, respectively. Language comprehension thus reflects the reuse of interoceptive, B-formatted motor representations. This suggests that 'higher-order thought is grounded in low-level representations of motor action' (Goldman 2014, 97). From here it is a short run to the type of work done by Glenberg (2010), Barsalou (1999) or by Lakoff and Johnson (1999), showing how, by simulation or metaphor, respectively, one can explain the embodied roots of abstract thought. Moreover, to the extent that memory involves activation of motor control circuits (Casasanto and Dijkstra 2010), or counting involves activation of motor areas related to the hand (Andres, Seron, and Oliver 2007), these cognitive activities should be considered as instances of embodied cognition.

Neural reuse means that neural areas or processes evolve in a way that allows them to be activated for tasks that were not the original tasks associated with such areas. Anderson (2010) and Goldman (2012) mention Broca's area as a good example of neural reuse. The homologous area in the monkey has motor and possibly action-recognition functions; Broca's area in the human continues to involve these original functions, including movement preparation, action sequencing, and action imitation. But, of course, in the human, the area in question has evolved linguistic function.

Clearly, the reuse hypothesis involves the evolutionary concept of exaptation which, as Vittorio Gallese rightly explains, 'refers to the shift in the course of evolution of a given trait or mechanism, which is later on reused to serve new purposes and functions' (2014, 6). In this strict sense, the reuse story applies to evolutionary processes rather than token activations or representational processes in individual brains. It refers to exaptation on an evolutionary timescale, not neural activations on an elementary timescale. In the case of a token activation of a specific brain area, the brain is not *reusing* for cognitive purposes neurons (or representations) that have a primary body-related purpose, although that is sometimes how Goldman seems to describe it. For example, he describes 'reusing or redeploying B-formats to execute a fundamentally non-bodily cognitive task' (2012, 83). 'Cognition (token) C is a specimen of embodied cognition if and only if C [re]uses some (internal) bodily format to help execute a cognitive task (whatever the task may be)' (2014, 103).[4] Likewise he references the mirror system where activation of mirror neurons 'as part of a representation of what another person is doing, or planning to do, [thereby involving] a different cognitive task than the fundamental [i.e., primary] one . . . constitutes a redeployment [reuse] of the motoric format in a novel, cognitively interpersonal, task' (2012, 79). He also suggests that the reuse principle can apply to cognitive strategies, e.g., people can use their imagination 'for a wide swath of novel applications' (2012, 78). Whether this is a proper use of the term 'reuse' is a question but likely not a major concern. Goldman is entitled to his own usage (or re-usage) of this concept. I return to this and more substantive issues concerning weak EC below (see section 2.5).

Goldman, as noted, regards the work of Lakoff and Johnson to be an instance of weak EC.

Consider the work of George Lakoff and Mark Johnson . . . Their dominant theme is the pervasive use of body-related metaphor in language and thought. The core idea here is the intensive use of representations of (parts of) the body in metaphor and associated uses of language . . . the core message . . . is that our conceptual structure is pervaded by representations of our bodies. Our conceptualization of objects is dominated by how we conceptually relate other objects to our own bodies. This is all, fundamentally, about representation.   (Goldman 2014, 95)

---

[4] Goldman's gloss on this statement justifies adding the bracketed 're' in '[re]use'. 'Instead of saying that it suffices for a cognition to qualify as embodied that it reuse a B-code, the test for embodiment (via reuse) should require both that the cognition reuse a B-code *and* that it reuse the B-code in question *because* this B-code has the function of representing certain bodily states. This might indeed be a helpful addition' (2014, 107).

Lakoff and Johnson, drawing primarily on cognitive and experimental linguistics and cultural anthropology, but also citing psychological, neuroscientific, and cognitive science research on mental rotation, mental imagery, gestures, and sign language, have famously argued that our conceptual life begins in spatial and motor behaviors, and derives meaning from bodily experience (Johnson 2010; Lakoff 2012). Accordingly, the 'peculiar nature of our bodies shapes our very possibilities for conceptualization and categorization' (Lakoff and Johnson 1999, 19). For them, the specific mechanism that bridges embodied experience and conceptual thought is metaphor.

Metaphors are built on basic and recurring image-schemas such as front–back, in–out, near–far, pushing, pulling, supporting, balance, etc., and the basic image-schemas are built on bodily experience. Thus, for example, 'the concepts of *front* and *back* are body-based. They make sense only for beings with fronts and back. If all beings on this planet were uniform stationary spheres floating in some medium and perceiving equally in all directions, they would have no concepts of *front* and *back*' (1999, 34). Similar things can be said for *up–down*, and so forth. These basic image-schemas then shape, metaphorically, our abstract conceptual thought in relation to planning and decision-making, for example. Thus, justice is conceived in terms of balance; virtue is conceived in terms of being upright; and planning for the future is conceived in terms of up and forward—'What's up?' 'What's coming up this week?' The *in* and *out* image-schema, and the containment metaphor, for example, range over a vast set of metaphors and concepts, from the close to literal: 'John went out of the room', to the abstract: 'She finally came out of her depression', or 'I don't want to leave any relevant data out of my argument', to the logically abstract, such as the law of the excluded middle in logic (Johnson 1987). This view has been extended to explanations of mathematical concepts as well (Lakoff and Núñez 2000).

On the one hand, consistent with Goldman's appropriation of this theory for weak EC, at least in some respects, Lakoff and Johnson place emphasis on neural processes. 'An embodied concept is a neural structure that is part of, or makes use of the sensorimotor system of our brains. Much of conceptual inference is, therefore, sensorimotor inference' (Lakoff and Johnson 1999, 20; Johnson 2017, 147). Moreover, on at least one interpretation (Zlatev 2010), their position is not inconsistent with classic cognitivism.

On the other hand, however, consistent with more enactivist views of EC, it may not be, as Goldman suggests, 'fundamentally about representation'.

As we said in *Philosophy in the Flesh*, the only workable theory of representations is one in which a representation is a flexible pattern of organism-environment interactions, and not some inner mental entity that somehow gets hooked up with parts of the external world by a strange relation called 'reference'. We reject such classic notions of representation, along with the views of meaning and reference that are built on then. Representation is a term that we try carefully to avoid.   (Johnson and Lakoff 2002: 249–50)

Weak EC defines embodiment and frames the problem in a way that precludes any significant contribution from the body as such. It champions an internalist view that is not inconsistent with the bodiless brain-in-a-vat conception of cognition. Although it's not clear how the reduction of the body to a set of brain processes remains consistent with Goldman and Vignemont's earlier elimination of the brain as part of what embodiment means, this strategy really brings us back to a model that is not inconsistent with a classic computational (CC) model—that is, a model opposed by more radical forms of EC.

Weak EC nonetheless presents a clear challenge to other versions of EC, and Goldman and Vignemont (2009, 158) make the challenge specific by providing a list of questions that EC theorists should answer in order to clarify their claims, and to help those who are not quite convinced. Here is their list.

1. Which interpretation of embodiment is at stake?
2. Which sectors of cognition, or which cognitive tasks, are claimed to be embodied; and how fully does each task involve embodiment?
3. How does the empirical evidence support the specific embodiment claims under the selected interpretation(s)?
4. How do the proffered claims depart substantially from CC?

Since a number of versions of EC reject representationalist theories of cognition, we can add a fifth question, closely related to (4).

5. Do mental representations play any role in this version of EC?

We can use these questions to guide us as we continue to survey the landscape of EC, and we can start by asking them of Goldman and Vignemont's 'most promising' but minimal or weak conception of EC. (1) They suggest a minimal, neural interpretation of embodiment, framed in terms of sanitized brain processes. (2) Originally, they suggested it applies to some (but not all) aspects of social cognition, and not much else: 'It is doubtful, however, that such a thesis can be generalized' (2009, 158). Goldman (2012; 2014), however, does generalize it by extending the notion of B-formatted representations to other aspects of cognition, including linguistically mediated cognition. (3) The empirical evidence in the social cognition context is tied to MN research, and evidence that lesions that affect B-formatted representations 'interfere with action and emotion recognition' (Goldman and Vignemont 2009, 156). (4) This weak version of EC is relatively consistent with CC. As Alsmith and Vignemont put it, ideas found in weak EC 'are but a hair's breadth away from the (also familiar) neurocentric idea that cognitive states are exclusively realized in neural hardware' (2012, 5). (5) This version of EC is obviously and strongly representational.

2.2 Functionalist EC and the Extended Mind

In some regards the notion of an embodied functionalism is either trivial, since even functionalist systems need to be physically embodied, or slightly contradictory, since one hallmark of functionalism is a certain indifference to the physicality that sustains the system (body neutrality, multiple realizability). The idea that functionalists should take notions of embodiment seriously, however, can be found in some discussions of the extended mind hypothesis (Clark 2008a; Wheeler 2005; Rowlands 2006; 2010). I'll focus on Clark as the main proponent of this view. On the one hand, Clark argues for a step back towards the idea of weak EC in the sense that he considers factors associated with anatomical determination and embodied semantics to be 'trivial and uninteresting' rather than deeply 'special' (2008b, 38). On the other hand, he defends the notion that the body plays an important role as part of the extended mechanisms of cognition. In this regard, the physical body, as well as aspects of, or objects in the environment, can function as non-neural vehicles for cognitive processes, performing a function similar to the processes of neurons, the primary vehicles of cognition in the classic view. The body is part of an extended cognitive system that starts with the brain and includes body and environment. As he puts it, 'the larger systemic wholes, incorporating brains, bodies, the motion of sense organs, and (under some conditions) the information-bearing states of non-biological props and aids, may sometimes constitute the *mechanistic supervenience base* for mental states and processes' (2008b, 38).

This view is not to be confused with the idea that the (human) body offers certain determining constraints (sensory–motor contingencies) that make (human) experience unique, an idea associated with O'Regan and Noë's (2001) theory of enactive perception. Clark is not convinced that animals with very different bodies could not experience certain aspects of the spatial environment in exactly the same way. Different types of bodies can compute or process information differently but still produce the same experience. The important thing for Clark (citing as evidence experiments by Ballard et al. 1997) is that part of the computing mechanism can include the body or the environment. In accomplishing certain tasks, for example, we could store task-relevant information in our brain-based memory system and consult the information in that store; alternatively, we could leave the information in the environment where it already is and simply use our bodies to perceptually consult it when needed. In the latter case, consistent with Rob Wilson's (1994) notion of 'exploitative representation' and 'wide computing', the perceiving body is playing a certain computational role that under some circumstances could be done fully 'in the head'; the body does this sort of thing frequently, and in effect operates as an 'external' vehicle for cognition. As Clark (2008a) makes clear, this view of an embodied extension of cognition (he calls it 'simple embodiment' [Clark 1999]) is also consistent with a robust representationalism for higher cognitive processes, as well as with a minimal representationalism (involving action-oriented representations) for action (see Clark and Grush 1999; and *Chapter 5*).

One way to split the difference between those who would argue for a special and essential role for material embodiment and those who would give the body only a 'simple' functional role, is to suggest that embodiment especially matters for phenomenal consciousness, even if it doesn't for cognition. Functionally equivalent cognitive states supervening on processes in a human body may feel different or register differently in phenomenal experience in a non-human body.

Clark hesitates to accept this kind of division of labor, however. He argues that even for experience one should allow the possibility that the cognitive system will provide 'compensatory downstream adjustments' that would, so to speak, even out differences in the experiential aspects that accompany cognition (Clark 2008a). There seems to be no strong reason to think this is the case (Clark cites no evidence to support this view), however, or even to think that it should be the case (after all, why should it matter that a frog's consciousness have the same phenomenal feel as a human's consciousness?). And there is some evidence against it. Wearing prism goggles changes visual experience by altering the angle of perspective on the visual field. A set of prism goggles may shift the visual field to the right by 40 degrees, or may even invert the visual field. It was once thought that the visual system eventually corrects for this distortion, because the subject, who is initially disoriented, eventually starts to engage with the world and to act in it as if she were not wearing the goggles. The thought was that the visual system makes compensatory downstream adjustments to restore visual–motor experience to normal parameters. But this has been shown not to be the case (Linden et al. 1999). Subjects make important adjustments in motor control processes, but their visual experience remains what it is. Prism glasses change the normal visual system at a basic bodily level (that is, the normal workings of the physical eye, plus the prism glasses, are equivalent to a different eye structure). Body-schematic processes that may allow adjustment in motor behavior to cope with this different visual experience, however, do not make compensatory downstream adjustments that restore upright visual experience (for more on the curious effects of prism glasses in cases of hemispatial neglect, see Rode et al. 2015; Rossetti et al. 2015). Even if this suggests that Clark might be wrong about the idea of compensatory effects with respect to experience, restoring the compromise division of labor (functionalist cognition vs embodied consciousness) it was meant to challenge is hardly consistent with stronger versions of EC.

2.3 A Biological Model of EC

In contrast to weak EC which regards anatomy and bodily movement as unimportant, trivial factors for cognition, other theorists suggest that anatomy and movement are important contributors to the shaping of cognition prior to and subsequent to brain processing ('pre-processing' and 'post-processing', respectively) of information in the cognitive system (e.g., Chiel and Beer 1997; Shapiro 2004; Straus 1966; see Gallagher 2005a). Embodiment in this case means that extra-neural structural features of the body shape our cognitive experience. For example, the fact that we have two eyes, positioned as they are, makes binocular vision possible, and allows us to see the relative depth of things. Similar things can be said about the position of our ears and our ability to tell the direction of sound. As Shapiro puts it, 'the point is not simply [or trivially] that perceptual processes fit bodily structure. Perceptual processes *depend on and include* bodily structures' (2004, 190).

Our sensory experience also depends on the way our head and body move, as one can see in the case of motion parallax (Churchland, Ramachandran, and Sejnowski 1994; Shapiro 2004). Furthermore, our motor responses, rather than fully determined at brain-level, are mediated by the design of muscles and tendons, their degrees of flexibility, their geometric relationships to other muscles and joints, and their prior history of activation (Zajac 1993). In the human, much of this depends, in evolutionary terms, on the attainment of the upright posture and the bodily changes that follow from that (see section 9.2). Moreover, movement is not always centrally planned; it is based on a competitive system that requires what Clark terms 'soft assembly'. The nervous system learns 'to modulate parameters (such as stiffness [of limb or joint]) which will then *interact* with intrinsic bodily and environmental constraints so as to yield desired outcomes' (Clark 1997, 45).

Many of these insights are still cast in terms of information processing, and as such may be consistent with the general principles of classic computational cognitivism. As Shapiro notes: 'steps in a cognitive process that a traditionalist would attribute to symbol manipulation might, from the perspective of EC, emerge from the physical attributes of the body' (2007, 340). In addition, even if the body is doing some of the work, cognitivists could easily claim that pre-processing is in fact feeding the more central processing which might be thought to be more constitutive of cognition, just as post-processing is to some degree determined by instructions from the brain as central processor.

More holistic, proprioceptive and affective processes, however, may pose more of a challenge to the classic conception. There is long-standing empirical evidence that peripheral and affective processes have a profound effect on perception and thinking (e.g., Aranyosi 2013). For example, vibration-induced proprioceptive patterns that change the posture of the whole body are interpreted as changes in the perceived environment (Roll and Roll 1988, 162). Proprioceptive adjustments of the body schema can help to resolve perceptual conflicts (Harris 1965; Rock and Harris 1967). Experimental alterations of the postural schema lead to alterations in space perception and perceptual shifts in external vertical and horizontal planes (Bauermeister 1964; Wapner and Werner 1965). Likewise hormonal changes—changes in body chemistry—as well as visceral and musculoskeletal processes, can bias perception, memory, attention, and decision-making (Bechara et al. 1997; Damasio 1994; Gallagher 2005a; Shapiro 2004). The regulation of body chemistry is not autonomous from cognitive processes, and vice versa. 'Body regulation, survival, and mind are intimately interwoven' (Damasio 1994, 123).

For example, in a token act of cognition in the individual human, the brain does what it does in tandem with the body. When the bodily system is fatigued or hungry, which is something more than just a neural state, these conditions influence brain function; the body regulates the brain as much as the brain regulates the body. Parts of the brain, e.g., the hypothalamus, operate on homeostatic principles rather than anything that can be construed as representational principles. Homeostatic regulation happens via mutual (largely chemical) influences between parts of the endocrine system, and signals from the autonomic system. Low glucose levels (hypoglycemia, which is a biological condition not caused by the brain) may mean slower or weaker brain function, or some brain functions turning off, or at the extreme, brain death. In cases of hypoglycemia, perception is not modulated because the brain *represents* hunger and fatigue, but because the perceptual system (brain and body) is chemically (materially) affected by the actual hunger and fatigue. There are real physical connections here in the complex chemistry of the body–brain system in its coupling with the environment, and in that complex chemistry one factor often modulates another. My hunger may not affect my perception so much if a sexually attractive person walks into the room; although this has something to do with processes in the hypothalamus (as well as in the social world), it is not the result of a confused hypothalamic B-representation.

On this biological reading of EC, the classic computational/functionalist thought experiment of the brain in the vat completely fails. The claim that cognitive function and experience would be similar, or even the same as for a fully embodied subject, if the appropriate inputs were delivered to a disembodied brain in a vat, fails to take into consideration the contributions of physical processes in peripheral and autonomic systems. As pointed out by a number of theorists, to be able to replicate human experience, or anything similar to it, experimenters would have to replicate everything that the biological body delivers in terms of pre- and post-processing, hormonal and neurotransmitter chemistry, and affective life. This, as Damasio suggests, would require the creation of a body surrogate 'and thus confirm that "body-type inputs" are required for a normally minded brain after all' (1994, 228; also see Aranyosi 2013; Cosmelli and Thompson 2010 Gallagher 2005b).

2.4 Enactivist EC and Radical Embodiment

Enactivist views on embodied cognition build on the biological model of EC, emphasize the idea that perception is *for action*, and that this action-orientation shapes most cognitive processes. This approach often comes with strong calls to radically change our ways of thinking about the mind and about how to do cognitive science (e.g., Gallagher and Varela 2003; Hutto and Myin 2013; Thompson 2007; Thompson and Varela 2001; Varela, Thompson, and Rosch 1991). Thompson and Varela (2001) endorse Clark's (1999) three-point summary of the enactivist model:

1. Understanding the complex interplay of brain, body and world requires the tools and methods of nonlinear dynamical systems theory.
2. Traditional notions of representation and computation are inadequate.
3. Traditional decompositions of the cognitive system into inner functional subsystems or modules ('boxology') are misleading, and blind us to arguably better decompositions into dynamical systems that cut across the brain–body–world divisions (Thompson and Varela 2001, 418; also see Chemero 2009, 29).

As we noted in Chapter 1, enactivist approaches are similar to concepts of extended mind or distributed cognition in arguing that cognition is not entirely 'in the head', but, instead, distributed across brain, body, and environment. Dynamical systems theory can be used to explain the complexities of brain function but can also capture the dynamical coupling between body and environment. The brain, taken as a dynamical system, operates as it does because it is a system coupled to a larger dynamical system of brain–body–environment. In contrast to Clarke's functionalist view, enactivists claim that bodily processes shape and contribute to the constitution of consciousness and cognition in an irreducible and irreplaceable way.

Specifically, on the enactivist view, biological aspects of bodily life, including organismic and emotion regulation of the entire body, have a permeating effect on cognition, as do processes of sensorimotor coupling between organism and environment. An enactivist account of perception highlights the integration of a variety of bodily factors into perception. First, perception depends on sensory–motor contingencies, as emphasized by O'Regan and Noë (2001) and Noë (2004). This means that perception is a pragmatic, exploratory activity, mediated by movement or action and constrained by contingency relations between sensory and motor processes. One can think of this in terms of ecological psychology where one's perception of the environment includes information about one's own posture and movement, and one's posture and movement will determine how one experiences the environment. In terms of body-schematic processes, agentive control over movement, our capacities and skills for moving around the environment, and for reaching and grabbing things, introduces specific biases into what we perceive. We see things in terms of what we can do with them, and how we can reach and manipulate them.

In a fuller sense, however, embodiment involves more than sensori-motor processes. An account that would focus only on sensorimotor contingencies would be incomplete since it would neglect the relevance of affective aspects of embodiment. These include 'non-representational internal states' (Perner and Ogden 1988): not only factors that pertain to mood and emotion, but also bodily states such as hunger, fatigue, and pain, as well as a complex motivational dimension that animates body-world interaction (Stapleton 2013; Colombetti 2013). As noted above, biological (hormonal and chemical) processes having to do with homeo-stasis modulate body–environment coupling, and become part of the reciprocal causal relations that shape cognitive processes. Accordingly, embodiment as it relates to cognition is not just about anatomical struc-ture, sensory–motor contingencies, and action capabilities; it involves a complex ensemble of factors that govern cognition and conscious life (see *Chapter 8*).

Moreover, on the enactivist view, to fully understand cognition, one has to consider not only non-representational and unruly processes complicated by autonomic and endocrine responses, but also the effects of intersubjective interaction in social and institutional environments (Gallagher 2013a). In contrast to weak EC where social interaction is explained in terms of mirror neuron activations that simulate or represent the other person's mental states, enactivists invoke fully embodied dynamical interactions that rely on facial expression, posture, movement, gestures, and distinct forms of sensory–motor couplings (Gallagher 2001; 2005a; Thompson and Varela 2001). The importance of embodied intersubjective practices for social cognition is supported by developmental studies that suggest infants engage in such practices from birth. Mirror neurons, rather than enacting a simulation or simple mirroring of mental states, may contribute to or develop within 'primary intersubjective' processes (Trevarthen 1979), as the neural part of an enactive social perception of another's intentions or emotions, framed in terms of the perceiver's own response preparation (Gallagher 2007). Context and social environment, including normative factors, also contribute to 'secondary intersubjective' practices starting at 9–12 months of age (Trevarthen and Hubley 1978). In the intersubjective context, perception is often *for interaction* with others, where perception-guided interaction becomes a principle of social cognition and generates meaning in a process that goes beyond what any individual brain can accomplish (De Jaegher and Di Paolo 2007; De Jaegher, Di Paolo, and Gallagher, 2010; Gallagher 2009).

Accordingly, on the enactivist view, the body's influence on cognition is, at least, three dimensional, including the influence of sensory–motor contingencies, affective factors, and intersubjective processes. The enactivist view incorporates many features of what I've termed, in the previous section, biological EC. It also borrows from the notion of affordances found in ecological psychology (Gibson 1977). This is already implicit in the phenomenological background to the notion of sensory–motor contingencies. For example, one finds an implicit theory of affordances in the idea that perception is guided by what Husserl (1989) calls the 'I can' (i.e., the idea that I see objects in terms of what 'I can' do), or what Heidegger (1962) calls the 'ready-to-hand' (i.e., that my primary relation to the world is a practical one rather than one of passive observational or theoretical contemplation). These ideas were taken up by Merleau-Ponty in his embodied approach to perception, and directly influenced Gibson's conception of affordance. This pragmatic orientation towards the environment, which is not just physical, but also social and cultural, can also incorporate insights from Material

Engagement Theory (Malafouris 2013), which emphasizes the role of material artifacts, architecture, and social practices in shaping our minds. In these respects, the enactivist approach claims to draw on a wealth of resources to help explain cognition.

2.5 Getting Down on All 4Es

It is often thought that EC approaches, even if they differ among themselves, are united in their opposition to traditional versions of computationalism and representationalism, but this is clearly not the case (see Table 2.1). Indeed, disagreements within the EC camp are primarily disagreements about just these issues. But perhaps one important outcome of EC is that these debates have moved the issues about computationalism and representationalism front and center, even in the minds of those who have taken less-embodied approaches. Thus there have been recent wholesale investigations into the concept of representation

Table 2.1. Different theories of embodied cognition

Interpretation	Weak EC	Functionalist EC	Biological EC	Enactivist EC
Sectors of cognition	Multiple, including social and higher-order cognition	Perception/ action and higher-order cognition	Perception/ action	Perception/ action, social cognition
Empirical evidence	Neuroscience, linguistics, psychology	Experimental psychology, robotics, engineering	Biology, experimental psychology	Developmental psychology, neuroscience, empirical psychology
CC Consistent	Yes	Yes	Neutral	No
Representations?	Strong yes	Yes for AORs and 'representation hungry' processes	Weak	No

(e.g., Chemero 2000; 2009; Hutto 2011a, 2011b; Hutto and Myin 2013; Gallagher 2008a; Ramsey 2007), as well as careful and somewhat defensive explanations of what representation means in analytic philosophy of mind (e.g., Burge 2010; and see Crane 2009 for a similar analysis).

Especially for the biological-ecological-enactivist approaches, it seems incumbent to deliver on some promissory notes. Chemero (2009), for example, makes clear that it will be important to 'scale up' dynamical systems approaches from the analysis of action and perception to higher cognitive performance in what are considered to be 'representation-hungry' tasks (Clark and Toribio 1994). 'It is still an open-question how far beyond minimally cognitive behaviors radical embodied cognitive science can get' (Chemero 2009, 43). Accordingly, within EC one of the most important and interesting debates is that between functionalist and radical enactivist versions, the first appealing to representations and eschewing any essentialist view of the body, the second dismissing representations and insisting on the ineliminable nature of the body. One of the leading theoretical questions in this field is whether it's possible to integrate these views (see Menary 2007).

There are clearly substantive differences in theoretical approaches between weak EC, i.e., internalist approaches focusing on B-formatted representations in the brain, and externalist theories that include the full body in its dynamical gestalt-like relations with its physical, social and cultural environments. One might think that we could opt for a hybrid theory that combines a B-formatted explanation of how the brain works internally with the externalist, ecological, enactive, and extended conceptions that would allow for some integration of neural and extra-neural elements involved in cognition.

A number of irreconcilable differences, however, define a strong opposition between weak EC and enactivist proposals, and count against the possibility of such a productive integration. I'll consider two of them here. Let me first mention again the minor problem about weak EC's application of the reuse hypothesis to token cognitive events. Recall that weak EC is a two-part theory. It depends on the notion of B-formatted representations, and on the reuse hypothesis. If we take the reuse hypothesis as applying to evolutionary timescales, as originally intended by Anderson (2010)—or if we take it to apply also to developmental timescales, following Dehaene's (2004) 'neuronal recycling' hypothesis, which explains ontogenetic changes in the visual system (specifically in the 'visual word form area') when a person learns to read—it does not strictly apply to the elementary or integrative timescales of token neuronal activations or token cognitive acts as Goldman seems to suggest in some of his statements.[5] As I indicated, this may be a minor point of terminological divergence. Rather than denying the extension of this concept to token cases, however, I suggest that the first irreconcilable difference between weak EC and enactivism applies equally in regard to weak EC's appropriation of reuse for phylogenetic, ontogenetic, and token dimensions of cognition, in a way that undermines the strong internalism of weak EC.

On the evolutionary timescale the human brain and the human body evolve together. Through the course of evolution the body gained the upright posture, leading to a restructuring of its skull and jaw to allow larger brain development and speech, along with many other morphological changes involving hands, feet, etc. (see Chapter 9). On the timescale of evolution, reuse has everything to do with the body—including changes in morphological features, which are dismissed as trivial by weak EC (Goldman and Vignemont 2009, 154). Changes in brain function, including those that fall under the category of reuse, are at least partially driven by changes in body.

Not only the body, but also physical, social, and cultural environments are important factors both evolutionarily and developmentally for any understanding of neural reuse or neuronal recycling. Brain evolution does not happen *in vitro* or in a vat. The role of the cultural environment, relevant especially in developmental contexts, for example, remains unstated, but implicit even in Goldman's discussion of neural reuse as it applies to Pulvermüller's work in neural linguistics. Citing this as one of the best examples of neural reuse, as Goldman does, however, comes along with the obvious connections between language and culture. That is, if we think of the reuse hypothesis in these terms, important parts of the story, even those parts that involve neural plasticity (*via*

---

[5] See section 2.1. This is not to deny that evolutionary and developmental factors account for how our brains may be set up and how they function. The brain is set up by such factors of reuse, but it is not set up to 'reuse' a particular brain area or representation in any particular instance. For example, mirror neuron activation due to my observation of your action is not a reuse of my mirror neurons. My mirror neurons are, so to speak, already set up by phylogenetic or ontogenetic processes of exaptation to function the way they function.

association, and Hebbian learning) in individuals, involve cultural learning (Overmann 2016). Even if Pulvermüller is right,[6] it should be clear that action words like *pick* and *kick* will not activate cortical areas that involve hand and foot, respectively, if we are scanning French speakers, or speakers of Urdu.

The role of culture and context (including bodily and environmental factors), however, applies equally even in token cases of cognition. Naumann (2012), for example, suggests that motor simulations related to word processing in the context of a sentence are more specific than the meaning represented by the abstract verb outside of a sentence. For example, the simulation of 'Bill grasped the needle' will be different from 'Bill grasped the barbell', since the shape of the grasp itself (as well as one's posture, the effort that would be expended during such an action, etc.) would be different and would involve differences in motor activation. Importantly, the simulation will take shape not only if one knows what a barbell is, or what a needle is, but also to some significant extent depending on the history of one's use of such items, and one's skill level. One can certainly ask about the difference between a novice and an expert seamstress or weightlifter with respect to their neural attunement in precisely those areas that would be activated by the use of words like 'needle' and 'barbell'. Likewise, what we mean by 'needle' can differ from one context to another (a sewing needle, a compass needle, a hypodermic needle), and with respect to how we plan to use it—the reach and grasp will in each case be different due to very basic body-schematic and intentional factors. In any case, things like barbells and needles are not entities that find appropriate explanation in the evolutionary framework. If there is relevant semantic somatopic function in this regard, it's a matter of plasticity and cultural learning—which means it's a matter of *metaplasticity* where not only neurons undergo plastic changes, but bodily and cultural practices do too (Malafouris 2013 Overmann 2016).

---

[6] There is some evidence against this type of semantic somatotopy. Not all neuroimaging studies have found increased activity for action-verbs in the motor system (Bedny and Caramazza 2011); activations found in premotor areas reflect no necessary overlap or match of neural areas correlated with motor action and neural areas that activate for the language task (Willems, Hagoort, and Casasanto 2009); Postle et al. (2008) showed the same general activation in premotor cortex in response to action-verbs related to leg, arm, and hand, with no somatotopical differentiation, suggesting that such activation may simply be related to general language use (Bedny and Caramazza 2011). Language use, after all, always does involve motoric processes. For fuller discussion, see Naumann (2012).

Reuse applies not only to neurons and brain structures, but also to the transformation of semiotic resources in embodied interaction with the environment and with others (Goodwin 2013).

Accordingly, that we are led directly to consider the role of body and environment, including cultural context, through considerations about the notion of reuse means that one would have to back off any strong statement of weak EC such as we find in Goldman.

A second irreconcilable difference between weak EC and enactivism is that there seems to be no way to mesh the extra-neural roles of peripheral, homeostatic/autonomic, and ecological aspects of embodiment, or the physical, social, and cultural aspects of the environment, with the notion of sanitized neural B-representations. Facing up to just such factors, the more radical biological-enactivist theories force us to rethink the way the brain works. They suggest that the brain or, rather, the system as a whole—in which the brain in its interwoven relations with body and environment is attuned by evolutionary pressures and by the individual's personal (social and cultural) experiences—*responds to* the world rather than *represents* it. Specifically, it responds not by representing, but through a dynamical participation in a large range of messy adjustments and readjustments that involve internal homeostasis, external appropriation and accommodation, and larger sets of normative practices, all of which have their own structural features that enable specific perception–action loops, that in turn shape the structure and functioning of the nervous system. The enactivists suggest that not just the brain, not just the body with its different systems, not just the physical and social environment—but all of these together play important roles in cognition in ways that are irreducible to B-representations (see Chapter 8). All of these factors undermine the explanatory role of B-representations, and mess up the sanitized picture presented by weak embodied cognition.

Even if some neat détente between weak EC and the enactivist camp is unlikely, what about the possibility of integrating functionalist EC's extended mind idea with a non-functionalist enactivism? In some regard this possibility points us back to issues raised in the discussion of predictive coding (in section 1.5), and forward to issues that concern intentionality (in *Chapters* 3 and 4).

3

Pragmatic Resources for Enactive and Extended Minds

Enactivist and extended mind approaches to cognition have different roots. Enactivist approaches typically point to phenomenology and theoretical biology; extended mind approaches are more influenced by analytic philosophy of mind, computational models, and cognitive science more generally. Rarely noted, however, or sometimes only noted in passing, pragmatism is something of a forerunner of both of these approaches. Clear statements of both extended and enactivist conceptions of cognition can be found in Charles Sanders Pierce, John Dewey, Georg Herbert Mead, and other pragmatists. Although today enactivist and extended mind approaches disagree with each other on a number of issues, the fact that pragmatists could embrace both views suggests that there may be resources in pragmatism that can help to adjudicate some of the current debate and allow us to develop a more integrated perspective. I will also suggest that one can draw on the same resources to address some of the strong objections that have been leveled at enactivist and extended models of the mind. My aim is not to provide a full historical account of how pragmatism anticipates the more recent developments; rather, my aim is to put pragmatism to work on clarifying and integrating these approaches, and thereby resolving some objections that have been raised against them. I'll begin, however, with some brief indication of the pragmatic anticipation of enactivist and extended mind approaches.

3.1 Pragmatism and Enactive Perception

The origin of the concept of enactive perception, and more generally, enactive cognition is often indicated by pointing to the work of Francisco

Varela (e.g., Varela, Thompson, and Rosch 1991), and then back to its phenomenological roots in Husserl, Heidegger, and Merleau-Ponty. Husserl (1989) had developed the idea of the 'I can' as part of the structure of embodied perception. On his view, I perceive things in my environment in terms of what *I can* do with them. Heidegger (1962) went further towards a pragmatic view in suggesting that our primary way of being-in-the-world—our way of relating to various events and objects—is in the mode of the ready-to-hand (*Zuhanden*) attitude. In almost all everyday engagements, I understand the world in terms of pre-reflective pragmatic, action-oriented use, rather than in reflective terms of an intellectual or overly cognitive attitude of conceptual contempla-tion or scientific observation. Merleau-Ponty (2012), drawing on both Husserl and Heidegger, works this out in some detail in his analysis of perception, and focuses on the important role played by the embodied motor system. A number of theorists who help to develop an enactivist view of cognition were influenced by Merleau-Ponty's account—not only the neurobiologist Varela, but also the psychologist J. J. Gibson (1977), who developed the notion of affordances,[1] the philosopher Hubert Dreyfus (1992), both in his critique of classic cognitivism and in his emphasis on embodied practice, and the neuropsychologist Marc Jean-nerod, who attended Merleau-Ponty's lectures and later developed a distinction between semantic and pragmatic perception (Jeannerod 1994; 1997; also see Noë 2004; Gallagher 2005a; Thompson 2007).[2]

That the roots of enactivism are to be found in phenomenology is an uncontroversial claim; the enactivists explicitly acknowledge this. More-over, anyone familiar with the phenomenologists will clearly see that certain pragmatic aspects of phenomenological philosophy are the ones that lead forward to the development of the enactivist approach. For that reason it is surprising that until recently the philosophical tradition of

---

[1] Anthony Chemero (private correspondence) notes that Gibson distributed copies of Merleau-Ponty's *Phenomenology of Perception* to his students. For a sustained discussion of Gibson from a pragmatist perspective see F. T. Burke (2013); Chemero (2009); Heft (2001); and Rockwell (2005).

[2] I'm leaving out Jerome Bruner (1966), who offers a concept of early developing enactive (action-based) representation involving motor memory as in some way basic to development. Bruner draws directly from Piaget, and was influenced by Dewey (see his 1961, 'After John Dewey, What?'); he came into contact with the work of Merleau-Ponty in discussion groups in Oxford around 1970 (see Shotter 2001).

pragmatism has been hardly mentioned by the enactivists. With the exception of William James (and usually his *Principles of Psychology*) the pragmatists have been rarely cited. There is no mention of Peirce, Dewey, or Mead, for example, in Noë (2004), Thompson (2007), or Hutto and Myin (2013). Varela, Thompson, and Rosch (1991, 30–1) make one general and undeveloped reference to pragmatism, but without direct relevance to the enactivist aspects of this work.[3]

Notwithstanding this lack of acknowledgment for the pragmatists, however, it's very clear that one can find the central concepts of enactivism already discussed by Peirce, Dewey, and Mead. Peirce, for example, foreshadows the externalist turn that is so important for enactivism: 'just as we say that a body is in motion, and not that motion is in a body, we ought to say that we are in thought, and not that thoughts are in us' (Peirce, CP 5.289, n. 1). Dewey, in turn, argues for an understanding of perception starting 'not with a sensory stimulus, but with a sensori-motor coordination . . . it is the movement which is primary, and the sensation which is secondary, the movement of body, head and eye muscles determining the quality of what is experienced' (1896, 358–9). Here, sensory–motor contingencies, which play a most obvious role in Noë's (2004; O'Regan and Noë 2001; also see Di Paolo, Buhrmann, and Barandiaran 2017) version of enactivism, are given a primacy in perception.

Re-echoing this idea, and building on the insight found in his famous essay, 'The reflex arc concept in psychology', that one's active response defines the nature of what the organism takes as a stimulus, Dewey offers

---

[3] My intent is not to do an exhaustive survey in this regard, but I will note the following. In the recent volume of essays, *Enaction: Toward a New Paradigm for Cognitive Science*, Andreas Engel (2010; also see Engel et al. 2013) does highlight the relevance of the pragmatists, but only in a most general way, and with an indication that this relevance deserves 'further exploitation' (222). Di Paolo, Rohde, and De Jaegher (2010), in the same volume, make a passing reference to Dewey. Richard Menary (2011) and Pierre Steiner (2008; 2010) point out the affinity between Dewey's account of experience and recent developments in externalist accounts of cognition including extended mind and enactivist accounts of cognition. Mark Johnson (2008) celebrates Dewey and at one point equates Dewey's notion of transaction with enaction (274). Johnson (2017, in press at the same time as this book) pursues these connections in detail; Di Paolo, Buhrmann and Barandiaran (2017 also in press at the same time as this book), do cite Dewey and Mead in important ways. Again, however, Chemero (2009) gives the clearest most insightful account connecting the radical embodied approach, with which he associates enactivism, with the pragmatists.

a characterization of the role of the brain in cognition that comes close to embodied-enactivist views today.

The advance of physiology and the psychology associated with it have shown the connection of mental activity with that of the nervous system. Too often recognition of connection has stopped short at this point; the older dualism of soul and body has been replaced by that of the brain and the rest of the body. But in fact the nervous system is only a specialized mechanism for keeping all bodily activities working together. Instead of being isolated from them, as an organ of knowing from organs of motor response, it is the organ by which they interact responsively with one another. The brain is essentially an organ for effecting the reciprocal adjustment to each other of the stimuli received from the environment and responses directed upon it. Note that the adjusting is reciprocal; the brain not only enables organic activity to be brought to bear upon any object of the environment in response to a sensory stimulation, but this response also determines what the next stimulus will be.   (Dewey 1916, 336–7)

This is fully consistent, for example, with enactivist arguments that cognition is not just a matter of brain processes—the cognitive agent is more than a brain in a vat; rather, the brain is one part of a body in which dynamical regulation goes both ways, with the brain both biologically and functionally dependent on the rest of the body, which is in dynamical interaction with the environment (see, e.g., Cosmelli and Thompson 2010; Gallagher 2005b).

Part of what it means for the body to be dynamically interacting or, as Dewey would say, *transacting* with the environment is captured by George Herbert Mead in his characterization of the reachable peripersonal space around the body, or what he called the 'manipulatory area'. He suggested, very much in the spirit of enactivism, that what is present in perception is not a copy (or representation) of the perceived, but 'the readiness to grasp' what is seen (1938, 103). Accordingly, the perception of objects outside of the manipulatory area is always relative to 'the readiness of the organism to act toward them as they will be if they come within the manipulatory area . . . We see the objects as we will handle them . . . We are only "conscious of" that in the perceptual world which suggests confirmation, direct or indirect, in fulfilled manipulation' (1938, 104–5; see section 9.5 for more on the manipulatory area).

Just as concepts like the manipulatory area, response-dependent stimulation, the contingent nature of sensory–motor coordination, and Peircean externalism prefigure related concepts in recent enactivism, other pragmatist concepts anticipate recent work on the extended mind.

3.2 Pragmatism and the Extended Mind

If extended mind theorists are somewhat better at acknowledging a foreshadowing in the pragmatists, this only goes so far. Although the classic paper by Clark and Chalmers (1998) that launched the discussion of extended mind makes no mention of the pragmatists, Clark's (2008a) book, *Supersizing the Mind*, begins with an invocation from Dewey.

Hands and feet, apparatus and appliances of all kinds are as much a part of it [thinking] as changes in the brain. Since these physical operations (including the cerebral events) and equipments are a part of thinking, thinking is mental, not because of a peculiar stuff which enters into it or of peculiar non-natural activities which constitute it, but because of what physical acts and appliances do: the distinctive purpose for which they are employed and the distinctive results which they accomplish.   (Dewey 1916, 8–9)

But this beginning is the end of it—there is no further discussion of Dewey or other pragmatists in the book.[4] Dewey's quote foreshadows much of what Clark wants to say, however. Richard Menary (2007) is perhaps the one figure closely associated with the extended mind approach who does understand its connection with pragmatism. Indeed, in his book, *Cognitive Integration*, he appeals to Dewey's notion of organism–environment transactions to work out a characterization of how embodied cognition incorporates the environment. I'll return to his analysis below. Menary also points to Peirce's 'continuity principle', which requires that there be no deep metaphysical discontinuity between the mind and the world, as an important source for understanding a neutral ground between internalist and externalist conceptions of representation (2007, 129). Indeed, I think it's quite clear that Peirce anticipates what was to become the extended mind.

A psychologist cuts out a lobe of my brain (*nihil animale a me alienum puto*) and then, when I find I cannot express myself, he says, 'You see, your faculty of language was localized in that lobe.' No doubt it was; and so, if he had filched my inkstand, I should not have been able to continue my discussion until I had got another. Yea, the very thoughts would not come to me. So my faculty of discussion is equally localized in my inkstand.   (Peirce, CP 7.366)

---

[4] One has the impression that this invocation, which precedes the foreword by Chalmers, is an afterthought motivated by Pierre Steiner calling Clark's attention to Dewey (Clark 2008a, xviii; see Steiner 2008; 2010). Also see Claudio Paolucci (2011) for the connection between extended mind and Pierce's semiotics.

It is a short distance from the inkstand to Clark and Chalmers' example of Otto's notebook, which Otto uses to keep and keep track of his memories. Peirce anticipates something similar. 'In my opinion it is much more true that the thoughts of a living writer are in any printed copy of his book than they are in his brain' (Peirce, CP 7.364).

Indeed, Peirce's notion that artifacts can play a cognitive role suggests an extension of the extended mind hypothesis into what Lambros Malafouris (2013, 9) calls 'material engagement theory',[5] and even further to include social practices and institutions, such as the institution of science (see Gallagher 2013a; Merritt and Varga 2013). For Peirce, 'it is no figure of speech to say that the alembics and cucurbits of the chemist are instruments of thought, or logical machines' (1887, 168). The manipulation of artifacts such as chemical flasks and tubing evokes a very specific way of thinking in the chemist. In this regard, 'thought is not just expressed in work, it is executed in work'.[6] For Peirce, as Aydin (2013, 16) explains, 'the mind has an artifactual character'.

Although Karl Popper is not usually considered a pragmatist in the classic sense, he was very much influenced by just these Peircean ideas, as Skagestad (1993; 1999) and Aydin (2013) suggest, and this is clearly reflected in a number of his statements, which may be considered an extension of Peirce. For example, Popper suggests that some cognition is exo- (but not necessarily extra-) somatic.

Yet the kind of exosomatic evolution which interests me here is this: instead of growing better memories and brains, we grow paper, pens, pencils, typewriters, dictaphones, the printing press, and libraries . . . The latest development (used mainly in support of our argumentative abilities) is the growth of computers.
(Popper 1972, 238–9; also see 225, n. 39)

Dewey's contention that the mind involves more than 'armchair' cognition follows directly from Peirce's artifactual externalism since not only

---

[5] Surprisingly Malafouris 2013 doesn't cite Peirce in this regard, nor does he mention Dewey or Mead.
[6] Peirce, cited in David Kirsh (2005, 157). Kirsh explains: 'C.S. Peirce, in his prescient way, was fond of saying that a chemist as much thinks with test tube and beaker as with his brain. His insight was that the activity of manipulating tools—in Peirce's case, manipulating representation rich tools and structures such as measuring devices, controllable flames, the lines in diagrams, written words—this activity is part of the overall process of thought. There is not the inner component, the true locus of thought, and its outer expression. The outer activity is a constituent of the thought process, though for Peirce it had to be continually re-interpreted to be meaningful.'

the body but apparatus and appliances of all kinds are involved, as much as the brain is. F. Thomas Burke (2014) points out that both Dewey and Mead, in the pre-computational age, promoted a more Darwinian conception of functionalism. Agents are inclined to use whatever is available to solve survival problems, and this extends to 'apparatus and appliances of all kinds'. The point is not to compute solutions on such instruments, but to incorporate them into the extended phenotype (Dawkins 1982), an idea that may be more consistent with Kim Sterelny's niche construction model of evolution, which emphasizes active agency in constructing an adaptive fit between agent and world (Sterelny 2010), than with Clark's functionalism. In this respect, the notion of reuse discussed in Chapter 2 should be extended via the concept of metaplasticity (Malafouris 2013) to the realm of cultural practices—we reuse not only our neurons for novel applications, but also our appliances.

3.3 Dewey's Notion of Situation

Turning from these historical connections, my focus in this section will be on Dewey's notion of situation. This concept will provide a productive way to motivate a rapprochement between enactivist and extended mind theories in section 3.4.

For Dewey's understanding of cognition, the unit of explanation is not the biological individual, the body by itself, or the brain, but the organism–environment. Organism and environment are not two self-sufficient or easily distinguishable items. Rather, they are always found together in a dynamical transactional relation.[7] They are, in effect, coupled in a way such that to pull them apart is to destroy them, or to treat them as theoretical abstractions. An organism never exists (and can never exist) apart from some environment; an environment is what it is only in conjunction with a particular organism that defines it. 'In actual experience, there is never any such isolated singular object or event; an object or event is always a special part, phase, or aspect, of an environing experienced world—a situation' (Dewey 1938a, 67). Although 'organism' seems a very biological term, by characterizing it in relation to the environment in this way Dewey's concept is very much akin to the notion of the lived

---

[7] For Dewey's anticipation of dynamical systems approaches, see Rockwell (2005).

body (*Leib*) as found in phenomenology and as distinguished from the objective body (*Körper*). Neither the organism nor the environment should be taken in strictly objective terms precisely because they are co-relational, defined relative to each other.

> The statement that individuals live in a world means, in the concrete, that they live in a series of situations. The meaning of the word 'in' is different from its meaning when it is said that pennies are 'in' a pocket or paint is 'in' a can. It means ... that interaction is going on between individuals and objects and other persons. The conceptions of situation and of interaction are inseparable from each other. (Dewey 1938b, 43)

The specific ways in which the coordinated coupling of organism–environment gets established is tied to how as a co-relational system it can successfully work for purposes of survival. Dewey's concept of situation arises when the coupling of the organism–environment becomes problematic or starts to break down. To the extent that the organism–environment is considered a self-organizing system, what some enactivists, following Varela, would call an 'autopoietic' system, even when functioning well it is in a precarious situation (see, e.g., Di Paolo, Buhrmann, and Barandiaran 2017, 236). When it starts to go wrong we have what Dewey calls a problematic situation and it calls for a kind of re-pairing, a reestablishment of a workable coupling. These are ongoing processes that give rise to experience. Cognition, in such cases, is a form of inquiry, understood as a hands-on practical activity through which we transform the problematic situation into one that is less confused and more comprehensible, and where ideas for successful action start to emerge. An idea is not primarily an intellectual entity in the head, but 'an organic anticipation of what will happen when certain operations are executed under and with respect to observed conditions' (Dewey 1938a, 109). In this regard, Dewey was influenced by Peirce's view that in coping with a problematic situation, we use physical tools as well as ideas to physically reshape the environment. This includes linguistic tools, which in communicative contexts may be used to reshape the dynamics of the situation. For Dewey, ideas, as well as gestures and speech acts, are themselves tools for this kind of interaction.

The important thing to note in Dewey's concept of situation is that the situation is not equivalent to the environment. That is, it is not that the organism is placed in a situation. Rather the situation is constituted by organism–environment, which means that the situation already includes the agent or experiencing subject. In this regard, for example, if I am in a problematic situation, I cannot strictly point to the situation because my pointing is part of the situation. I cannot speak of it as some kind of objective set of factors because my speaking is part of it. My movement is a movement of the situation. Accordingly, the trick to solving a problematic situation is not simply to rearrange objects in the environment, but to rearrange oneself as well—to make adjustments to one's own behaviors. Indeed, any adjustment one makes to objects, artifacts, tools, practices, social relations, or institutions is equally an adjustment of oneself.[8]

Another important thing to note about this concept of situation is that, for Dewey, it is almost always social. That is, for the human agent the environment is never just the physical environment; it is physical and social. Even if there are no others present in a particular environment, in a literal or objective sense, it still involves social dimensions because it is coupled to a social organism (i.e., the agent). Likewise, as we attempt to resolve a problematic situation, our action involves a social dimension even if we are going it alone. This idea is taken over and made clear by Mead.

[I]t is not necessary that we should talk to another to have these ideas. We can talk to ourselves, and this we do in the inner forum of what we call thought. We are in possession of selves just insofar as we can and do take the attitudes of others toward ourselves and respond to those attitudes . . . We assume the generalized attitude of the group, in the censor that stands at the door of our imagery and inner conversations, and in the affirmation of the laws and axioms of the universe of discourse . . . Our thinking is an inner conversation in which we may be taking the roles of specific acquaintances over against ourselves, but usually it is with what I have termed the 'generalized other' that we converse, and so attain to the levels of abstract thinking, and that impersonality, that so-called objectivity that we cherish.   (Mead 1964, 287–8)

Thus, for Mead, one's self and one's mind arise in human behavior in a way that is shot through with sociality. As Burke (2014) points out, the pragmatists are espousing a form of social externalism. This means what counts as important in any situation will depend on how the living

---

[8] The notion of *active inference* in predictive coding doesn't really come close to this complex articulation of organism–environment in coupled or mutual adjustment, not only because it is characterized as a form of inference, but because it's pictured simply as the organism moving to gain information about the external environment.

organisms are dynamically coupled to each other and to their environments. What counts as an object, for example, depends on what it *affords*, to use Gibson's term. An affordance, however, is defined, not objectively, but always relative to the animal—to the kind of body one has. A chair affords sitting (or solving a problematic situation) only if the organism has bendable joints. Various affordances are also modified in some way by who else may be around. A chair is less of an affordance if someone else is already sitting in it. A heavy object may afford lifting, and that may resolve the problematic situation, but only if someone else is around to help lift it. My action, or our conjoint action, or a collective action can define what a particular object means in relation to the situation. 'Objects exist in nature as patterns of our actions' (Mead 1964, 289).

This is clearly consistent with an enactivist viewpoint; we enact the meaning of the world through our individual and joint actions. It is also clearly consistent with an extended mind concept. Otto's notebook, in Clark and Chalmers' (1998) famous example, affords him the ability to resolve a problematic situation. Other people can and often do serve the same function, and in larger ways, Mead's notion of the generalized other can act as an extended archive of knowledge. This indeed leads to the notion of a socially extended mind where we can dynamically engage with complex social institutions and social practices to accomplish certain cognitive tasks or to solve problems (Gallagher 2013a).

3.4 Rapprochement

As represented in the common refrain that takes embodied, embedded, enactive, and extended cognition as a unitary '4E' alternative to classic, computational, cerebral, cognitivism, enactivist approaches are often associated with the extended mind hypothesis. Yet there are important differences between enactivist and extended models, and as we saw in *Chapter 2*, specific differences about how essential the notion of embodiment is for understanding cognition. Enactivists argue against the functionalism of extended mind theorists who discount any special role of the living body in cognition, given that one may be able to substitute prosthetic parts to take over or augment bodily functions (see, e.g., Thompson and Stapleton 2009). A related disagreement concerns the role of representation in action-oriented perception and basic cognition (see *Chapter 5*), or the role of higher-order representations in transforming processes that are specific to bodily action (e.g., Clark 2008a). Whether such differences will continue to be pivots of an uneasy détente, or whether one could work out an enactivist version of extended mind might find some clarification by turning to the pragmatists, who not only express enactivist leanings, but also embrace the notion of an extended mind.

In many regards much depends on how we understand the coupling relation between organism–environment. The fact that most extended mind proponents adopt a functionalist framework, which includes representational mechanisms that discount the role of the body, does not mean that this is the only way to understand the extended mind. If we follow Clark, then we have to accept that higher-order representations, which 'float free of the full spectrum of fine sensorimotor detail' (2008, 179), accomplish the coupling at stake. Internal representations sort out differences in input signals that may be due to bodily differences. So animals (or robots) with different bodies may, in principle, experience the same world as long as a certain set of representations (apparently running different algorithms in these respective cases) filter or properly adjust, for example, visual input that may be different because of different eye structure. Differences are ironed out at the representational level, in which case the same shape, structure, or design of the body is not so important. In contrast, if we follow Thompson and Varela's (2001) notion of radical enactive embodiment, the body makes all the difference and it reaches into the agent's experience. That is, as the theoretical biologists (from von Uexküll to Maturana and Varela) tell us, each species of animal enacts a different world (see Chemero 2009, 185ff. for discussion). What the frog perceives is quite different from what the human perceives, primarily because the frog has a different body (which includes different eye structure and a very different brain), which defines different affordances.

Can a pragmatist like Dewey adjudicate on this issue? Notions like organism–environment and situation, as defined by Dewey, suggest that one can have a theory of extended mind that is based on enactivist principles rather than functionalist principles. The life-worlds of frogs, robots, and humans will differ insofar as they are constituted by different types of organism–environment transactions. Pragmatically speaking it would make no evolutionary sense to think that frogs, robots, and humans would need to inhabit the same meaningful perceptual world rather than an organism-relative world. Organism and environment must be thought together in a dynamical relation, so that if differences or adjustments in organism are made, one finds correlative adjustments and differences in the experienced environment. Accordingly the animal enacts an ecological-cognitive niche appropriate to its embodied needs; the organism defines the manipulatory area of its reach and therefore the practical valence of things in its surrounding world. For the animal, in any case, a change in its neural representations will not change the very physical fact of how far its limb or (in the case of the frog) its tongue reaches into the environment. Changes in neural representations (if there be such things) will normally reflect the parameters of the shape and structure of the body, and plastic changes in the brain will occur only in correlation to bodily changes and what bodily structure allows. This, at least, is a matter of pragmatic (and evolutionary) principle. This may be different for non-enactive (non-Brooksian) robots where representations are the rule. In the case of cyborg existence it may depend on whether the principles of operation follow biological plasticity (like our human operating systems) or computationally rigid processing. If, indeed, unrealistically, executive control were (or became) for some reason computationally rigid, either biological plasticity in some other part of the system will accommodate the difference, or the system will likely stop working, or will work in a pathological way. One way or another, however, the organism will be doing important work.[9]

In no way, however, does a substitution of enactivist principles for functionalist principles rule out the concept of extended mind. Rather, it simply reinforces one of the main points behind both approaches, namely that we need to think of the mind differently from the traditional internalist models. As extended and enactive, the mind is *situated* in the way that Dewey defines this notion. The situation includes not just our notebooks, computers, and other cognitive technologies, and not just the social and cultural practices and institutions that help us solve a variety of cognitive problems, it also includes *us*. We are *in the world* in a way that is not reducible to occupying an objective position in the geography of surrounding space, and in a way such that the world is irreducible to an abstraction of itself represented in one's brain. We, as minded beings, are definitively 'out there', dynamically coupled to artifacts, tools,

---

[9] See Menary (2013) for more on neural and phenotypic plasticity.

technologies, social practices, and institutions that extend our cognitive processes. Enactivist and extended mind conceptions are, or at least should be, of one mind in this regard.

3.5 Responding to Objections

Can these considerations about the pragmatist precursors of enactive-extended cognition provide a response to the current criticism of such approaches? Pragmatism reinforces in many ways the enactivist-extended model, and champions an integrative approach that follows along the lines of proposals made by theorists like Menary (2007). Menary, who is much influenced by pragmatism, proposes his own integrationist responses to objections raised against the extended mind (and by implication, the enactivist) approach to cognition.

Consider again the coupling-constitution objection (Adams and Aizawa 2008). The objection is that extended mind proposals confuse causal relations with constitutive relations. Adams and Aizawa characterize the position they criticize as follows: 'If a cognitive agent causally interacts with some object in the external world in some "important" way—if that agent is coupled to an object—then that agent's cognitive processing is constituted by processes extending into that object' (Adams and Aizawa 2010, 582). Menary (2010a) rightly replies that this characterization of extended mind assumes a pre-formed cognitive agent, fitted out with internal mental representations, causally interacting with an external world that is supposedly independent of them. Then the problem becomes one of explaining how that agent can incorporate elements of the environment into its own cognitive apparatus. The pragmatist would ask why one should assume that agents are cognitively independent of, or merely in a causal relation to, their environment. For the pragmatist, the organism and environment are not two things that are merely causally related to each other, but are mutually constituted in this relation—organism–environment (as explained in section 3.4). The organism is not a cognitive agent before coupling to an environment; the environment is an essential, constitutive, element in making the organism what it is. Specifically, the organism's cognitive capacities are transformed by the way it is coupled with (transacts with, or manipulates) structures available in the environment.

Adams and Aizawa's idea that the cognitive agent is pre-formed independently of the environment is tied to their view that all cognition is in the brain. Unless one accepts a form of identity theory, however, neural processing is itself a causal factor. This does not rule out the idea that it could also be constitutive, since, as suggested in section 1.3, causal factors may be constitutive and not *merely* causal. The question then is what makes neural processes (or any factor) constitutive? Menary (2010a) suggests that Adams and Aizawa fail to provide a way to distinguish merely causal from constitutional relations.

I think there are three things to say in this regard. First, Adams and Aizawa do have a theory of what distinguishes mental from non-mental phenomena, namely non-derived intentionality. In that sense they point to an answer about what makes something constitutive of mind, even if they don't provide a general principle about what distinguishes the merely causal from the constitutive. Second, however, whether one should think of non-derived intentionality as something that is reducible to brain processes is a separate question. Brains, as noted above, do what they do only by being integrated in the system of brain–body–environment, and only in their dynamical, non-linear transactions with bodily and environmental processes.[10] In this regard there is no in-principle reason to think of cognition as belonging to anything less than the system as a dynamical whole. Third, even if non-derived intentionality were a mark of the mental, and even if we could agree on what non-derived intentionality is, it's not clear that there is only *one* mark of the mental rather than a pattern of elemental marks that constitute the mind.

What is non-derived intentionality? And is it *the* mark of the mental, or only one, non-necessary aspect of the mental? One can raise such questions because, as I'll make clear in the next chapter, the notion of intentionality is not completely settled. Some mental phenomena may be non-intentional, e.g., certain affective states (Husserl 1982a, §36; Searle 1992). Tim Crane (1998), for example, points out that the experience of pain is a mental experience, but is not necessarily intentional. As Shapiro (2009, 268) notes, the notion of original content remains ambiguous. Accordingly, there are debates about what is derived versus non-derived

---

[10] Chemero (2009) argues that the presence of just such non-linear relations, or, as Orestis Palermos (2014; 2012, 58ff.) argues, the continuous mutual interactions which entail such relations, may count as an objective criterion of constitution.

or original intentionality. Adams and Aizawa would argue that something like beliefs and other propositional attitudes are characterized by non-derived intentionality; but pragmatists and neo-pragmatists would argue that the intentionality of propositional attitudes is itself derived from a more original form of embodied intentionality, what phenomenologists like Husserl and Merleau-Ponty call operative or 'motor intentionality' (see section 4.4). Robert Brandom makes this point very clearly with reference to classic pragmatism.

A founding idea of pragmatism is that the most fundamental kind of intentionality (in the sense of directedness towards objects) is the *practical* involvement with objects exhibited by a sentient creature dealing skillfully with its world.
(2008, 178)

Brandom, as a neo-pragmatist, pictures this intentionality as more basic than propositional-based '*semantic* intentionality'. It involves feedback-governed processes that extend across body and environment, and which exhibit 'a complexity [that] cannot in principle be specified without reference to the changes in the world that are both produced by the system's responses and responded to . . . [Such practices] are "thick," in the sense of essentially involving objects, events, and worldly states of affairs. Bits of the world are *incorporated* in such practices' (178). On this view, non-derived intentionality may not be what Adams and Aizawa think it is.

One can also ask whether intentionality, whether derived or non-derived, is necessarily the only mark of the mental. If one carefully considers such phenomena as emotions and self-experience, one can argue that these phenomena, and more generally the mind itself, are really constituted by a pattern of factors, no one of which is necessary, but some number of which are sufficient for that constitution (Gallagher 2013b). Emotion, for example, can be characterized as involving the following elements: autonomic processes (e.g., James 1884), action and action-tendencies (Frijda 1986); overt expressions; phenomenal feeling; cognitive aspects such as attitudes, shifts of attention, and changes to perception; and intentionality (Goldie 2000). Is any one of these the unique mark of emotion? Newen, Welpinghus, and Jukel (2015) argue that not every emotion has a distinct autonomic pattern, and different emotions need not have different autonomic patterns (Prinz 2004); furthermore, some emotions, e.g., happiness, may not include action tendencies; some may not include expressive features; and in some, albeit rare, cases, typical physiological, expressive, and psychological aspects may be present without the phenomenal aspect (e.g., in those disposed to repress fear [Sparks, Pellechia, and Irvine 1999]). Indeed, any particular feature, including psychological and intentional features, may or may not be present, and yet the presence of a variable number of these features would be sufficient to constitute a particular emotion. In that case, a pattern of marks rather than one unique mark may delineate mental from non-mental phenomena.

Similar considerations apply to the concept of self where we may find a plurality of factors organized in typical patterns that include embodied, minimal experiential, affective, intersubjective, psychological/cognitive, and/or narrative elements (Gallagher 2013b). James (1890) discussed *extended* aspects of self, suggesting that what we call self may include physical pieces of property, such as clothes, homes, and various things that we own, since we identify ourselves with our stuff and perhaps with the cognitive technologies we use, or the cognitive institutions we work within.

One could argue that more generally this same pattern theory applies to the mind itself. The mind (or the mental) is constituted by a pattern of aspects or elements not all of which are necessary in every case, but some of which are constitutionally sufficient. This puts pressure on the idea that there is one unique mark of the mental. To complete the pragmatist picture in this regard, let me add that emotion, self, and more generally what we call mind constitutionally involve *situational* aspects. For example, Dewey, in his early essays on a theory of emotion (1894; 1895), not only emphasized the action-oriented aspect of emotion, but also pointed out that emotions are not reducible to a set of bodily states since the body is always coupled to an environment, and always includes situational aspects. In regard to the self, these are aspects that play some (major or minor) role in shaping who we are. They may include the kind of family structure and environment where we grew up; cultural and normative practices that define our way of thinking and living, and so on. Even in defining something like belief, we should not think that it is reducible to functional states of the brain, since belief may be constituted in terms of dispositions or action-tendencies that vary across different situations.

In this chapter I have shown that many of the insights of enactivist and extended mind approaches to cognition were foreshadowed in pragmatists such as Peirce, Dewey, and Mead. This is more than an interesting historical fact, however. The work of the pragmatists fleshes out the various embodied and situated accounts of cognition in ways that suggest that enactivist and extended mind versions are not necessarily in conflict. I've argued that Dewey's notions of situation and organism–environment may offer a way to develop a theory of the extended mind that is based on enactivist rather than functionalist principles. Furthermore, this pragmatist-enactivist version of extended cognition can better respond to objections raised by critics who actually share some of the functionalist views of the original extended mind hypothesis. Specifically, a pragmatist view would argue that non-derived intentionality is not reducible to either physical or functional processes in the brain, but that it is better understood as a more embodied form of transaction with the environment. Non-derived intentionality, as a basic motor intentionality, *is* the action-oriented coupling of organism–environment. Furthermore, even on this notion of intentionality, neither non-derived nor derived intentionality is the sole mark of the mental. As pragmatists like Dewey demonstrate, intentionality is only one possible element of a pattern that constitutes the mind.

4

Enactive Intentionality

As indicated in *Chapter 3*, one of the central and most contested issues in philosophy of mind concerns the nature of intentionality. In some cases intentionality is simply reduced to the notion of representation; in some cases, in what is claimed to be its original or non-derived form, it is defined as the mark of the mental. The concept of intentionality, however, is a complicated one, with a long history. Both the phenomenological and the analytic traditions can trace their views back to Brentano's definition of intentionality as a starting point. Brentano, in turn, took his orientation from medieval sources.

> Every mental phenomenon is characterized by what the Scholastics of the Middle Ages called the intentional (or mental) inexistence of an object, and what we might call, though not wholly unambiguously, reference to a content, direction toward an object (which is not to be understood here as meaning a thing), or immanent objectivity. Every mental phenomenon includes something as object within itself . . . (Brentano 2008, 88)

In this regard, Brentano understood intentionality to be the distinguishing mark that differentiated the mental from the physical. Intentionality is the mark of the mental, and Brentano understood the mental to include psychological acts, their content, and the relation between them.

In this chapter I explore several conceptions of intentionality and sketch out some arguments that will take on more structure in later chapters. I argue that (1) although both enactivist and extended mind approaches champion a non-Cartesian, non-internalist conception of mind, we only start to see what this conception of mind is when we adopt an enactivist conception of intentionality; (2) only by adopting this model of intentionality will the proponents of the extended mind hypothesis be able to fend off those critics who insist on defining the 'mark of the mental' in terms of non-derivative (narrow or internal) content (e.g., Adams and Aizawa 2001; 2009); and (3) any account of intentionality will be closely tied to a number of contentious issues in the area of social cognition.

4.1 Intentionality in Mind and Action

The Brentanian view, or what John Haugeland (1990) called a neo-Cartesian concept of intentionality, has been recently defended by Terry Horgan and Uriah Kriegel; they refer to it as a 'traditional, strongly internalist, broadly Cartesian picture of the mind' (2008, 353). On this view the mind is in some way discontinuous with everything around it, but at the same time, naturalistically continuous with the brain. Horgan and Kriegel (2008) summarize this internalist view in six propositions:

1. The mind exhibits intentionality in virtue of its nature as phenomenal consciousness (intrinsic phenomenal intentionality).
2. Intentional content is narrow—i.e., internal, and could be instantiated in a brain in a vat, reflecting the fact that prototypical mental states have strict neural correlates.
3. Intentionality is subjective—access is given only to the experiencing subject.
4. Intentionality applies to both sensory and cognitive states.
5. Intentionality is non-derivative.
6. Intentionality is the mark of the mental.

This is clearly a view that locates intentionality in the head, limits it to traditionally defined internal mental states, and identifies non-derived intentionality as the mark of the mental (Horgan and Kriegel 2008; also Horgan and Tienson 2002).

The concept of non-derived intentionality (or non-derived content), however, is not on settled ground. There are disagreements about what is or is not intentional on the neo-Cartesian picture. Husserl (1982a, §36) and Searle (1992) have argued that not all mental experiences are intentional. The experience of pain, for example, is a mental experience, but is not necessarily intentional (Crane 1998). Moreover, as Shapiro (2009, 268) notes, 'there is today no received theory of how original content comes to be in the first place'.

Furthermore, in regard to the internalist argument against the extended mind hypothesis the question about what constitutes the mark of the mental, or what constitutes non-derived intentionality, is not a question that can be answered without begging the question of whether some cognitive processes are extended. That is, as suggested in *Chapter 3*, it seems possible that there could be a theory of non-derived intentionality consistent with the very different conception of the mind suggested by enactivist and extended mind accounts of cognition.

Tellingly, the discussion of intentionality goes beyond a narrow discussion of mental state intentionality in both phenomenology and analytic philosophy of mind. In phenomenology, Husserl introduced the concept of operative (*fungierende*) intentionality in contrast to act intentionality. The latter includes the intentionality of an act of perception, or remembering or imaging, etc. The former attempts to capture the fact that the experiencing agent is intentionally engaged with the world through actions and projects that are not reducible to simple internal mental states, but involve what Husserl refers to as bodily intentionality (1977, §39). Merleau-Ponty (2012) takes up the analysis of intentionality just at this point. Bodily (motoric) actions are intentional, not only in the sense that they are willed, but also in the sense that they are directed at some goal or project. Moreover, this intentionality of action is something that can be perceived by others.

Likewise, in analytic philosophy of mind, we find discussions of agent intentionality that go beyond the notion of mental state intentionality. Haugeland (1990), for example, contrasts the neo-Cartesian concept of intentionality to neo-behaviorist and neo-pragmatist conceptions. Both the neo-behaviorist and the neo-pragmatist conceptions of intentionality share a common feature: an externalist view that intentionality is something that we can discern in behavior, and is not necessarily hidden away inside the head. In this respect they seem to be good candidates for the kind of intentionality needed to support the enactivist and extended concepts of mind.

4.2 Neo-behaviorism and Theory of Mind

The neo-behaviorist view is exemplified in Dennett's intentional stance, which he explains in terms of observing an agent engaged in rational behavior, and on that basis ascribing intentionality, i.e., treating the agent as someone 'who harbors beliefs and desires and other mental states that exhibit intentionality or "aboutness", and whose actions can be explained (or predicted) on the basis of the content of these states' (1991, 76).[1] Note two things in this account: first, this conception of an intentional agent (or system) starts with considerations about the agent's behavior, but almost immediately leads us back to questions about mental state intentionality. Second, this conception of intentionality raises questions about social cognition or theory of mind (ToM)—that is, about attributing mental states to the other person. Phillip Pettit provides a similar explanation: intentional agents 'are agents that engage with their environment in such a way that we ascribe beliefs and desires to them' (1996, 10). We ascribe beliefs and desires to them on the basis of observed regularities in their behavior, most commonly identified as 'rational regularities' (11).

In contrast to claims made by the neo-behaviorist model, however, in our actual practice of intentional ascription, we do not always treat another agent's meaningful action as a rational behavior, or as an instrumental action directed at a particular desired goal. If, for example, we see someone gesturing or nodding their head as they listen to a lecture, we do not fail to attribute a certain intentionality to them in this respect, even though we do not always understand the intentionality expressed in gesturing or head-nodding as motivated by specific beliefs (e.g., about the meaning of the gesturing or head-nodding) or desires (e.g., to impress the lecturer) (Miyahara 2011).

Another example involves the intentionality associated with sexuality. Merleau-Ponty puts us more in the neighborhood of operational (or bodily) intentionality in his description.

Erotic perception is not a cogitatio that intends a cogitatum; through one body it aims at another body, and it is accomplished in the world, not within consciousness. For me, a scene does not have a sexual signification when I imagine, even confusedly, its possible relation to my sexual organs or to my states of pleasure, but rather when it exists for my body, for this always ready power of tying together the given stimuli into an erotic situation and for adapting a sexual behavior to it. (Merleau-Ponty 2012, 159)

---

[1] Here is Dennett's original formulation. 'Here is how it works: first you decide to treat the object whose behavior is to be predicted as a rational agent; then you figure out what beliefs that agent ought to have, given its place in the world and its purpose. Then you figure out what desires it ought to have, on the same considerations, and finally you predict that this rational agent will act to further its goals in the light of its beliefs. A little practical reasoning from the chosen set of beliefs and desires will in most instances yield a decision about what the agent ought to do; that is what you predict the agent will do' (Dennett 1987, 17).

Erotic intentionality is not a matter of a propositional attitude or an instrumental rationality; nor is it reducible to a set of observable behaviors, or, even if it does have something to do with desire, to some attributional/inferential link between behavior and belief. It's a form of intentionality that seemingly goes beyond the terms of folk psychology.

As the descriptions of the intentional stance suggest, however, neo-behaviorists rely on a commonsense or folk psychology involving mental states (or mental state intentionality) as the basis for ascribing intentionality to the agent. In addition, neo-behaviorism asserts that we take an agent as having intentionality 'only in relation to the strategies of someone who is trying to explain and predict its behavior' (Dennett 1971, 87). On this view, it's not clear that there is anything like original intentionality in the perceived agent. Accordingly, an agent is said to have intentionality only relative to its being ascribed by an external observer, and this fails to explain how an agent might have intentionality on her own (or how one might ascribe intentionality to oneself) without the presence of an observer (or without trying to explain and predict one's own behavior). This, however, seemingly goes against the very same folk or commonsense psychology to which we supposedly appeal in order to understand ourselves or others. For we do usually think we can have intentional states on our own. Furthermore, the idea that an agent might not have intentionality on her own seemingly undermines the idea that the external observer's attribution has its own intentionality. If subject A takes the intentional stance towards subject B, B may or may not have genuine intentionality, but A certainly does have intentionality. On the neo-behaviorist logic, however, to think of A's attribution as a case of intentionality, we would have to appeal to a second observer who attributes the first observer's attributional behavior. The intentionality of the second observer, however, would require a third observer, and so on. Adams and Aizawa (2001) point out that for the neo-behaviorist account to get off the ground, it would be more reasonable to suppose an internalist story of non-derived intentionality for the first observer, or, indeed, for the agent whose intentionality was originally in question. This, of course, would return us to the traditional internalist position about mental state intentionality. The other alternative is to think of A's attributional intentionality as operative in the very activity of attribution—and this would bring us to the phenomenological concept of operative intentionality.

More generally, with respect to the attribution of mental states—that is, with respect to social cognition or ToM—the neo-behaviorist model of intentionality goes hand in hand with a theory theory (TT) approach: that is, an approach that conceives of intersubjective understanding as a form of inference based on folk psychology. Like other indications associated with the neo-behaviorist position, TT depends on a framework that endorses an internalist conception of mental states. That is, both the neo-behaviorist approach to understanding intentionality, and the TT approach to social cognition, still depend on a rather standard model of the mind as a set of mental states 'in the head', hidden behind behavior. Such hidden mental processes are said to constitute the canonical type of explanation of the intentional behaviors that we observe.

Surprisingly, some defenders of the extended mind hypothesis, including Clark and Chalmers (1998; Clark 2008a), seem to adopt this neo-behaviorist conception of intentionality.[2] For them, it is reasonable to ascribe intentionality to extended processes only insofar as it allows us to gain explanatory and predictive advantage by doing so. In the case of extended mind, some aspects of intentionality require external physical vehicles for their realization. Yet, a trace of the internalist idea remains in the extended mind theorists' appeal to the 'Parity Principle' (Clark and Chalmers 1998; Clark 2008a) or to 'functional isomorphism' (Clark 1997). The principle is that we should take non-neural processes to be a part of the vehicle of cognition only to the extent that the functional contribution they make to a cognitive activity is isomorphic or similar enough to a contribution that could be made by neural processes in the brain. A notebook containing information which guides an agent's behavior, for example, constitutes a part of the agent's mind because the function it plays is on a par with the function biological memory might play (Clark and Chalmers 1998). The Parity Principle has invited troubling arguments against the extended mind hypothesis. Adams and Aizawa (2001), for example, reject the general hypothesis, while still endorsing the Parity Principle, by arguing that, as a matter of empirical

---

[2] The neo-behaviorist view is quite consistent with the functionalist position defended by Clark. Indeed, Horgan and Kriegel (2008) contend that the neo-behaviorist position would be the only viable option for the extended mind hypothesis, although more generally they think the extended mind hypothesis is not viable.

fact, external processes are functionally dissimilar to internal, neural processes (see also Rupert 2004 for a similar argument). Therefore they do not have intentionality in the right way. Extended mind proponents, as well as extended mind critics, agree on what intentionality is; they just disagree about where it can be found. Whether or not the extended mind theorists can provide viable responses to such criticisms, I'll argue that neither neo-Cartesian nor neo-behaviorist conceptions of intentionality will work for enactivist and extended mind theorists who want to push toward an alternative conception of mind.[3]

4.3 Neo-pragmatism

In contrast to neo-behaviorists, some neo-pragmatists, like Robert Brandom (1994; 2000), appeal to an account of intentionality that depends on social/normative concepts. Brandom explains the concept of intentionality in terms of what he calls the practice of *deontic score-keeping*, i.e., our mutual implicit practice of keeping track of each other's and our own actions in terms of *normative status* (1994, ch. 3). On this view we understand the intentionality of the other implicitly in terms of certain commitments or entitlements specified by social norms, although we do not always *acknowledge* such normative statuses *explicitly*. If, for example, I promise to play chess with you at a certain time and place, neither you nor I necessarily think of this in explicit terms of my loss of entitlement to be someplace else at that time, or my commitment to playing through the whole game. However, we keep score or keep track of such things implicitly, and this is revealed in the way we act. Thus, if I fail to meet you or decide to quit half way through, I will apologize

---

[3] Adams and Aizawa (2009) contend that we can understand 'why even transcranialists [i.e., enactivist and extended mind theorists] maintain that cognition extends from brains into the extraorganismal world rather than from the extraorganismal world into brains' (92) based on the fact that non-neural external processes are actually non-cognitive. One can agree that it is misleading for the extended mind theorists to describe the mind as *extending from brains into the world*, but that does not mean that such misleading descriptions constitute evidence in support of the standard model of the mind as 'in the head'; rather, such descriptions reflect remnants of the old model in the extended mind literature, which need to be removed in order to fully appreciate the potential of the claim. See the alternative idea that the mind is 'extensive' rather than extended (Hutto, Kirchhoff, and Myin 2014).

and you may blame me because I am breaking my commitments. This kind of interaction reveals that we were both implicitly tracking the normative status of our actions.

Accordingly, we ascribe intentionality to an entity capable of having a particular set of commitments and entitlements, namely those that can be *articulated* and discursively instituted by social linguistic norms—the implicit norms that determine the social appropriateness of our linguistic practices including inferential reasonings. In this regard Brandom thinks it's 'norms all the way down' and that 'only communities, not individuals, can be interpreted as having original intentionality . . . [T]he practices that institute the sort of normative status characteristic of intentional states must be *social* practices' (Brandom 1994, 61). That is, we track, and occasionally acknowledge, other people's intentionality in virtue of what they are doing and saying, what they are expected to do or say, what roles they play, what kind of place and time it is, and what such factors mean to us in the shared social situation, rather than by somehow looking for mental states hidden behind their behaviors.[4] We ascribe intentionality to actions to the extent that we have a practical grasp on their socially instituted significance.

On this basis, returning to a previous example, we have no problem in ascribing intentionality to gestures and head nods. According to neo-pragmatism, gestures have socially instituted significance and normative status, and they are part of what we track in the other's behavior, even if many times non-consciously. In understanding another's head-nodding, for example, we attribute to that person a discursive commitment to the

---

[4] Mason Cash (2010, 650) describes this idea as follows: 'On this normative view . . . the paradigmatic cases of such ascriptions are made by another member of the agent's linguistic and normative community; the ascriptions abide by, and are justified by, the norms of that community's practice of giving intentional states as reasons for actions. This practice is firmly situated in and supported by that community's shared, public language, with its norms regulating the appropriate uses of words to give content to intentional states . . . This practice constrains what ascriptions an observer is licensed to ascribe according to the agent's behavior. But they also normatively constrain the further actions of the agent. Agents who recognize that observers are licensed to ascribe particular intentional states to them ought to take themselves to be committed to further actions consistent with those intentional states. If I say to you that I intend to go for a walk, I should recognize that this utterance licenses you to ascribe to me the intention to go for a walk; I have licensed you to expect me to go for a walk, and thus I have placed myself under a commitment (ceteris paribus) to go for a walk.'

claim that the lecturer made, which he or she may or may not explicitly acknowledge; tracking the gesture is sufficient to grasp the intentionality in the other's behavior, and we don't have to posit, in addition, a belief or internal mental state. Furthermore, since we can keep track of our own normative status by relying on the social significance of our own circumstance, typically including our own previous sayings and doings, there is no problem about understanding my own intentionality as a social agent. In this regard, intentionality is not something internal or merely neuro-based; it's in the agent's actions, scaffolded by social and institutional practices.

Thus, the neo-pragmatist account of intentionality avoids some of the problems found in the neo-behaviorist account. Neo-pragmatists, however, run into a different problem, namely in their attempt to account for our commonsense ability to recognize intentionality in the behavior of a variety of non- or pre-social entities, e.g., in non-human animals, human infants, or even our inclinations to attribute intentions to geometrical figures moving in certain patterns on a computer screen. According to neo-pragmatism, something is an intentional agent only if it acts according to norms that are socially based. Certain insulting gestures, for example, are culturally relative, and we should not understand someone from a different culture, or an infant, who accidentally made an insulting gesture, to be acting as an insulting intentional agent. More generally, if a creature (e.g., a non-human animal) *completely* lacks understanding of social norms, and is not expected to act in accordance with such norms, it seems that the ascribing of intentionality itself would be inappropriate. And yet we do ascribe intentionality to animals, and others who lack understanding of social norms (e.g., pre-social infants). Empirical studies show that we also tend to see intentionality even in geometric figures if they make particular kinds of movements (Heider and Simmel 1944; Michotte 1963). Neo-pragmatists, then, seemingly fail to explain our everyday practices of ascribing intentionality in such instances.

One suggestion for resolving this problem points to a more basic issue. Cash (2008; 2009) suggests that on a neo-pragmatist account, we can ascribe intentionality to animals and infants 'based on the similarity of *their movement* to the kind of actions, which if performed by a person would entitle us to ascribe such intentional states as reasons' (2008, 101; *emphasis* added). That is, neo-pragmatists can ascribe intentionality to a non-social entity, but only by recognizing some kind of similarity between that entity's behavior and the behavior of a socialized human. What this proposal entails, however, is not clear. Moreover, this lack of clarity extends back to the processes that are involved in ascribing intentionality to humans as well. That is, neo-pragmatism doesn't make it clear how things work even in the human case—how precisely we recognize agents to be acting in accordance with social norms.

There seem to be two possibilities in the case of ascribing intentionality to non-human entities, if, as Cash indicates, similarity is the operative concept. The first would be a form of pattern recognition plus inference from analogy. That is, we might take certain non-social agents to have intentionality by detecting a common dynamic pattern between their movements and behaviors displayed by social agents. This solution fails, however, based on the simple fact that at least in some instances where we ascribe intentionality to animals or moving geometrical figures on a computer screen, there is no behavioral similarity to humans involved (Miyahara 2011). Alternatively, if we take ourselves to be the model on which to base the comparison, we can understand the emphasis on similarity as a move in the direction of the simulation theory of social cognition (ST). Goldman, for example, calls the following view, as described by Dennett, a version of ST: 'the view that when we attribute beliefs and other intentional states to others, we do this by comparing them to ourselves, by projecting ourselves into their states of mind' (Dennett 1987, 98–9; see Goldman 2006, 57).

ST contends that we rely, not on folk psychological inferences, but on modeling the other person's mental states using our own minds to simulate what we would do if we were in their shoes. Mindreading on this view involves the projection of our own first-person pretend beliefs and desires onto the minds of others based on a similarity that we see between their actions and our own. The recent neuroscience of mirror neurons (MNs) has motivated a reconceptualization of simulation (see Gallese 2014; Gallese and Goldman 1998; Rizzolatti, Fogassi, and Gallese 2001). According to this view, MNs are characterized as simulating the actions of others since they are specific neurons that are activated in two circumstances: either when I perform an action or when I see the other person perform an action. In this regard, the claim is that the observer's motor system goes into a matching state with the observed action of others. Simulation on this view would be equivalent to my system *matching* or establishing a *similarity* with the system that I observe—sometimes referred to as the matching hypothesis (Goldman 2006; Rizzolatti, Fogassi, and Gallese 2001). On this view, mindreading, or at least action comprehension, would be the result of an automatic mechanism that works entirely on a subpersonal level.

On the one hand, this move to neural ST looks promising for neo-pragmatism since it focuses on action understanding and treats intention as something implicit in the action itself. Theoretically, one can certainly stop short of stronger claims about MNs being a basis for mindreading, rather than just action understanding. Note, however, that with respect to the issue of intention attribution to non-human entities, MN activation is limited to very few cases of cross-species action perception—that is, MNs cannot explain why we would attribute intentions to dogs, cats, roaches, geometrical figures, etc., since MNs are not activated in these cases, although they may explain intention attribution to monkeys and apes (see Buccino et al. 2004). Supposedly, the bodily action similarity is strong enough between humans and monkeys. Outside of these limited cases, we run into an objection similar to the one about simple pattern recognition—insufficient behavioral (bodily action) similarity.

On the other hand, it's not clear how subpersonal, automatic processes scale up to the kinds of normative structures that neo-pragmatism emphasizes. Furthermore, ST, like TT, remains too closely tied to internalist models of intentionality. For example, ST shares two important assumptions with TT. (1) The unobservability principle, i.e., that the problem that needs solving is that the other's mind is inaccessible, hidden away inside the other's head. Both approaches assume that the central problem of social cognition is best posed as one that involves mindreading—a capacity that allows us to address our lack of access to other minds, characterized as hidden mental states that explain manifest behavior. In other words, we easily find ourselves packing the mind back inside the head. If some proponents of neural ST sometimes move away from this mindreading model to focus on action understanding (e.g., Gallese 2009), many others understand neural ST to be nothing more than a form of mindreading (e.g., Oberman and Ramachandran 2007) or a support for mindreading (e.g. Keysers and Gazzola 2006). This assumption goes against neo-pragmatic claims that intentionality has a status specified by social norms, and is, at least in part, publicly accessible to other people.

(2) The assumption of methodological individualism—that is, the assumption that access to knowledge about the minds of others depends on cognitive capabilities or mechanisms found within the individual, or on processes that take place inside an individual brain (Froese and Gallagher 2012). In other words, for TT and ST, the solution has to come by some cognitive ('in the head') operation (theoretical inference, introspective modeling, or neuronal process), or theory-of-mind mechanism (ToMM), or mirror system, that would allow us to grasp the other person's mental states. Thus, both the attribution process and the intentionality that is attributed are narrowed down to the workings of internal mental states or brain states.

According to neo-pragmatism, however, the cognitive understanding of others, or the explicit attribution of intentionality is secondary, and is possible only on the background of implicit shared practices; the basic mode of understanding others is not supported by the individual's cognitive capacities for acknowledging others' mental states as such, but rather by actual or potential interaction with others. Thus, according to neo-pragmatism, some agents (or pre-agents, such as young infants) may be capable of tracking another's intentionality in pragmatic interactions, even if they are unable to understand it abstractly—that is, without engaging in an actual social interaction.

Accordingly, neither TT nor ST models of intentionality attribution and social cognition provide a good fit with either the neo-pragmatist view or the enactivist or extended mind theories of cognition. This still leaves us searching for a fuller account of intentionality consistent with the alternative concept of mind suggested by enactivist and extended mind approaches. I've suggested that we rule out the Brentanian, the neo-Cartesian, and the neo-behaviorist views of intentionality for a variety of reasons. But versions of neo-pragmatism that would depend on analogical and simulationist accounts would also be problematic. An alternative proposal is to see the phenomenological conception of operative intentionality as consistent with neo-pragmatism, and as supported by a conception of social cognition that focuses more on interaction. Specifically, this would give us a conception of intentionality that is enactive, and, as I will argue, this is precisely the view of intentionality needed by extended mind theorists to counter the arguments concerning non-derived content and the mark of the mental.

4.4 Enactive Intentionality

Evidence from developmental psychology shows that from birth or very early infancy the interactions of infants and caregivers register in a shared motoric 'language', a cross-modal sensory–motor system that, in each individual, is directly attuned to the actions and gestures of other humans (Meltzoff and Moore 1994; Gallagher and Meltzoff 1996). Phenomenology, however, goes a bit further; it suggests that in this kind of interaction there is a bodily intentionality distributed across the interacting agents, an intentionality that couldn't be realized without there being an actual interaction. Merleau-Ponty calls this 'intercorporeity', and characterizes it in this way: 'There is . . . between this phenomenal body and the other person's phenomenal body such as I see it from the outside, an internal relation that makes the other person appear as the completion of the system' (2012, 368; see 1968, 141, 143). Intercorporeity involves a mutual influence of body schemas, but not in an isomorphic format, where one mirrors, or maps the other's actions onto one's own motor representations. Rather, intercorporeity involves a reciprocal, dynamic, and enactive response to the other's action, taking that action as an affordance for further action rather than as the occasion for replication (simulation). This enactivist approach offers an alternative (non-simulationist) interpretation of MN activation in the social cognition process. Consistent with the suggestion made by Newman-Norlund et al. (2007), activation of the broadly congruent MNs may be preparatory for an enactive response rather than a matching action.

The evidence for this type of intersubjective interaction—found in developmental studies of infant interaction with caregivers (e.g., Trevarthen 1979), in communication studies that look at the detailed give-and-take dynamics of posture, gesture, and speech (e.g., Goodwin 2000), as well as in behavioral and perceptual studies that specify what we attend to in our interactions (e.g. Bayliss et al. 2006; 2007)—shows that social cognition is both dynamic and enactive in nature. On the enactive view, we engage with others in ways that depend on embodied sensori-motor processes. We do not first perceive non-intentional movements, and then make inferences to what they mean. We enactively perceive the actions and emotional expressions of others as forms of intentionality—i.e., as meaningful and directed. Enactive perception of others means that we see their emotional expressions and contextualized actions as meaningful in terms of how we might respond to or interact with them. Others present us with social affordances. Accordingly, our understanding of others is pragmatic and it references their actions in context: it is not indexed to Cartesian mental states that would explain their actions.

Another way to say this is that we ordinarily perceive another's intentionality in the form of operative intentionality rather than infer or simulate mental act intentionality. As indicated above, the concept of operative intentionality attempts to capture the fact that the experiencing agent is intentionally engaged with the world through actions and projects that are not reducible to simple mental states, but involve an intentionality that is motoric and bodily. Actions have intentionality because they are directed at some goal or project, and this is something that we can see in the actions of others (see Gallagher 2008b). Actions that are seemingly identical in their mechanical details are subtly different in kinematic details corresponding to different intentions, and we can see these differences. Thus, subjects who see only the first reaching part of grasping an apple (1) in order to eat it, or (2) to offer it to another person, or (3) to throw it at that other person, are able to discriminate these different intentions in a significant number (70%) of cases (Becchio et al. 2012), even outside of interactive contexts. This perceivable, motoric, operative intentionality is quite different from mental state or act intentionality (associated with a belief or desire or distal intention, for example), which would be garnered in reflective inference or judgment (Merleau-Ponty 2012, lxxxii). The latter seems to be what we appreciate when we try to explain or predict others' behaviors from a detached, observational standpoint, or reflect upon others' behaviors rather than when we enactively engage with their intentional behavior. In contrast, we usually experience both others and ourselves in terms of operative intentionality, an intentionality 'that establishes the natural and prepredicative unity of the world and of our life, the intentionality that appears in our desires, our evaluations, and our landscape more clearly than it does in objective knowledge' (Merleau-Ponty 2012, lxxxii). With respect to social cognition, we normally grasp the other's intentionality in terms of its appropriateness, its pragmatic and/or emotional value for our particular way of being, constituted by the particular goals or projects we have (or share) at the time, our implicit take on cultural norms, our social role or status, etc., rather than as reflecting inner mental states, or as constituting explanatory reasons for the other's further thoughts and actions.

Consider the following example (from Miyahara 2011). Suppose you are driving a car along a busy street where there are no crosswalks and see a person at the edge of the street restlessly looking left and right. You slow down a little in case he runs onto the street, or at least you ready yourself to press the brake pedal. If the passenger in the car with you asks you why you slowed down, you might answer that the person looked like he *wanted* to cross the road. In this reflective explanation it seems as if the person had been experienced in terms of his mental states, i.e., his *desire* to cross the road, which constitutes a reason for a further action of crossing the road. This, however, is a way of putting it that is motivated in the reflective attitude or the subsequent giving of reasons. In fact, in the original action, placing your foot on the brake pedal just is part of what it means to experience the intentionality of the person at the edge of the road. As Merleau-Ponty puts it:

The body's motoric experience is not a particular case of knowledge; rather, it offers us a manner of reaching the world and the object, a 'praktognosia', that must be recognized as original, and perhaps as originary. My body has its world, or understands its world without having to go through 'representations', or without being subordinated to a 'symbolic' or 'objectifying function'.

(2012, 141, trans. revised).

Making such bodily responses to the world or to an object, or in social contexts, to others, is a way of encountering such entities, which not only cannot be reduced to actions guided by the mediation of reasonings, but is also more primitive than the kind of recognition of the world that guides action only indirectly.

Enactivists claim that this intersubjective and pragmatic understanding is the basic kind of understanding we have of others' and our own intentionality, and that this operative intentionality is what we should consider to be primary and non-derived. On this notion of intentionality 'the unity of the world, prior to being posited by knowledge through an explicit act of identification, is lived as already accomplished or as already there' (Merleau-Ponty 2012, lxxxi). Intentionality is determined by what the agent is doing and what the agent is ready to do, and is constrained, for example, by the agent's sensorimotor skills relevant to coping with the situation at hand, whether that's stepping off a curb or stepping on the brake, or any interaction that might follow.

4.5 Enactive and Extended Minds

On the enactivist view, one doesn't need to go to the realm of mental states (propositional attitudes, beliefs, desires), inside the head, to encounter intentionality—operative intentionality is intrinsic to the movement; it is in one's action, in one's environmentally attuned responses. This operative intentionality is the real non-derived, primary intentionality. Anything like attributed or reflectively given intentional states, what we come to recognize as beliefs, desires, or other folk psychological states, are derived from this and, in most cases of everyday interaction, are redundant and arise only in instances where explanation or justification is called for. Moreover, operative intentionality is clearly distributed over brain–body–environment—and so it is precisely the concept of intentionality that enactivist and extended accounts need.

My own intentions are operable, and quite often only emerge, within my perception of the other's intentions. I see the other's actions as an affordance for my own possible responsive action (which may be very different from hers); I see the other's action as inter-actionable or as calling forth a response on my part. This notion of intentionality under-pins an embodied-enactive account of everyday social cognition and joint action. In contrast to neo-Cartesian and the neo-behaviorist approaches discussed earlier, for example, this enactivist, neo-pragmatist explanation also provides a better account of erotic intentionality. In erotic perception, which is not a *cogitatio* but a sexual significance for me 'when it exists for my body', as Merleau-Ponty puts it,

we discover, at one strike, sexual life as a form of original intentionality, and the vital origins of perception, motility and [symbolic] representation, by basing all these processes on an intentional arc . . .

(Merleau-Ponty 2012, 160, trans. revised)

Erotic intentionality, as an instance of original operative intentionality is not an '*I think that* . . .', and is even more than a pragmatic '*I can* . . .' It draws on a certain form of affective interest (see section 8.1).

This account is also consistent with a non-simulationist version of neo-pragmatism. Indeed, it shows us how to connect very basic opera-tive intentionality with the neo-pragmatist emphasis on social/norma-tive aspects of behavior. As noted in *Chapter 3*, Brandom makes the connection between operative intentionality and neo-pragmatism very

clear. He associates pragmatism with the idea that the most fundamental, non-derived form of intentionality is our practical and often skillful
involvement with the world (2008, 178). For Brandom this intentionality is more basic than language-based '*semantic* intentionality'. It
involves feedback-governed processes that extend into the world.
It exhibits 'a complexity [that] cannot in principle be specified without
reference to the changes in the world that are both produced by the
system's responses and responded to'. Accordingly, such practices are
'thick', i.e., they involve artifacts, events, and worldly states of affairs.
'Bits of the world are *incorporated* in such practices' (178).

There is reason to think that this kind of intentionality (and the
possibility of recognizing and attributing such intentionality to others)
comes into play ontogenetically earlier than any standard discussion of
social norms might indicate, namely in the intercorporeity of primary
intersubjectivity in early infancy. One might think that from the perspective of the infant, social norms are not yet operative. Yet from the
perspective of the interaction itself, since caregivers, family members,
and strangers are already involved in normative practices in the way that
they treat infants, then normative aspects are already pervasive, even if
they are clearly prior to what develops as more explicit social/normative
aspects of behavior that depend on communicative and narrative practices later in childhood (Gallagher and Hutto 2008).

The enactive, neo-pragmatic, operative concept of intentionality is
precisely the relevant concept needed to support the extended mind
hypothesis. As Dewey made clear long before the proponents of the
extended mind formed their hypothesis, this is a pragmatic concept of
mind: The mind 'is formed out of commerce with the world and is set
toward that world'; it should never be regarded as 'something self-
contained and self-enclosed' (1934, 269). That this concept of mind is
intersubjective from the very start means that there is no mystery about
where this non-derived intentionality comes from. It comes from the
others with whom we interact, or more precisely, it is generated in our
interaction. To the extent that we are all born into a community,
our environment is full of intentional practices from the very beginning
of our life. We develop and shape our own intentionality by being
initiated into this communal practice in virtue of actual interactions
with other people, primarily with our caregivers, and in virtue of our
innate or early-learned sensitivity to them or to opportunities for such

interactions. This means that non-derived intentionality is not something that is first generated in my own isolated mind, or in brain processes that are not already directed to and by others. What Adams and Aizawa call non-derived content is surely derived from these originary inter-active practices. In this regard, the mind is constituted by our enactive engagements with the environment, which is both social and physical; and intentionality means that we are 'in the world', distributed over brain–body–environment, and extended in pragmatic and communi-cative practices that may further supervene on the tools, technologies, and institutional practices through which we engage with the world.

5

Action without Representations

In philosophy of mind, the concept of intentionality is often thought of as equivalent to the concept of representation; or sometimes representation is thought of as the primary form of intentionality. Enactivist approaches argue against representationalist interpretations of intentionality and hold that one can have intentionality without representation. In this chapter I want defend the anti-representationalist argument, and do so especially in regard to the idea of operative intentionality discussed in *Chapter 4*. For this reason I focus on the question of intentionality in action, without, at this point, making any claims about the more general question of representational accounts of cognition. Others have gone into these questions in some detail (e.g., Hutto and Myin 2013; Ramsey 2007). I also want to set aside the question of whether representation plays a role in deliberation about action, or the planning of action, or the working out of prior intentions, and so forth. I'll consider what I take to be the strongest models for the involvement of representations in action. The question is simple: Is the concept of representation required for an account of action? Is there anything representational *in* action, as part of action itself?

5.1 Representation in Action

Consider the classic concept of representation. The following characteristics are based on a list provided by Mark Rowlands (2006, 5ff.) who points out that the classic concept is modeled on language.

1. Representation is internal (an image, symbol, or neural configuration).
2. Representation has duration (it's a discrete identifiable thing).

3. Representation bears content that references something external to itself (it refers to or is about something other than itself).
4. Representation requires interpretation—its meaning derives from a certain processing that takes place in the subject—like a word or an image its meaning gets fixed in context.
5. Representation is passive (it is produced or called forth by some particular situation).
6. Representation is decouplable from its current context.[1]

The idea of decouplability is that one can take the representation 'offline' and, for example, imagine or remember an action or context. Representation in such cases involves a form of decoupling away from action, away from the target of action, or away from the current context. One question is whether this kind of offline or decoupled activity may still be involved in aspects of action (a point to which I return below).

We find agreement concerning elements on this list in both proponents and critics of representation. For example, Ramsey (2007), who notes 'there is nothing even remotely like a consensus on the nature of mental representation', describes the common understanding of mental representation as involving 'content-bearing internal states' and 'structures that serve to stand for something else' (xi). 'Mental representations are states that have some sort of non-derived intentionality and that interact with other cognitive states in specific sorts of ways' (19). We find some disagreement as well. Rather than taking representations to be passive (as in 5), representations are often considered causally active—'mental representations are states that *do* various things' (Ramsey 2007, 18).

Nico Orlandi (2014) rehearses a conception of representation understood as an explanatory or theoretical posit that functions abstractly under a particular description, and specifically under a description that does not explain precisely how a system does what it does. Representations 'figure in explanations that concern behavior described at a fairly abstract level, a level that ignores details of how the behavior is

[1] Rowlands does not include decouplability as part of the classic conception, but others certainly do. As he notes: 'It is often thought that for an item to be regarded as genuinely representational it must be *decouplable* from its wider environment and, in particular, from the state of affairs that it purports to represent' (2006, 157). Rowlands, however, does include this characteristic in his more action-oriented definition of representation.

carried out' (2014, 8). In partial agreement with the list above, she suggests that representations have the following features: (1) they stand in for something else—that is, they are internal mediators that stand between the physical (e.g., neuronal) system and what is represented; (2) they inform—that is, they bear content that semantically references something other than themselves, i.e., they 'state' something (or provide propositional information) about the world, and have accuracy conditions (they can be correct or incorrect); and (3) they function to guide the system's behavior.

One thing that all of these authors agree on is that there is no deep agreement about what counts as a representation. As Orlandi puts it, '*Standing in, content*, and agent-level *performance contribution* are then some basic features of representations. What more specific attributes internal states and structures need to possess in order to have these features is a matter of dispute' (2014, 11). At the same time, she notes that the account of what is seemingly the most important aspect—the idea that representations inform or have content—varies and is also 'a matter of dispute' (9), perhaps because the notion of content is 'ambiguous' (10), on some models resembling language (hence, propositional content); on other models resembling maps that are isomorphic to what they reference; and on other (deflationary) models simply co-varying with what it references, in the way that mercury in a thermometer co-varies with the temperature.

Specifying characteristics of representation in this way contrasts to the views of some theorists who would define representation in extremely loose terms—for example, construing a representation as any internal change caused by experience. In these terms, 'to assume the existence of a representation is rather innocuous and should rarely be an issue for theoretical dispute' (Roitblat 1982, 355). This seems to be the deflated concept of representation—for example, a neural pattern that co-varies with some feature of the environment, in the case of perception—and as Orlandi notes, this is a common understanding one finds in cognitive neuroscience (2014, 12–13). In much of mainstream cognitive science and philosophy of mind, however, the concept of representation is not so innocuous. In spite of variations in definition (including or excluding some of the characteristics on the list above), the notion of representation appears to occupy a significant place within many models of cognition.

In contrast to this ubiquitous presence of representation in the analysis of cognition, Hubert Dreyfus (2002) famously takes up an anti-representationalist view, and argues that for practiced or skillful intentional action one does not require representation.

A phenomenology of skill acquisition confirms that, as one acquires expertise, the acquired know-how is experienced as finer and finer discriminations of situations paired with the appropriate response to each. Maximal grip [a concept drawn from Merleau-Ponty] names the body's tendency to refine its responses so as to bring the current situation closer to an optimal gestalt. Thus, successful learning and action do not require propositional mental representations. They do not require semantically interpretable brain representations either.   (2002, 367)

Dreyfus associates the idea of representation with a failed Cartesian philosophy—the concept of representation (as used in AI, for example) remains context-independent and bound up with epistemic states of *knowing-that* (propositional knowledge), when everything about intelligent action and *knowing-how* depends on being-in-the-world (rather than standing back and representing the world) and on context—both background and immediate context.[2]

The limitations of representationalism can be seen in the commonsense knowledge problem and the frame problem in AI. Representational approaches to the problem of commonsense knowledge (pictured as an interconnected system of representations) leads to 'a vicious combinatorial explosion' (Wheeler 2005), as propositional (representational) knowledge of one aspect of the world presupposes propositional knowledge of other aspects, etc. etc. The frame problem—roughly, how does a system adjust itself to recognize relevant features in a changing environment?—remains unsolved in a representationalist model. To claim that the system uses appropriate representations is just to push the problem back—how does the system know what representations are appropriate/relevant to the particular context?—and we still get an infinite regress.

It's important to note that what is involved here is not simply the immediate context of a well-ordered task. One might think that a

---

[2] Berthoz and Petit (2006) provide a similar anti-representationalist argument, holding that the brain is an organ for action rather than an organ for language-centered representation. 'By applying this representational filter, everything in the external as well as in the internal world appears frozen, fixed and stabilized by the projection of the propositional form, which implicitly structures representation' (Berthoz and Petit 2006, 23).

connectionist model, where a system is trained in a rich environment, could generate distributed representations that are context-sensitive. But the problem also involves the *background* context that informs the particular system's abilities and decisions. Whereas a background context is not required for a robot that does one (or a limited set of) pre-defined task(s) (my household robot does a great job at vacuuming, but it can't do the dishes), the human context is not defined by narrowly circumscribed actualities; it is also defined by finite but extensive possibilities, including possibilities about flexibility, style, and timing in relation to many other projects.

What takes the place of representations in non-representationalist accounts of action is a form of dynamical perception/affordance-based online intelligence which generates action 'through complex causal interactions in an extended-body-environment system' (Wheeler 2005, 193). But can this sort of system do everything it needs to do for the basic scale of perception–action without representation?

5.2 Minimal Representations

Michael Wheeler (2005), a friend of the Dreyfus anti-representationalist view, nonetheless follows Clark (1997, 47ff., 149ff.), suggesting that certain actions require 'action-oriented representations' (AORs). AORs are temporary egocentric motor maps of the environment that are fully determined by the situation-specific action required of the agent (organism or robot).[3] On this model, it is not that the AORs re-present the objectively pre-existing world in an internal image, or that they map it out in a neuronal pattern: rather, 'how the world is *is itself encoded in terms of* possibilities for action' (197). What is represented in AORs is not knowledge that the environment is x, but knowledge of how to negotiate the environment. AORs are action specific, egocentric relative to the agent, and context dependent. If there were any such thing as an enactive representation, clearly this would be it.

---

[3] Clark (1997, 47) first explicates the concept of the AOR in the example of Mataric's robot rat and a robot crab (pp. 153ff.). I don't plan to address the issue of whether robots require AORs for certain purposes. In this chapter my focus is on human action. Clark suggests that AORs count as some version of Millikan's 'pushmi-pullyu' representations.

But what sort of thing can count as an AOR? Is it a neural firing pattern (in which case, it may be what Goldman (2012) calls a B-formatted representation in contrast to propositional-formatted representation [see section 2.1]), a motor schema, or something like a bodily movement? Before we consider Wheeler's answer to this, let's consider something that he rules out, namely bodily movement itself (2005, 209). According to Wheeler, bodily movements do not have representational status because in the relevant contexts of action, they play a role that can be given a fully causal and specifically non-representational explanation. Rowlands (2006), in contrast, defends the idea that certain bodily movements that are elements of action can be representational. He argues that the classic concept of representation, modeled on language—internal but with content externality, in need of interpretation, and passive—is not adequate to capture the concept of representation in action. To get to a more adequate action concept of representation (or AOR) he gives up some of the aspects on the list presented in the previous section (2006, 11). Indeed, Rowlands (2012) criticizes the classic concept of representation and offers a revised list of characteristics or constraints that make something representational (see 2006, 113–14).

1. *The informational constraint*: If something is representational it carries information about something other than itself (x)—it has content.[4]
2. *The teleological (or normativity) constraint*: If something is representational it is teleological—it tracks or has a specific function towards x.
3. *The misrepresentation constraint*: If something is representational it can misrepresent x.
4. *The decouplability constraint*: If something is representational it is decouplable from x (x may be represented even when x is absent).
5. *The combinatorial constraint*: If something is representational it can be *combined* into a more general representational framework.

---

[4] Although Rowlands suggests that on some alternative account of representation content may be internal to representation (2006, 11), when it comes to explaining the idea that representation carries information (pp. 115ff.) in Rowlands' account it is difficult to distinguish it from the traditional concept that representation bears content that is external to itself (it refers to or is about something other than itself).

In order to see how these constraints apply in the case of action, Rowlands distinguishes between intentional actions, sub-intentional acts, and pre-intentional acts. Sub-intentional acts (O'Shaughnessy 1980) are non-intentional movements, e.g., of tongue or fingers, of which we are not aware, for which there is no reason, and which serve no purpose connected with action. Pre-intentional acts (PIAs), or 'deeds' in Rowlands' terminology, do have a purpose with respect to intentional action and include such things as the positioning of fingers in catching a ball that is flying towards you at a high rate of speed, or the movement of your fingers while playing Chopin's *Fantasie Impromptu in C# Minor* on the piano. PIAs include an array of 'on-line, feedback-modulated adjustments that take place below the level of intention, but collectively promote the satisfaction of [an] antecedent intention' (103).

Rowlands provides a detailed example: Yarbus's (1967) experiments on saccadic eye movements (see Figure 5.1). Yarbus presents subjects with a painting that shows six women and the arrival of a male visitor; subjects are then asked to do certain tasks.

1. View the picture at will.
2. Estimate the family's wealth.
3. Judge the age of the people in the painting.
4. Guess what the people had been doing prior to the arrival of the visitor.
5. Remember the clothing worn.
6. Remember the position of the objects in the room.
7. Estimate how long it had been since the visitor was last seen by the people in the painting.

Yarbus found that the visual scan paths varied systematically with the nature of the task. Thus, the saccades are in some way governed by the intention/task, but they are not intentional in the sense that we do not decide to use this visual tactic, and we are not conscious we are doing the saccades: they are PIAs.

Rowlands argues that PIAs are representational and meet all of the constraints listed above: they *carry information* about x (the trajectory, shape, size of ball, the keyboard, a specific aspect of people in painting); they *track* x or function in a way that allows me to accomplish something in virtue of tracking x; they can *misrepresent* (get it wrong); they *can be combined* into a more general representational structure (I catch the ball

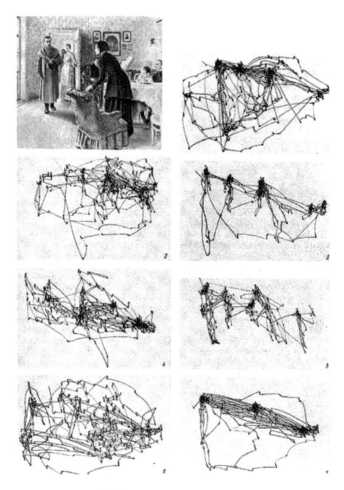

Figure 5.1. Seven records of eye movements by one subject (from Yarbus 1967, 174, Fig. 109, with permission).

and throw it back; I continue to play the music; I can systematically scan a painting); they are *decouplable* from x (x may be absent from the immediate environment—e.g., I can later remember or simulate how I caught the ball, replicating the same act).

On some interpretations (e.g., Anscombe 1957; Merleau-Ponty 2012), PIAs are intentional just insofar as they subserve and are part of the intentional action. For example, in regard to playing the piano or catching the ball, if you ask me did I intend to posture my fingers in just such a position, I could say yes in so far as I intended to play this piece, or catch the ball. On this view, intentionality reaches down into the motor elements that serve the intentional action. In regard to the Yarbus example, one might ask: 'Did you mean to focus on the faces when you were answering that question?' I might respond that I wasn't conscious of doing so, or of controlling my eyes in any explicit way (and in that sense I might claim that it was unintentional). Or I might say: 'Yes, since I was trying to answer a question about the picture, I was intentionally scanning it.' My intentional scanning includes my saccadic eye movements. The issue of whether PIAs are pre-intentional or in some sense share in the intentional nature of the action can be set aside for our purposes. For simplicity, I'll follow Rowlands and continue to refer to them as pre-intentional.

5.3 Decouplability and Causal Spread

Representations, by definition, are decouplable from x (I can represent x even if x is absent from the immediate environment). But once we decouple a PIA from x (the ball, the piano keys, the painting), I suggest that we are no longer talking about action in the same sense. Indeed, it is difficult to see how PIAs or AORs can decouple from x (the ball, the piano keys, the painting) or the context, without becoming something entirely different from an element of the action at stake. Offline cognition, imagining, remembering, or even re-enacting an action decoupled from its original context and absent x, may (or may not) require representation—but this says nothing about representation *in action*.

An advocate of representation in action, however, could appeal to the model developed by Andy Clark and Rick Grush (1999). They offer a model that puts representational decouplability directly into action at a sub-personal level. They propose that anticipation in motor control, specifically the 'internal' neural circuitry used for predictive/anticipatory purposes in a forward emulator, involves a Minimal Robust Representation (MRR). The circuitry is a model, a 'decouplable surrogate' that *stands in* for a future state of some extra-neural aspect of the movement—a body position (or proprioceptive feedback connected with a body position) just about to be accomplished, e.g., in the action of catching a ball. Since the emulator anticipates (represents) an x that is not yet there—a future position of the ball, for example, or a predicted motor state—it is in some sense off-line, 'disengaged', or certainly decoupled from the current x or the current movement.

For Clark and Grush, this MRR is an 'inner state' that does not depend 'on a constant physical linkage' between it and the extra-neural states which it is about. Thus, 'emulators seem to be a nice, biologically detailed example of the sort of disengagement that Brian Cantwell Smith . . . has recently argued to be crucial for understanding representation' (Clark and Grush 1999, 7). But it is difficult to see how an aspect of motor control that is a constitutive part of the action can be considered decoupled from x, which it may be tracking, or, for that matter, from the context, or the action itself. Isn't this kind of anticipation fully situated in the action context? Doesn't the anticipation of a future state or location of x (e.g., anticipating where the ball will be in the next second), or of the predicted motor state (anticipating where to strike the keyboard in the next measure) require reference to the present state or location of x and of my hand, or to the current motor command (via efference copy)—that is, the current state of the system? It is true that, as anticipatory, it is one step ahead of real-world proprioceptive feedback from the just-future movement—but it is also at the same time one step behind the just-previous feedback—informed and updated by it—and it depends on the ongoing perception of relevant objects in the world. To put it simply, I can't anticipate where the ball is going or in what direction my hand should move unless the mechanism responsible for this anticipatory aspect is currently tracking where the ball or my hand is right now. Moreover, if it is going to play a part in the control of movement, doesn't this have to be a physical linkage—relying on the physical processes of my eyes tracking the ball, activating extraocular muscles and kinaesthetic sense, and my hand already in movement, generating its own proprioceptive/kinaesthetic feedback? To think that the anticipatory emulator involves a decoupled process is to think that such anticipations can be detached from perceptual and proprioceptive input, which they clearly cannot be. They are part of the online process of action; as such they register not simply some future state, but the trajectory of the action (from present to future).

This characterization depends on the notion that the emulation process is tracking an environmental feature, and in the minimal sense is co-varying with it. If one does decouple the emulation process—if one disengages it from the action itself—it ceases to be part of a forward motor control mechanism, although it supposedly turns into part of a truly offline representation-process, a decoupled emulation process in memory or imagination (see, e.g., Grush and Mandik 2002, for the example of moving on an imaginary chessboard).

Of course the argument may not be that the representation in action *is* decoupled from action; rather, the argument may be that the representation is *decouplable*. So one might admit that once it is decoupled it no longer has any direct function in action itself. Perhaps, as decoupled, it operates as a simulation that can assist action planning. Nonetheless, it is not clear at all that *in action* it functions in a representational manner, or whether it only takes on a representational role once it is decoupled. Clark and Grush acknowledge this issue: 'full-blooded internal representations' are fully decouplable inner surrogates for extra-neural states of affairs. But the 'case of basic motor emulation does indeed fall short of meeting this stricter criterion . . . the surrogate states are not fully decoupleable from ongoing environmental input' (1999, 10). So the neural circuitry correlating to the anticipatory aspect in the emulator turns out not to be a full-blooded representation; it is at best, as Clark and Grush suggest, the most minimal entity that we might consider a representation.

It is not clear, however, why some mechanism that may (or may not) operate in a representational way in a non-action (so-called higher-order cognitive) context, means that it is necessarily operating in a representational way in the perception–action context. Even if it were the case that an emulation process can take on representational duties outside of action, this does not require that it be representational in action. Indeed, one could run this question inversely: if an emulation process is not operating in a representational way in action, why does that *same process* become representational when it is run offline?

Wheeler, for one,[5] gives up the criterion of decouplability as part of the concept of a minimal representation (2005, 219); and both Wheeler and Rowlands suggest that minimal representations involve aspects of a system that is brain, body . . . but also environment. 'The vehicles

---

[5] Clark (1997) also states, in reference to Haugeland's definition of representation, 'the role of decouplability (the capacity to use the inner states to guide behavior in the absence of the environmental feature) is, I think, somewhat overplayed' (144).

of representation do not stop at the skin; they extend all the way out into the world' (Rowlands 2006, 224). Here Rowlands joins Clark and Wheeler, and some version of the extended mind hypothesis, where actions are characterized by complex causal interactions that involve a dynamical coupling of body and environment, and where the causality is spread across all these elements.

Wheeler here calls our attention to the 'threat [to representationalism] from [non-trivial] causal spread' (2005, 200). Indeed, the commitment to some version of this idea of extended or situated cognition is what motivated anti-representationalism in the first place. On this view, the environment itself does some of the causal work, and it does so in a way that undermines the notion of decouplability and eliminates the need for representations. Consider, for example, driving from Memphis to New Orleans (see Haugeland 1985). It involves following some kind of strategy.

> Strategy 1: I have a stored inner representation of the directions in my memory.
>
> Strategy 2: I follow a map and road signs, which are external representations.
>
> Strategy 3: Having decided to go to New Orleans, I jump in the car and start off, and having done it many times before, I go on automatic pilot and allow the landscape and roads to guide me (no representations required since the actual road and landscape do the cognitive work usually attributed to representations).

This third situation depends on neither internal nor external representations and involves non-trivial causal spread. But, according to Wheeler, this does not rule out AORs. He argues that to go fully anti-representationalist in an extended cognition paradigm one needs to reject (1) strong instructionalism (i.e., the idea that representations provide a full and detailed description of how to achieve the outcome); and (2) the neural assumption (i.e., the idea that neuronal processes play a central and close to exclusive role in cognition). On the extended mind hypothesis, the neural assumption is clearly weakened. For Wheeler, however, if we maintain a neural assumption, even if sufficiently weakened (which he specifies as the claim that 'if intelligent action is to be explained in representational terms, then whatever criteria are proposed as sufficient conditions for representation-hood, they should not be satisfied by any extra-neural elements for which it would be unreasonable, extravagant, or explanatorily inefficacious to claim that the contribution to intelligent action made by those elements is representational in character' [2005, 209]), then we don't need to rule out a minimal form of representation. Extra-neural factors can't do all the work, so AORs may still have a role to play as functioning neural representations.

The idea of strong instructionalism was already given up by Dreyfus in his discussion of background knowledge—a representation no matter how strongly instructional can never be adequate to meet the background knowledge problem or the frame problem—it can never specify everything necessary to determine an unruly contextualized action; indeed it would lead to the frame problem, a paralyzed system and inaction if the system attempted to specify everything required. The context and background knowledge problems are not solvable by appeal to representations. Dreyfus (2007a) thus appeals to Merleau-Ponty's phenomenology, which offers a nonrepresentational account of the way the body and the world are coupled and suggests a way of avoiding the frame problem. According to Merleau-Ponty, as an agent acquires skills, those skills are 'stored', not as representations in the agent's mind, but as dispositional embodied responses to the solicitations of situations in the world. What the learner acquires through experience is not by way of representations at all but by way of more finely discriminated situations. If the situation does not clearly solicit a single response, or if the response does not produce a satisfactory result, the learner is led to further refine his discriminations, which, in turn, may solicit ever more refined responses.

Wheeler too appeals to a non-representational solution to the frame problem. Evolutionary and cultural contributions to the already situated subject inform a perception-based account of action (which also involves a crucial appeal to continuous reciprocal causation to explain fast and fluid context-switching). Lions, and tigers, and bears as well as other people, and specific objects in the environment, e.g., bombs, have either an evolutionary or culturally based valence that solicits a particular response. Intentional life is keyed into relevant aspects of the environment in a way that shapes our subpersonal processes, and the latter come to serve the intentional aspects of action. In this sense, the frame problem is solved not by a network of representations, but by intuitive and emotionally informed responses. This is why it is still a problem for AI and top-down robotics. We try to get the robot to recognize the bomb as a threat by providing it with a cold propositional algorithm to that effect. The robot thus has to represent the bomb as a threat and then has to represent what action to take and then has to represent what parts of its own mechanisms to activate. In contrast, we culturally attuned non-robots *see* that the bomb is a threat and we run for our lives.

5.4 Where's the Representation?

Rowlands (2012), taking issue with the above characterization of decouplability, suggests that decouplability does not mean being offline or detached from the action. Following Ruth Millikan (1984), he maintains that the decouplability constraint is tied to the misrepresentation constraint, which in turn is governed by the teleological (normativity) constraint: 'all the decouplability we can reasonably require can be found in misrepresentation, if this is properly understood' (2012, 141). The perception–action system can become decoupled from its object by misrepresenting it. Millikan links Brentano's notion that intentionality explains 'the capacity of the mind to "intend" the nonexistent' (as in the case of imagining something that does not exist) with 'an explanation of how misrepresentation can occur'. Thus she argues 'that misrepresentation is best understood by embedding the theory of intentionality within a theory of function that allows us to understand, more generally, what malfunction is' (2005, 168). Proper function is captured by the teleological constraint. By accepting the teleological/normativity constraint, we get the misrepresentation and decouplability constraints for free. In subsuming the decouplability constraint under the misrepresentation constraint, and subsuming the latter under the teleological/normativity constraint, Rowlands is suggesting that decouplability is a form of misrepresentation, and misrepresentation consists in failing to track x properly. In trying to catch the ball, if I turn my fingers up rather than down, thereby missing the ball, my fingers fail to track the ball properly; then the PIA or AOR is misrepresenting and is decoupled from what it is supposed to be representing.

It's not clear, however, that decouplability can be reduced to misrepresentation, in contrast to what Rowlands and Millikan claim. If misrepresentation is one way of being decoupled from the action, not all forms of decoupling are misrepresentations. Significantly, Millikan acknowledges the compatibility of pushmi-pullyu representations with evidence, from Marc Jeannerod's work, that imagining ourselves acting activates the same representations as engaging in the action. The representation of a possibility for action is, according to Millikan, a 'directive' representation (2005, 166). This is because it actually serves a proper function only if and when it is acted upon. On this view, there is no reason to represent what can be done unless this sometimes effects its being done. But Brentano can also imagine an action that he should *not* do and that he *will not* do—and there may be a good reason to imagine it. Does this mean that he is misrepresenting the action, or that engaging his imagination in this way involves a malfunction? It is not at all clear that imagining an action offline—in a way that is decoupled from action—is misrepresenting it. Rowlands may want to claim that for PIAs to be representational it is enough that they can be decoupled in the sense of misrepresenting. Rowlands, however, with respect to PIAs, shouldn't (and I think, doesn't) object to ditching decouplability in the classic sense. And we've already seen that Clark and Grush, as well as Wheeler, already go some distance in this direction in regard to MRRs and AORs.

On a non-representational model we can indeed get things wrong, but not because our representation of the world *mis*represents the world. Rather, the world itself is ambiguous in the light of our particular abilities and projects. From a particular distance and perspective, or in a specific light, the mountain appears to be climbable. Once I get closer, or begin to climb, however, I can discover that the mountain is not climbable. On the representationalist view this is explained by saying that my original representation of the mountain was wrong. On the embodied, non-representationalist view, at a particular distance, in a specific kind of light, and from a particular perspective the mountain affords a certain climbing possibility relative to my embodied skills. Change the distance, the light, the perspective, and/or my bodily condition, and the affordance may disappear—that is, the dynamical coupling of body and environment changes. These things are physically determined factors that involve a real mountain, light conditions, and my bodily position, strength, and capabilities; they are not representational. The affordance doesn't disappear because I change *the representation of* my distance from the mountain—I actually have to change *my distance*, and when I do so, the body–mountain relation, which defines the affordance, and my perception, changes.

I don't deny that a representationalist could provide a representational description of this same situation.[6] For example, from a particular distance and perspective I 'represent' (or misrepresent) the mountain as climbable. Clark (also following Millikan) suggests that affordances are in fact AORs (1997, 50), which, of course, goes precisely against Gibson's concept of affordances. For Millikan, the perceived layout of the environment is a representation of this sort (a pushmi-pullyu represen-tation or PPR), because it describes 'how things out there are arranged', and at the same time represents 'possible ways of moving within that environment' (Millikan 1996, 151). But this is simply to redefine affor-dances in representational terms and to presume that the perceptual layout of the environment is something different from the layout of the environment that I perceive, i.e., that a 'percept', which is something over and above the perceiving, is located in the perceiving subject. If the landscape is right there in front of me, affording me the opportunity to act, or if in perceiving the other's gesture I am shaping my own response accordingly, then the system (including both neural and extra-neural elements), the situation (in Dewey's sense of the term [see section 3.3]), is already organized for action and there seems no reason to reduplicate it representationally.

Within an embodied-situated approach, then, what role can a minimal representation play? Wheeler defends AORs as perception-based, short-lived, egocentric (spatial) mappings of the environment calibrated strictly in terms of possible actions. Clark and Grush suggest that the anticipation that is built into a forward emulator for online motor control is representational. Rowlands argues that PIAs governed by the

---

[6] It seems that if one is committed to representationalism then any process can be described in terms of representation. Thus Chemero (2000) is able to offer a representa-tional description of the Watt governor, which van Gelder considers to be purely a dynamical mechanism. Chemero argues that the angle of a control arm designed to modulate engine speed is to be considered a valve's AOR. Indeed, he does so on a relatively restrictive three-point definition of representation, which differs, as he notes, from van Gelder's (1995), and from Wheeler's (1996); and we note it differs from Rowlands' (2006) and Clark's (1997), which Clark differentiates from Haugeland's (1985) three-point defin-ition, which is also different from Chemero's. Even if there were some consensus on a definition of representation, what Chemero shows at best is the possibility of taking a 'representational stance' (a version of Dennett's intentional stance)—that is, we can treat any mechanism 'as if' it were representational. But as Chemero goes on to suggest, the representationalist account is superfluous or redundant since the non-representational dynamical account tells us everything important about the system.

intentional action are representational. When we consider these aspects of action together we should notice that they reflect nothing more nor less than the dynamical temporal structure of action itself. On a phenomenological, non-representational model of this temporal structure (on the integrative timescale), action involves a coherent trajectory held together in the tightly coupled perception–action structure: (1) an online pragmatic retentional maintenance of the relevant aspects of the environment as it is being experienced (a holding in perceptual presence of those factors that have just defined my possible actions); (2) an anticipatory or protentional aspect that is an implicit characteristic of my immediate project-determined coupling with the environment, and (3) the ongoing movements that constitute the current dynamical state of the system.[7]

This retentional–protentional structure, which is characteristic of action as well as consciousness, is fully 'online' in what Husserl calls the 'living present'. The retentional tracking of the just-past details of body and environment is, in the present moment of the integrative timescale, neither a recollection nor a representation which would (re)duplicate them; it is rather part of the action structure in its ongoing experienced directionality. The protentional anticipation of what comes next points to where the action is heading, not in the sense that it maps or represents where it is heading, but in the sense that the ongoing action has a heading—that the action is already going, and experienced as going, in a certain direction, heading toward a completion (that it may or may not attain). An action is not a momentary or frozen snapshot supplemented by representations of past and future movements; it has a unity over time that is accounted for by (and integrated into) the intentional structure of the action itself. Nothing in this dynamically dissipating process amounts to a representation, if, returning to our original list, we take representation to involve:

• An internal image or symbol or sign
• A discrete duration
• Decouplability

[7] For an interpretation of Husserl's analysis of the retentional–protentional temporal structure of experience in terms of non-representationalist dynamic systems theory, and its application to motor control, see Gallagher (2011; 2016); Gallagher and Varela (2003); Thompson (2007); Van Gelder (1999); Varela (1999).

Wheeler, when he ditches decouplability, endorses Clark's idea that an AOR can 'simultaneously be viewed simply as a smaller dynamical system linked to the one that hooks directly into the real-world' (2005, 219). The problem with the classic conception of representation is that it's difficult to say how a representation 'hooks directly' into the physical environment since in some sense a representation, as defined, seems more decoupled than coupled to begin with—if, for example, it stands in for something (or some part of the action) not present (Orlandi 2014, 97). As Rowlands puts it, classic representations 'can be instantiated independently of what is going on in the outside world'. But even more so than AORs and MRRs, on Rowlands' conception, PIAs *are* the things that hook directly into the real world—'through complex causal inter-actions in an extended-body-environment system' (Wheeler 2005, 193); they are, after all, already, extra-neural events in the world—things like hands shaping and moving in a certain direction, and eyes saccadically tracking what they need to track. Even more than Wheeler's AORs, Rowland's PIAs fit well with an embodied, *enactive* action/perception model, where perception and action are linked to the world in a tem-poral, dynamical structure.

A representationalist might reply that even if this describes the absence of mental representations in the *experience* of action, there are certainly subpersonal representations, in the elemental timescale, that underlie this dynamical structure. The conception of a dynamical system is always open to a representational interpretation. The representation-alist might claim that the action itself depends on certain B-formatted neural representations that operate at a subpersonal level, outside of or below the threshold of experience. There is no doubt that there are neural processes involved in body-schematic motor control, but these subper-sonal body-schematic processes operate on the same dynamical model reflected in experience (Gallagher 2011; Gallagher and Zahavi 2014). The ubiquity of anticipatory mechanisms in the sensory–motor system (sometimes specified in terms of efferent 'anticipation for the conse-quences of the action' [Georgieff and Jeannerod 1998]) is well known (Berthoz 2000; Berthoz and Petit 2006). Body-schematic processes are not static, but include a retentional component that dynamically organ-izes sensory–motor feedback in such a way that the current motor state is 'charged with a relation to something that has happened before' (Head 1920, 606). Neither the relations nor the *relata* in this process, however,

are discrete or decouplable. Neither body schemata nor neuronal patterns have discrete durations. Neurons, of course, are part of the highly
connected complex system of the brain in which connections are effected
causally by chemical, physical processes, rather than by representational
processes. If body schemas were reducible to neuronal firing patterns,
they would be characterized in the same way. Alternatively, if body
schemas are complex processes that extend over brain and body (including the peripheral nervous system), and are in all cases specified by
environmental contexts (see Gallagher 2005a), they are not constituted
by one part of the system representing another part, or by one part
interpreting the other as a representation. In such neuronal and body-
schematic systems whatever could count as representation would be
purely the result of an explanatory representationalist interpretation;
not an interpretation by the system, agent, or subject, but by the scientist
abstracting (drawing discrete lines between one schema and the next;
claiming decouplability, etc.) from the system.[8]

Wheeler, as we noted, gives up the criterion of decouplability in
his characterization of a minimal representation (2005, 219). On his
account, a minimal representation (1) is richly adaptive, (2) is 'arbitrary'
(which means that the equivalence class of different inner elements that
could perform a particular systemic function is fixed by their capacity,
when organized and exploited in the right ways, to carry specific
behavior-guiding information about the world, rather than by any
non-informational physical properties of those elements, such as their
shape or weight [Wheeler, private correspondence]), and (3) employs a
homuncular mechanism, i.e., a mechanism that is hierarchically com-
partmentalized but contributes to a collective achievement. With the

---

[8] Borrowing on Menary's (2007) reading of Peirce's semiotics, one simple way to put this is
that one of the triadic elements of the representational process is missing in the case of
neuronal events or subpersonal processes more generally. For Peirce, 'representation necessarily involves a genuine triad' (1931, 1.480). It involves a *vehicle* (sign) mediating between an
object and an *interpreter*. A neuronal pattern or event might be considered a representational
vehicle, but only in connection with an object (some event in the environment, perhaps) and a
consumer or interpreter (to produce an interpretant or meaning). The missing element is the
consumer (interpreter). The experiencing subject is not an interpreter of its own brain events,
but neither is the brain itself, unless one is willing to substitute for causal vocabulary the idea
that one process in the brain interprets another process in the brain as a sign of something
happening in the environment (see the next paragraph). On the Peircean model, if one of the
elements is missing, there is no representation.

idea of the homuncular mechanism Wheeler attempts to preserve the criterion of interpretability within the system itself. Representational interpretation can be conceived of as involving modularity—processing in one module independent of processing in another, but each communicating results to (and mutually interpreting) another module. The homuncular mechanism thus takes some information off-line (but, according to Wheeler, without decoupling it from the action itself) and manipulates it to anticipate possible actions. This is similar to Clark and Grush's emulator *sans* decoupability. At the same time it is not clear what offline but not decoupled means, or, as I indicated above, how an anticipation of possible action can be formed without reference or integral connections to the current and just-past situation. In fact, in the case of action, modularity can be given up for the dynamical systems concept of a self-organizing continuous reciprocal causation which Wheeler himself favors in most instances. Online sensory–motor processes that are serving intentional action and are temporally structured in dynamical relation to the environment are in fact richly adaptive and arbitrary in the relevant sense, but are not homuncular, which means they involve no interpretational element. The dynamical process (being causal rather than communicative) does not require the idea that one discrete part of the mechanism interprets in isolation (or off-line) the information presented by another part. Rather, the protentional/anticipatory aspect that characterizes action itself, on the dynamical model, functions only in relation to the ongoing, online, project-determined coupling with the environment.

Even if, however, instead of outright ditching some minimal form of decoupability (defined perhaps in terms of misrepresentation), we wanted to allow that these conditions may be governed by the normativity condition (i.e., that we can somehow get it wrong), as Rowlands wants, still, it is possible that the normativity constraint can be fully explained in terms of non-representational dynamical processes. This connects with a re-conceptualization of the notion of the teleological found in the recent biological sciences and explicated by Jonas, Varela, Thompson, and others. If you think of the mind purely in terms of mechanistic processes (or machine states, or emulators), you miss something fundamental about the life-aspect of the mind—the embodied mind. On this view, intentional directedness is the default of action; not something to be accomplished in representational processes (*Chapter 4*; also Thompson 2007; Weber and Varela 2002). This is the deeper sense of operational intentionality, captured by the concept of motor intentionality (Merleau-Ponty 2012) or motor intention (Pacherie 2006). If PIAs are 'pre-intentional', they are so, as Rowlands indicates, only in the sense that they are not consciously controlled or decided. But to the extent that they are elements within an intentional action, they are not pre-intentional in any deeper sense.

Concerning the teleological or normativity condition, then, we can maintain the idea that a movement or process qualifies as a PIA 'only if it has the *proper function* either of tracking the feature or state-of-affairs *s* that *produces* it, or of enabling an organism . . . to achieve some (benefi-cial) task in virtue of tracking *s*' (Rowlands 2012, 138). But it does so only as a dynamical process where an organism is properly coupled to an environment (enactively hooked into the world).

5.5   What's Left of the Idea of Representation in Action?

We can summarize what we have learned in this chapter in a detailed negative characterization of what we have been calling minimal repre-sentations, including MMRs, AORs, and PIAs.

1. Minimal representation is not internal—it extends to include embodied-environmental aspects and is only 'weakly' neuronal.
2. Minimal representation is not a discrete, identifiable, enduring thing—it's more like a temporal, dynamical, distributed process.
3. Minimal representation is not passive—it's pragmatically enactive, proactively contributing to the adaptability of the system.
4. Minimal representation is not decouplable—indeed, if it is to remain teleological, it has to continue tracking x or it has to involve a continuing and online anticipation of a predicted motor state.
5. Minimal representation is not strongly instructional—even if it can be combined into a more general representational framework, it is never sufficiently detailed to solve the commonsense knowledge or the frame problem.
6. Minimal representation is not homuncular and does not involve interpretation.

In effect, the idea of a minimal representation no longer conforms to the criteria that would make it a representation. At this point we can surely ask, what's the point in retaining the term 'representation' in the case of action? What work does the concept of representation really do since nothing is being re-presented to the subject; since it is not consistent with the classic notion of representation; and since in explicating the 'job description' (Ramsey 2007, 25) that representation is meant to fulfill, one is already explaining action in non-representational terms of perception-based complex causal interactions in an embodied-situated system. A facetious economic argument against representationalism would suggest that the explanatory work that the concept of representation does is less than the work it takes to justify the use of the term 'representation'.

Actions do involve processes that are *intentional*, certainly at the personal level, and in a way that contributes to the organization of the subpersonal processes that support the intentional action (motor control processes and PIAs that contribute to the accomplishment of actions). But if representation is one form of intentionality, not all intentionality is representational. The kind of motor intentionality described in terms of body-schematic processes by Merleau-Ponty (2012), for example, is a non-representational dynamical process. Actions do involve *teleological* functions insofar as they require tracking something in the world. This is an enactive perceptual tracking—I see the ball that I want to catch, I see the ball-at-A-moving-towards-B, and my bodily posture and movements go into dynamical relation to the changing conditions of its trajectory. Even if tracking involves co-variance, this doesn't mean it's a representational process. I think Orlandi gets this right.

Tracking states are states that are close to their informational origin, and they are typically implicated only in subpersonal transitions. They do not *inform* organism-level behavior. Thinking that they are representational betrays a misunderstanding of the notion, since representation requires both independence from causal or statistical correlates and performance-contribution.

(Orlandi 2014, 96; *emphasis* added)

Actions are also *fallible*—actions can fail, not because of a misrepresentation, but because perception is finite and the world can be a rough place: things look climbable but turn out not to be; things look catchable, but often turn out not to be, etc.

There is thus an intentionality of the body-in-action that is not characterized in terms of representations understood as internal, decouplable, or instructional; an intentionality that does not involve interpretation in the relevant sense; and that is accordingly non-representational. This kind of intentionality is dynamically linked with the environment in a way that reflects a specific temporal structure at the subpersonal level. As Wheeler puts it:

as the brain becomes ever more bound up in complex distributed [and extended] causal interchanges with the non-neural body and the wider physical environment, it seems likely that the temporal character of those interchanges will become increasingly rich.   (Wheeler 2005, 244)

Action involves temporal processes that can be better explained in terms of dynamical systems of self-organizing continuous reciprocal causation. Accordingly, one can characterize the intentionality that contributes to the constitution of actions as conforming to the following constraints:

1. *The teleological/normative constraint*: actions *fallibly* track things in the world. But this can be explained in terms of an enactive perceptual tracking. In this regard, Rowlands rightly states:

The true locus of normativity does not, or does not necessarily, reside on the inside, in the form of inner representations. Rather, it is also to be found on the outside. Our behaviour is infused with a form of normativity that is *sui generis* and does not derive from the inner states of a subject.   (2012, 136)

Once we get this far, I suggest, the problem of explaining our normative grip is no longer the problem of representation; it's rather the problem of explaining how we are dynamically coupled to the world.

2. *The dynamical constraint*: actions are dynamically related to (coupled or hooked directly into) environmental contexts. Processes that make up an action may refer to something or some state of affairs other than the action itself, but only in pragmatic terms of the action. But this doesn't mean that they represent that state of affairs. Even if they objectively register information about that state of affairs (e.g., if the shape of my grasp reflects the shape of the thing that I am reaching for), taking this as information about the world is the result of an external interpretation, and is available only from an observational perspective. It doesn't play the role of information for the system itself.

3. *The combinatorial constraint*: PIAs and basic actions reflect integrated temporal and kinematic patterns of intentionality that can form more complex, dynamical, goal-related, intentional actions.

5.6 Scientific Pragmatism about Representations

Do representational accounts provide a helpful shortcut for explaining action? Does the concept of representation offer 'very real explanatory leverage' (Clark 1997, 145; see Chemero 2000)? Or does it explain anything about action at all? Clark and Grush (1999, 8) put the question in precisely the right way:

> It is, of course, true that the emulator circuitry can also and simultaneously be viewed simply as a smaller dynamical system linked to the one that hooks directly into the real-world. But that is just as it should be . . . The question is, which of these descriptions is most useful for Cognitive Science?

I suggest that, at best, representationalism is just one way—a scientifically abstract way—of explaining the action process. But a representation is not an *explanans* that does any work itself. It's a concept under which one still needs all the explanation to be made. Furthermore, the risk is that representational accounts lead to the temptation of bestowing ontological status, i.e., the idea that there really are discrete representations in the system and that they are something more than what a motor control system does as part of the action itself.

One important problem is that a majority of cognitive scientists continue to use the R-word and do so in ways that are not often clear. In the case of action it is nothing more than a handy, but often confused and misleading term, a bad piece of heuristics, an awkward place-holder for an explanation that still needs to be given in dynamical terms of an embodied, environmentally embedded, and enactive model.

In this regard, however, even if one thinks that the concept of representation does do some explanatory work, what I identified as the facetious economic argument against representationalism also counts as a very pragmatic argument. It may take more energy to define and distinguish any legitimate sense of representation from amongst the plethora of uses of that term, and to justify its use, than it would take to explain the phenomenon in non-representationalist terms. And if one can explain the phenomenon in non-representationalist terms, then the concept of representation is at best redundant.

6

Perception without Inferences

In *Chapter 5* I looked at the notion of representation in action; in this chapter I'll look at the question of inference in perception. Are there inferences involved in perception, and if so, what does that mean, and where should we locate them? Here I'll join several others in arguing against an inference model of perception (e.g., Bruineberg, Kiverstein, and Rietveld 2016; Orlandi 2014) and I'll defend an enactivist alternative. I'll explore how the enactivist approach can respond to issues related to cognitive penetration and the effects of culture on perception. This approach, however, will raise some challenges in regard to how we might pursue a science of perception. Accordingly, I'll end by returning to considerations mentioned in *Chapter 1*, concerning enactivism understood as a philosophy of nature.

6.1 Inference Models of Perception

There is a long tradition in which perception is understood to involve inference. One can think immediately of Helmholtz, but also the more recently developed models of predictive coding. In between, but seemingly consistent with both of these approaches, we find the computationalist view, expressed, for example, by Fodor and Pylyshyn in their 'Establishment' critique of Gibson's notion of direct perception.

The current Establishment theory (sometimes referred to as the 'information processing' view) is that perception depends, in several respects...upon inferences. Since inference is a process in which premises are displayed and consequences derived, and since that takes time, it is part and parcel of the information processing view that there is an intrinsic connection between perception and memory. And since, finally, the Establishment holds that the psychological mechanism of inference is the transformation of mental representations, it follows that perception is in relevant respects a computational process.

(Fodor and Pylyshyn 1981, 139–40)

One question is whether we should take the notion of inference literally or metaphorically (see Hatfield 2002 for review). For example, Helmholtz contends that the processes of perception 'are *like inferences* insofar as we from the observed effect on our senses arrive at an idea of the cause of this effect' (Helmholtz 1867, 430). Likewise, Palmer, expressing what Fodor and Pylyshyn describe as the Establishment view, states:

Using the term 'inference' to describe such a process may seem to be somewhat metaphorical and thus to undercut the force of the claim that perception works by unconscious inference. But, as we said at the outset, unconscious inference must be at least somewhat metaphorical, since normal inference is quite clearly slow, laborious, and conscious, whereas perception is fast, easy, and unconscious. The important point for present purposes is that perception relies on processes that can be usefully viewed as inferences that require heuristic assumptions.

(Palmer 1999, 83).

Finally, in the predictive coding camp, Jakob Hohwy sometimes makes the same gesture.

The problem of perception is the problem of using the effects—that is, the sensory data that is all the brain has access to—to figure out the causes. It is then a problem of causal inference for the brain, *analogous* in many respects to our everyday reasoning about cause and effect, and to scientific methods of causal inference...There is a sense in which, in spite of being Bayesian, [prediction error minimization] is more mechanical than it is inferential...The 'neuronal hardware' of the mechanism itself is not literally inferential: neuronal populations are just trying to generate activity that anticipates their input.

(Hohwy 2013, 13, 55)

The pervasive claim that brain processes are best understood as inferences, if sometimes regarded as metaphorical, is nonetheless often treated as a substantive claim. If the claim is that perceptual processes operate *as if* they were inferential (computational, representational), it would be difficult to disagree: many things can be viewed as if they operated inferentially—thermostats, smoke detectors, etc. But this would mean that it's just one way of characterizing the subpersonal brain processes of perception, and if we can find a different and simpler, i.e., more parsimonious, way of characterizing such processes, or one that has equal or greater explanatory power, we should consider it as a viable alternative.

What motivates the idea that brain processes are inferential?

1.   A general unobservability principle (UP).

The brain has no direct access to the world. Helmholtz (1867, 430) expressed this well: 'We always in fact only have direct access to the events at the nerves, that is, we sense the effects, never the external objects'. Or as Jacob Hohwy puts it, 'the sensory data ... is all the brain has access to' (2013, 13). Predictive coders, including Hohwy, should in fact deny the last proposition since they would also argue that the brain has access to a set of priors (memory), based on prior experience. But this is only further explication of why they think perception is inferential, since inference seems to be the best mechanism to explain how priors, which may be conceptual in format, get integrated with sensory information. A more specialized version of UP motivates the idea that social cognition involves theoretical inference—because what we want to know (the other's mental state) is hidden from us. Just as we have no direct access to the other person's mind, our own brain, more generally, has no direct access to the world.

The assumptions are clear. First, assume that all cognition (including perception) happens in the brain. Second, assume that the brain is locked up in the darkness of the skull and has no access to the outside world. It's a mystery how it could gain knowledge of current worldly affairs without drawing inferences from the clues provided by sensory data—the only clues it seemingly has available. Andy Clark summarizes:

For, the task of the brain, when viewed from a certain distance, can seem impossible: it must discover information about the likely causes of impinging signals without any form of direct access to their source ... [A]ll that it 'knows', in any direct sense, are the ways its own states (e.g., spike trains) flow and alter. In that (restricted) sense, all the system has direct access to is its own states. The world itself is thus off-limits (though [it] can, importantly, issue motor commands and await developments) ... How, simply on the basis of patterns of changes in its own internal states, is it to alter and adapt its responses so as to tune itself to act as a useful node (one that merits its relatively huge metabolic expense) for the origination of adaptive responses? ... The task is ... to infer the nature of the signal source (the world) from just the varying input signal itself.
(Clark 2013a, 183)

Because the brain is isolated from the world—locked up in the skull—we are led to ascribe a complex structure or procedure involving computations, inferences, and representations, a structured process that helps the system (the brain) work out a solution.

This is precisely the predictive coding view. The brain is pictured as having no direct access to the outside world; accordingly, it needs to represent that world by some internal model that it constructs by decoding sensory input (Hohwy 2013). This process involves synaptic inhibition based on empirical priors. Based on priors (i.e., memories, assumptions, or prior experiences) and given a certain sensory input, the brain is pictured as making top-down probabilistic inferences about the causes of that input. Predictions are then matched against ongoing sensory input. Mismatches generate prediction errors that are sent back up the line; the brain corrects for those errors, and the system adjusts dynamically back and forth until there is a relatively good fit.

2.   A second motivation for the inference explanation is that it offers sufficient explanatory power to resolve the poverty of stimulus problem.

This is based on the assumption that the stimulus does not provide all the information needed for perception—the so-called poverty of stimulus problem. For example, the pattern of light that hits the retina is ambiguous—compatible with the production of a variety of visual representations of the world. Note that this again depends on (1), i.e., the brain has no access to the world.

This fact predicts that we should see the world in a radically unstable way: but this is patently false. The inferential view explains stability by supposing that the visual system makes use of some stored assumptions that help reduce the representations produced in response to the retinal stimulus.   (Orlandi 2013, 743)

On the predictive coding model, priors, based on Bayesian statistical processes, feed and constrain a process of inference (prediction) formation. For example, visual light discontinuities might be caused by various environmental features—edges, cracks, shadows, etc. But since edges are statistically the more frequent cause of light discontinuities, that is the prior that informs the inference. Unless that inference generates prediction errors, the brain settles in a stable way on this being a perception of an edge.

6.2 An Example from Social Cognition

Whether inference is a necessary ingredient of perception has been the subject of recent debates about direct (i.e., non-inferential) perception in the context of social cognition. There has been, in fact, a surprising turn in this debate. Some proponents of theory of mind (ToM), a position that has traditionally held to the Unobservability Principle (UP), have given up this principle and have embraced the idea of direct social perception for some mental states (e.g. Carruthers 2015; Lavelle 2012). UP has been seemingly one of the central assumptions leading to the idea that one requires inference for ToM processes, precisely because, as traditionally held, we do not have perceptual access to the other's mind. Alan Leslie (of many who could be cited) gives clear expression of this position: 'Because the mental states of others (and indeed ourselves) are completely hidden from the senses, they can only ever be inferred' (Leslie 2004, 164). In giving up UP it might seem that we should give up the idea that we need inference to understand others, and that our knowledge of other minds via perception could be non-inferential. But that's not how it turns out.

Carruthers (2015, 3), for instance, argues 'the mental states of other people are often represented *in the content of perception* [and] this conclusion is consistent with many forms of theory-theory [inferential] accounts of our mindreading abilities'. It remains consistent with ToM because, according to Carruthers, perception itself is shaped by a tacit set of ToM inferences.

Indeed, one might think that *any* adequate account of our perception of mental states (assuming that the latter is real) would need to appeal to a set of tacit inferences underlying such perceptions, which might then qualify as a form of theory-theory.   (Carruthers 2015, 2)

Inferences are required because mental states cannot be perceived independently of concepts and acquired knowledge of the world. 'We have no idea how to explain the causal processes involved except by appealing to something amounting to a tacit *theory*, I suggest...even enactivism cannot obviate the need for tacit theory' (Carruthers 2015, 3).

In conceiving of perception in this context, there are at least three possibilities.

1. We need perceptual processes plus extra-perceptual inferential processes; the inferences are conceptual/theoretical and the integration happens so fast it *seems* to be purely perceptual (this is the position defended by Lavelle and Carruthers).
2. Perception is itself an inferential process (Helmholtz and the predictive coding view); it is not that we add a cognitive process to perceptual processes; perception is already cognitive.
3. Perception is enactive (action-oriented, affordance driven, and not inferential), but is nonetheless epistemic and 'smart' because it is attuned to context and can take direction.

Lavelle (2012), for example, makes it clear that to grasp another person's mental states (e.g., intentions, emotions), perception must be supplemented by extra-perceptual inferential processes. This does not occur on the phenomenological level of our conscious experiences (i.e., on the integrative timescale), but subpersonally (on the elemental timescale). We need not add an extra step to our conscious experience; but that's because the extra (inferential) step is already in the mix—already added at the subpersonal level.

Lavelle rejects, for example, Gallese's proposal that low-level mirror neuron processes are sufficient for understanding actions. Gallese had argued that '[W]e don't need to suppose an over-arching top-down influence in order to have a neural mechanism that maps the goal. We already have it in the premotor [or parietal] system. We don't need to imply a further mechanism that maps the goal' (Gallese 2007, 15). In contrast, Lavelle sticks to the idea that beliefs are represented in non-perceptual areas and are introduced via inferential processes. 'The moral is that while theoretical entities need not be unobservable, one requires a theory in order to observe them' (2012, 228).

Carruthers (2015), in agreement with Lavelle, still wants to distinguish between perception and inference, but also suggests that perception is never '*encapsulated* from the remainder of one's beliefs and goals. This way of thinking of the perception/cognition boundary presumes that there is a stage in visual processing—sometimes called "early vision"—that is beyond any direct influence from one's other mental states . . . it is doubtful whether there is any such stage' (2015, 3). While this almost suggests a perceptual process that is fully integrated with the conceptual, in a way that would not require inference—a perception that is cognitively penetrated *simpliciter*—Carruthers still wants to retain the inference process. He regards it as a fast, online process.

Acquiring concepts that classify a set of arbitrary similar-seeming shapes into two distinct categories, for example, transforms the perceived similarity spaces among the shapes. Those that seemed similar before now seem distinctively different as a result of category acquisition. Until recently, however, it was unclear to what extent these effects reflect a late decision-like stage in processing, or whether sensory experience is altered by concepts in an online manner. But there is now ample evidence of the latter.   (Carruthers 2015, 5)

Another example that he cites suggests the same thing. The Greek language has two words for 'blue' (light blue [*ghalazio*] vs dark blue [*ble*]), but only one for 'green'. Thierry et al. (2009), using EEG, measured a specific neuronal signal, *visual mismatch negativity* (vMMN) over the visual cortex, in Greek and English speakers. This signal occurs *c.*200 milliseconds following the presentation of an oddball stimulus (for example, a square in a series of circles, or a dark blue circle in a series of light blue circles). On this elemental timescale, this signal is pre-attentive and an unconscious stage of visual processing. For blue contrasts, vMMN showed significant difference in Greek speakers, but no significant difference for English speakers. That is, the conceptual difference between different shades of blue shows up directly in visual processing. Thus, Carruthers concludes: 'Because Greek speakers have distinct *concepts* for light blue and dark blue, they see the two colors as more unlike one another and they do so from quite early stages in visual processing, prior to the impact of attention or judgment' (2015, 5).

It's not clear that these examples settle the question completely since we can still ask whether the influence on early visual processing could not be the result of plastic changes to early sensory areas. Carruthers, however, prefers a speedy online binding process between strict sensory/perceptual processing and culturally related concepts—something that still leaves room for unconscious inferences infecting the perceptual process. Carruthers doesn't mention that Thierry et al. (2009) also show differences between Greek and English speakers in P1 (the first, earliest positive peak elicited by visual stimuli over parietooccipital regions of the scalp at 100–130 milliseconds (100 milliseconds prior to vMMN). Given this, the inferential integration would have to be extremely speedy.

For Carruthers, however, the point is that *via* speed of processing, perceptual and conceptual processes are integrated by the time perception reaches consciousness.

Conceptual information is processed within the window of a few hundred milliseconds that elapses between the presentation of a stimulus and its subsequent global broadcast. This could well be a function of expertise. While you or I might be capable of slowly figuring out, from the configuration of pieces on a chess board, that White has a winning position, a chess grandmaster may immediately *see* it as such ... [In the case of social cognition, the] only limit will be whether *mindreading inferences* can be drawn fast enough for binding to take place. Since many forms of mental-state awareness are seemingly simultaneous with awareness of the behavior and/or circumstances that cause them, we can presume that ordinary mindreaders *can* draw the requisite inferences fast enough. (2015, 6–7)

In that case, even if I say that I see that you are upset, or that you intend to take a sip from your glass, this seeing (which on a conscious level seems direct) is really the result of subpersonally inferring your emotional state or intention on the basis of some perceptual cues and some basic rules of folk psychology. So, for Carruthers, this is still perception *plus* fast (indeed, very fast at 100 milliseconds if, following Thierry et al., we consider the earliest positive peak) theoretical inference, at the subpersonal level where a tacit ToM operates. What Lavelle and Carruthers suggest, then, is that perception and tacit theory are two separate things that need to be combined in quick inferential processes on the elemental timescale. This is not perception that is inferential, as in predictive coding (PC), but perception *plus* extra-perceptual inference.

Accordingly, this type of proposal contrasts with the PC or Helmholzian model, which considers perception itself to be inferential. Moreover, in PC models, as we noted, there is a more basic unobservability principle at work. This is the Helmholtzian idea, mentioned above, that the brain only has direct access to the events 'at the nerves', and never to the perceptual objects. The implication is that perception is not really direct. Rather, 'perceptual phenomenology [is] at one remove from the world ... Interspersed between you and the world is a process of using models to explain away sensory input [i.e., to resolve prediction errors]' (Hohwy 2013, 48). This is 'a kind of indirectness'. Perception 'is indirect in the sense that what you experience *now* is given in your top-down prediction of your ongoing sensory input, rather than the bottom-up signal from the states of affairs themselves' (48).

6.3 The Enactivist Alternative

Enactivist approaches start with different assumptions and suggest a different vocabulary. The human brain not only evolved along with the human body, and works the way it does because of that; it's also not isolated, but rather is dynamically coupled to a body that is dynamically coupled to an environment. The organism (the brain–body system) is operating within the situation itself rather than on a model of the situation inferred by the brain. This coupling of brain–body–environment is structured by the physical aspects of neuronal processes, bodily movements, affects, anatomy and function, and environmental regularities.

Co-variance is physical variance across all parameters—brain, body, environment. For example, an object such as a piece of food in the near environment activates not only the visual cortex, but also other sensory areas, and the premotor and gustatory cortexes the way it does because I have hands and the object is reachable, and there is motivating interest (hunger) and an anticipation of reward. Change in any of these factors means that perception changes. If the human body evolved without hands, if I were aplasic (born without hands), or even if I lost my hands to amputation, to different degrees the whole system would perform differently and my perception would be different.

On the enactivist view, neural plasticity mitigates to some degree the need to think that subpersonal processes are inferential. The neural networks of perception are set up by previous experience—'set up to be set off', to borrow a phrase from Jesse Prinz (2004, 55). Whatever plastic changes have been effected in the visual cortex, or in the perceptual network constituted by early sensory and association areas, such changes constrain and shape the current response to visual stimuli. Neural networks are attuned to situated environmental events. Consider, in addition, that networked patterns of neuronal activation in premotor, parietal, and limbic areas modulate the dynamics of visual processing (Kranczioch et al. 2005; see Engel 2010, 233–5 for discussion).

For example, the limitations of my reach are determined not by my brain's representations of my arm, but by the physical length of my arm, which has grown as I have grown to adulthood, and to which my visual system has already physically accommodated itself. What this means is not that there is a fact or assumption about my arm length stored somewhere acting as a prior, and activated in an inference when the brain has to decide whether it's possible to reach the food. Rather, it means that there are physical changes that have occurred in visual cortical areas and in their connections with premotor and motor areas, so that when a hand-to-food-to-mouth action is called for, the system is activated in a dynamical causal fashion—it has already been set up to be set off in the right way. The physical length of my arm, which changes over the developmental timescale, together with my prior reaching practices, tune brain processes so that neuronal activations, rather than inferring anything, are attuning to my embodied physical possibilities and the physical affordances in a particular environment where something is either within reach or not, graspable or not, of interest or not, etc. I perceive things in terms of these sensory–motor contingencies and in terms of what those things pragmatically afford in relation to a body like mine, in the situation, also defined in part, for example, by my gustatory and more general interest conditions.

Many accounts of perception restrict the analysis to questions of recognition. As we've seen, the question in PC is often about how the visual system recognizes what is out there in the world, given that its access is limited to sensory input. This leads to the idea that the function of perception is to solve a puzzle, and what better way to solve a puzzle than to use inferential logic. But perception's function is never purely recognitional; vision, for example, involves more than recognition and motor control. The senses are not charged with just identifying or recognizing objects or just guiding bodily movement in the world. Response involves more than that; there are always ulterior motives. Because the organism desires food or rest or sex or aesthetic enjoyment or understanding, etc. the eye is never innocent. Consider that neuronal activity in the earliest of perceptual processing areas, such as V1, reflects more than simple feature detection. V1 neurons anticipate reward if they have been tuned by prior experience (Shuler and Bear 2006). This is not sensory data first, followed by inferential processes that conclude to reward possibility (an additional neural or cognitive function added on to sensory activation)—it's an intrinsically reward-oriented response or attunement to stimuli due to prior experiences and plastic changes— there's no room for or need for inferences in this respect. Perception is already attuned to reward possibilities.

Furthermore, with perception, autonomic and peripheral nervous systems are activated in dynamic patterns in synchrony with central processes—but in a way that makes it unclear what is regulating what. As we noted in section 1.5, along with the earliest visual processing, the medial orbital frontal cortex is activated initiating a train of muscular and hormonal changes throughout the body, modulating processes in organs, muscles, and joints associated with prior experience, and integrated with current sensory information (Barrett and Bar 2009). Just such modulations help to guide affective and action response. Integrated with affective and sensory–motor processes tied to the current situation, visual stimulation generates not just brain activation, but also specific bodily affective changes. Consider further that perception of another's face activates not just the face recognition area and ventral stream, but, importantly, the dorsal visual pathway that informs our motor system— suggesting that we perceive action affordances in the face of the other (Debruille, Brodeur, and Porras 2012). That is, we don't simply perceive the snapshot of a face in an instant with the task of recognizing it, we perceptually *respond* over time to affordances offered by the others' emotions as well as their actions.

Face perception presents not just objective patterns that we might recognize conceptually as emotions. It involves complex interactive behavioral and response patterns arising out of an active engagement with the other's face—not simple recognition of objective features, but interactive perception that constitutes an experience of significance or valence that shapes response. Social perception is affective in ways different from object perception. The experience of the gaze of another person directed back at you *affects* you, and your perception of the other's emotion *affects* you, even if this affect is not consciously recognized. Even when presented with masked, subliminal images of angry or happy faces or bodies, one's autonomic and peripheral systems register the emotion and respond (Tamietto 2013), and this response is part of what the perception is, as Barrett and Bar (2009) suggest. The perception of emotion is itself affective.

Is this best described as an inference process, perhaps a hierarchically organized set of inferential steps, a complex syllogistic argument that loops through the body to reach the conclusion that I'm attracted to or repulsed by what I see? It's one thing to think that the best way to talk about conceptual factors or folk psychological rules having an influence on perception is in terms of inferential processes, whether that is meant in a metaphorical or literal way. Likewise, if the only thing perceptually at stake for the organism were the task of recognition—of some object, a face, or another person—then it might seem intuitive to think that inference might do the job. But we (or our brains) are not simply trying to solve a puzzle that involves guessing or recognizing what is outside the skull. It seems less intuitive to think that broadly affective factors—including various autonomic and homeostatic factors—fit neatly into an inferential structure. Even a strong proponent of predictive coding, like Jakob Hohwy, can have doubts. '[T]he Bayesian, inferential approach to perception...seems rather intellectualistic...There is also something slightly odd about saying that the brain "infers", or "believes" things. In what sense does the brain know Bayes, if we don't? For that matter, a Bayesian approach to perception does not seem to directly concern the full richness of perceptual phenomenology...' (Hohwy 2013, 18–19).

We've already seen (in *Chapter 2*) that it was impossible to fit all sorts of unruly bodily processes into a set of B-formatted representations, and we'll see (in *Chapter 8*) that all kinds of affective processes, and even variations in circulation and heartbeat, can influence perception (Garfinkel et al. 2014). Add to this the fact that respiration is not simply artifactual for perception but a causal factor contributing to the variability of neuronal responses to sensory stimuli and behavioral performance. We know, for example, that the obstruction or willful interruption of breathing increases cortical neuronal activity in sensory, motor, limbic, and association areas (e.g., Peiffer et al. 2008). It's also the case that MEG-measured changes in beta, delta, and theta oscillations and ongoing gamma power modulations in somatosensory cortex are driven by corresponding respiratory phase (a causal link via sensory input from the olfactory bulb), with the result that reaction time to a visual stimulus changes significantly, taking longer during inspiration than during the resting phase (Liu, Papanicolaou, and Heck 2014; see Heck et al. 2016).[1]

Such things as affects and the effects of respiration and heart rate are not *represented* as part of my perception; they are non-representational

---

[1] There are many other relevant effects that are tied to respiration; it affects movement and perceptual tracking (Rassler 2000); visual and auditory signal detection (Flexman, Demaree, and Simpson 1974; Li, Park, and Borg, 2012); emotion perception (Zelano et al., 2016); and pain perception (Iwabe, Ozaki, and Hashizume 2014; Zautra et al. 2010). Thanks to Somogy Varga for these references.

factors that have an effect on perceptual response. I (the experiencing agent) see what's in the world when my eyes are open, light is present, chemical changes happen on my retina, there's neural activation in visual cortex that connects to neural activation in premotor cortex and other areas that loop through affective, peripheral, autonomic, and other fully embodied systems. On the enactivist view, the perceptual system is not just in the brain; it includes the organism (brain–body) embedded in or engaged with an environment that is characterized by certain regularities and affordances and action possibilities. Take away some of the oxygen in the air and the entire system is affected—respiration, heart rate, digestion, postural balance, motor control. These are some symptoms of altitude sickness—which can also include double vision and irrational behavior.

The poverty of stimulus problem—the second motivation for the inference model—is addressed by the possibility of bodily movement— reflected in what enactivists call sensory–motor contingencies, and pre-dictive coders call 'active inference'—moving around the environment provides more information and reduces the ambiguity. The point in such action is that the environment specifies itself (the environment is what it is)—*it* is not impoverished; the poverty only arises if we think that the brain has no access to the rich structure of the environment. It disap-pears if we acknowledge that the organism has access—is attuned or coupled—to the environment over time and is not only capable of movement, but is almost always moving. One can manufacture the poverty of stimulus problem by staying as still as possible—but this requires either some work or falling asleep.

Nico Orlandi has a nice argument in this context. The inferential view suggests that a default assumption informing the visual system is that edges are more statistically common than shadows or perhaps more evolutionarily important to detect. Given sensory stimulation by light discontinuity, the system goes to this default and forms the inference that it is perceiving an edge. In other words, to explain why the visual system infers what it does, the inferentialists must appeal to external environ-mental facts. Orlandi asks, 'why not do this from the get-go? If edges are more common or more typical or more important than other entities, then *that* is why we see them' (2014, 41). The visual system does not require an inference since, given evolutionary pressure or experience-driven plasticity, it 'can simply be wired by the environmental fact in question to produce states that track edges when exposed to discontinuities' (41). The system is physically attuned to such things, 'set up to be set off' by such visual discontinuities.

Just as there is more in the environment 'than meets the eye', there is also more in the environment that *does* meet the eye; that is, more than simple sensory cues such as visual discontinuities or colors. Visual cues taken together form a visual context, and integrated inter-modally with other sense modalities, including interoceptive proprioceptive, vestibular factors, etc. they capture a richer embodied and environmental context. This fact mitigates the need to think that what we call cognitive penetration works by fast knowledge-based inferences. If my visual system is wired to track edges, it should also be expected that, given the evolutionary and developmental significance of social relations, my perceptual system is (or comes to be) wired to track patterns of facial expressions, postures, movements, vocal intonations, and so forth. The tracking, which just is the co-variant activation of my perceptual system, is entirely perceptual, and the pattern that is perceived just is a sufficient part of the other person's emotion or intention to allow us to say that, without intervention of folk psychological inferences even at the subpersonal level, we perceive the emotion or intention (see Gallagher 2008b; Newen, Welpinghus, and Juckel 2015).

Along this line Orlandi (2014, 192ff.) shows, for the visual system, how context-sensitivity rather than knowledge-based inference can explain why we see a banana as more yellow than it actually is, or see African-American faces as darker than Caucasian faces even when they are exactly the same skin color (Levin and Banaji 2006). In the latter case, for example, it is not because we know factually that one face is African-American and infer that skin color must be comparatively darker, and so see it as such, but because we never see skin color all by itself; we also see shapes of noses and mouths—elements of a face pattern that we associate with darker skin color because of statistical regularity. If it were the result of knowledge-based inference, then we would expect the perceived difference to disappear once we knew that the skin color was identical—but it doesn't. As Orlandi goes on to show, one can explain such typical examples of cognitive penetration by reference to context sensitivity or semantic effects on attention—which is to say that these are not necessarily examples of cognitive penetration as this phenomenon is conceived by the inferentialists (also see Firestone and Scholl 2015).

Neural processes, coupled with non-neural processes, may co-vary with environmental regularities—certain light dispersals, certain tasty chemical patterns, certain textures, certain sound waves that the organism comes into contact with—but there's no reason to think of this in representational terms, or to think that such contact requires the mediation of inference making. Inferences are unmotivated if the organism (brain–body) is thought of as having access to, being attuning to, or being dynamically coupled to the environment. Attunement means that the organism is sensitive to certain environmental features—in part for evolutionary reasons (see *Chapter 9* for a more complex story), but also for reasons tied to ontogenetic development as well as to metaplastic effects of social and cultural factors. Such attuned sensitivity of organism to environment (shaped by reward patterns and affect patterns tied to learned responses and developed skills, which are themselves shaped by bodily details and environmental affordances) is sufficient for the perception of a significant world without requiring inferential processes seemingly tasked with constructing hypotheses about a world it cannot access.

6.4 Cultural Penetration

What is it that penetrates perception? Top-down, cognitive assumptions or beliefs? ToMish, folk psychological concepts or platitudes? Or some broader features of human (social) life? Moods, affects, traits, practices, and skills also can modulate perception (Siegel 2011). Some of these involve cultural factors. Perceiving others is not constrained simply by abstract differences in emotion patterns, but by situated affective attitudes towards out-group (*versus* in-group) members (Gutsell and Inzlicht 2010). Whether a person is able to respond to the emotions and intentions of another is crucially dependent on the person's attitudes (often implicit and nonconscious) about the racial or ethnic group to which the other belongs.

Evidence for this can be found in cross-cultural experiments on the perception of pain in others. A study by Xu et al. (2009) dramatically demonstrates the neural effects of implicit racial bias and shows that empathic neural responses to the other person's pain are modulated by the racial in-group/out-group relationship. fMRI brain imaging showed significant decreased activation in the anterior cingulate cortex (ACC), an area thought to correlate with empathic response, when subjects (Caucasians or Chinese) viewed racial out-group members (Chinese or Caucasian respectively) undergoing painful stimulations (needle penetration) to the face, compared to ACC activation when they viewed the same stimulations applied to racial in-group members. Differences in attitudes and biases are shaped by social and cultural experiences that likely cause plastic changes in ACC and SMA, and that clearly have some connectivity to our sensory systems. We are simply less responsive to out-group members and we display significantly less motor cortex activity when observing out-group members (Molnar-Szakacs et al. 2007). Most strikingly, in-group members fail to understand out-group member actions, and this is particularly prominent for disliked and dehumanized out-groups. The more dehumanized the out-group is, the less intuitive the grasp of out-group member intentions and actions (Gutsell and Inzlicht 2010).

On the inferentialist view, it is best to think of social and cultural factors in terms of theory-laden perception, as if the way our experience is (in)formed by social and cultural factors translates into the possession of a theory (a knowledge in the form of folk psychological beliefs or platitudes) that needs to be added to perception to formulate an extra inferential step in understanding others. The frequent example in discussions of cognitive penetrability involves beliefs. When you know that bananas are yellow, this knowledge affects what color you see bananas to be, so that an achromatic banana will appear to be yellow (Gegenfurtner, Olkkonen, and Walter 2006). This leads too quickly to the idea that perceptions are 'theory laden', a concept borrowed loosely from philosophy of science. Inferentialists will cite research to show that beliefs, and especially negative beliefs, about out-group members can interfere with one's ability to recognize emotions (Gutsell and Inzlicht 2010). In these cases making sense of the emotions of others is not constrained by cultural differences in emotion patterns, but by specific beliefs about the out-group member. On some conceptions it is not just a matter of 'having a belief' but of having a set of beliefs or a set of platitudes about the out-group that constitute part of folk psychology. On this view, the kind of subpersonal inferential processes suggested by Lavelle (2012) and Carruthers (2015) seem a possible explanation.

In contrast, rather than adding extra-perceptual inferential processing to perception, there is good evidence that perceptual processes at the subpersonal level are already shaped, via mechanisms of plasticity, by bodily and environmental (including social and cultural) factors and prior experience. For example, consider the now well-known difference between the way Westerners and Asians perceive and attend to visual objects and contexts (Goh and Park 2009). Westerners pay more attention to individual objects, while East Asians have an attentional bias toward backgrounds. These differences are not about the effects of particular beliefs or pieces of knowledge; they're regarded as differences in cognitive style that correlate not only with culture but also with age, and involve differences in the ventral visual areas of the brain (Goh et al. 2007). One also finds, for example, not only brain processes that are different relative to the use of different cultural tools and practices, but also cultural variations in brain mechanisms specifically underlying person perception and emotion regulation (Kitayama and Park 2010). For example, relative to European Americans, Asians show different neural processing in response to images of faces that represent a social-evaluative threat (Park and Kitayama 2014). In very specific ways, social and cultural factors have a physical, plastic effect on brain processes that shape basic perceptual experience and emotional responses.

   This can help to explain why individuals are more accurate at recognizing the intentions and the emotions of members of their own culture versus those of other cultures (Elfenbein and Ambady 2002a, 2002b; Matsumoto 2002). There are subtle differences in emotional 'dialects' (or embodied interactional dynamics) across cultures, which reduce cross-cultural emotion recognition (Elfenbein et al. 2007). Research also shows that the in-group advantage in emotion recognition is largely independent of genetic or ethnic factors. It seems that individuals make best sense of emotions expressed by a member's own cultural group, regardless of race and ethnicity (Elfenbein and Ambady 2003). Again, however, if we regard emotion perception not simply as objective identification or intellectual recognition of the other's emotion, but as itself an embodied and affective process for the perceiver, as discussed in the previous section, it's not clear that theoretical inference will be sufficient to explain these phenomena. Moreover, theorists, like Carruthers, who defend the notion of innate, modular ToM mechanisms, or those who defend preprogrammed mirror systems operating in an automatic and context-independent fashion, have an especially difficult time explaining cultural differences in perception. For example, Scholl and Leslie (1999,

136–7) leave no room at all for these types of cultural effects, which may involve not only plastic changes in the brain but also metaplastic changes across the brain–body–environment system.

One hallmark of the development of a modular cognitive capacity is that the end-state of the capacity is often strikingly uniform across individuals. Although the particulars of environmental interaction may affect the precise timetable with which the modular capacity manifests itself, what is eventually manifested is largely identical for all individuals. As the modular account thus predicts, the acquisition of ToM is largely uniform across both individuals and cultures. The essential character of ToM a person develops does not seem to depend on the character of their environment at all. It is at least plausible, prima facie, that we all have the same basic ToM!... The point is that the development of beliefs about beliefs seems remarkably uniform and stable.

Others maintain that the pattern of ToM development is identical across a species (e.g., Segal 1996), which is in marked contrast to the uneven and culturally dependent development of many other capacities. Again, however, cross-cultural studies of social cognition (see Domínguez et al. 2009 for a summary) and results from studies of racial bias and dehumanization (see Gallagher and Varga 2014) are inconsistent with these expectations, and show that mechanisms of social cognition are constitutively dependent upon historical-cultural situatedness and group membership. This suggests that the fundamental perceptual level of understanding others as persons is essentially dependent on cultural context—an aspect that any theory of social cognition must account for.

To deny that cultural factors have such effects on social perception, or perception in general, would only make sense if one were to accept the thesis of the 'cognitive impenetrability of perception' (Pylyshyn 1999). Both cognitive impenetrability and cognitive penetrability, however, conceive of the problem in the same way, because they conceive of the cognitive in the same way. In both cases, the cognitive is considered something that is stored on the upper floors of the brain, and then either inferentially injected, or not, into early perceptual areas of the brain. It's as if developmental and learning processes had an effect only on pre-frontal or higher association areas and somehow passed through perceptual and motor areas without lasting effect. The effect only comes later when, in the case of cognitive penetration, there is 'just in time' delivery to effect the fast integration of conceptual information with sensory input.

In contrast, however, cultural aspects seem more pervasive. Not only beliefs, but also moods, traits, practices, and skills can modulate perception. For example, to the newly trained reader of Russian, a sheet of Cyrillic script looks different than it looked to her before she had the skill to read it (Siegel 2011). As Siegel points out, penetrated perceptions are confirmatory of the mood, trait, skill, etc. in a way that reinforces such things and can be epistemically pernicious. In fact there is a continuity of perniciousness from the cultural to the neurological. Cultural biases can reinforce neuronal firing patterns and result in plastic changes, reinforcing embodied practices and postures, behavioral habits, and intersubjective interactions. On the enactivist view, however, none of this counts against the idea that my perception of another's intentions and emotions is direct, requiring no extra-perceptual inference that would take us beyond what we perceive. All such changes, pernicious or not, are not additions to perception, an added-on set of inferences; rather, they transform the perceptual process itself.

6.5 Rethinking Nature: From Free-Energy to Autopoiesis

I return now to a theme I raised in section 1.6. Enactivist approaches present a challenge for science. As I indicated there, by focusing on not just the brain, not just the environment, not just behavior, but on the rich dynamics of brain–body–environment, where environment includes social and cultural factors, enactivism offers a holistic conception of cognition that is difficult to operationalize. Various practices and institutional arrangements that seem essential to good science—experimental controls, divisions of labor, disciplinary divisions—prevent taking all factors into consideration at once.

What would it mean to take up the distinction, suggested by Peter Godfrey-Smith (2001), between a 'scientific research programme' and a 'philosophy of nature', placing enactivism on the side of a philosophy of nature. As Godfrey-Smith suggests, a philosophy of nature would not necessarily have to share the same vocabulary as science. It 'can use its own categories and concepts, concepts developed for the task of describing the world as accurately as possible when a range of scientific descriptions are to be taken into account, and when a philosophical

concern with the underlying structure of theories is appropriate'
(Godfrey-Smith 2001, 284).

For a philosophy of nature to take scientific data seriously does not
require that it take any particular scientific interpretation as necessary
truth. Neuroscientific data, for example, tell us that certain neurons
activate under certain circumstances. The open question is whether we
have to interpret such activations in the standard scientific vocabulary of
representations, inferences, simulations, computations, etc., all such
interpretations predicated on a major internalist assumption (all cognition happens in the brain) that flies in the face of other data that point to
the ongoing dynamical integration of such activations with bodily
(affective, peripheral, and autonomic) and environmental (physical,
social, and cultural) processes.

Being a pragmatist about the vocabulary of representation (as suggested in section 5.6), or about the vocabulary of inference, is at best only
a temporary stance toward a set of placeholders that need ultimately to
be cashed out not just in a different conception of brain function, but in a
different philosophy of nature. An alternative way of thinking about
nature should push hard on cognitive scientific practice in a way that
makes doing science more difficult, but also more productive.

In this regard, enactivism involves not only a rethinking of the nature
of mind and brain, but also a rethinking of the concept of nature itself
(see Di Paolo 2005; Thompson 2007, 78ff.). Rethinking nature, as well as
the nature of cognition, perception, and action, in terms of a continuity
and integration of dynamical self-organizing adaptive systems where the
distinction between physical and mental is deconstructed, where nature
is not conceived purely in terms of objectivity, devoid of subjectivity,
may further motivate a rethinking of science. As Daniel Hutto indicates,

[E]nactivism is committed to the idea that mentality is something that emerges
from the autopoietic, self-organizing and self-creating, activities of organisms.
The activities in question are themselves thought of as essentially embedded and
embodied interactions between organisms and their environments, interactions
that occur and are themselves shaped in new ways over time.   (2011, 22)

This transformation of the explanatory unit from brain to brain–
body–environment is central to the challenge that faces the sciences of
the mind. On one reading of predictive coding, the model of Bayesian
inference entails a strong epistemic boundary that divides the brain from

the rest of the body and the world (Hohwy 2013). On a different reading, the free-energy principle, which seems foundational for the PC approach as developed by Friston, points to a broader theoretical framework that links up with the concept of autopoiesis, which, in turn, plays a similar role for enactivism (Bruineberg, Kiverstein, and Rietveld 2016; Gallagher and Allen 2016; see Clark 2013a). Thinking in these broader terms affords a way to move closer to a philosophy of nature, or at least to a theoretical biology that might allow new insight into the more specialized problems of cognitive science.

The free-energy principle applies to any biological system that resists a tendency to disorder (Friston, Kilner, and Harrison 2006). It states that for an adaptive self-organizing (i.e., autopoietic) system to maintain itself it needs to minimize entropy or free-energy (or in PC terms, prediction errors). Variational free-energy, a mathematical concept, is, roughly, an information theoretic measure (the upper bound) of disorder or surprise. In theoretical biological terms, if we think of the living organism as a self-organizing system, it survives by anticipating sensory input or by taking action, which in turn changes its sensory input. Accordingly it needs to be attuned to its ecological niche in such a way that it minimizes surprise and 'the coupled dynamics of the organism-environment system remain within a relatively small subset of states that maintain the organism's viability in its econiche' (Bruineberg, Kiverstein, and Rietveld 2016, 2; see Friston 2011). Living systems and cognitive systems share this same organizational principle.

One important question is: how precisely does any particular system accomplish this minimization of surprise; how does it keep itself within the viability zone? Predictive coding is one possible answer, and, as we've seen, this particular answer is framed in terms of the Helmholtzian notion of unconscious inference, prediction error minimization, and active inference. This answer cuts the brain off from the world, however, at least theoretically. The brain has access only to its own processes and it has to predict its way to viability. The Markov blanket diagram represents this situation (Figure 6.1). The Markov blanket is a concept derived from formal treatments of Bayesian networks and causal dependency.

A Markov blanket defines a network or ensemble of nodes or subsystems that are interconnected by local deterministic forces. Markov blankets thus behave in a fashion similar to a cell wall, separating internal and external states to create stable dynamics that do not themselves directly

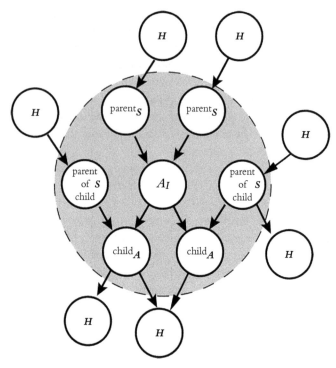

Figure 6.1. Markov blanket. The circle shaded in gray represents the Markov blanket of Node *A*, consisting of A, its children, parents, and parents of children, with parent/child being understood in terms of cause/effect. In small script, the sub-partition of internal and external states according to the Free Energy Principle (Friston 2013a); *H*, hidden external states, *I* internal states, *A* internal active states, and *S* internal sensory states. (Figure by M. Allen, from Gallagher and Allen 2016.)

impinge upon the local coupling responsible for their emergence. On the predictive coding interpretation, states external to the blanket can only be known indirectly (*via* inference). The blanket thus constitutes a partition between the world and the organism. Internal states themselves can be subdivided into those that are either the children of external states (sensations) or children of internal states (actions). Internal states have the capacity to probabilistically represent or infer hidden (external) states, which are themselves influenced by changes in the environment caused by active states. The inherent circularity of this scheme means that actions (which cause changes in the external world, but not sensory states) place an upper bound on the entropy of biological states, serving to maintain a homeostatic equilibrium constrained by internal states (Friston 2013a).

The predictive coding interpretation imposes a vocabulary of inference and representation on these dynamical, co-varying biological processes. As Bruineberg, Kiverstein, and Rietveld (2016) suggest, however, Friston's emphasis on circular causality and active inference leaves open another possible interpretation—the enactivist account, which emphasizes dynamical coupling of the organism with its environment, and works out the free-energy principle in terms of autopoiesis. In an autopoietic system, the boundary, represented in the Markov blanket, does not cut the system off from its environment but defines a coupling of organism–environment. 'The importance of such a boundary for living organisms has been central in the autopoietic approach from the very start... If this is the only kind of boundary that stems from the free-energy principle, then there seems to be nothing in the idea of probabilistic inference per se that challenges enactive cognitive science' (Bruineberg, Kiverstein, and Rietveld 2016, 22; see Bruineberg and Rietveld, 2014; Clark, 2015).

The organism, to minimize entropy, maintains internal homeostasis by hovering around an equilibrium point that keeps a balance among the conditions necessary for its viability and survival. It needs to minimize any surprises by anticipating possible threats and taking action to avoid or reduce them. Bruineberg, Kiverstein, and Rietveld (2016), citing Dewey's notion of organism–environment, mention an example that shows the importance of biological factors: 'For whales, being in deep sea is an event with low *surprisal*, and being on shore has high *surprisal*, while this is reversed for humans. Hence, the particular embodiment or biological organization of an animal and the environmental conditions of the animal necessary for its viability constrain each other' (p. 6). This general conception can be specified in terms of defining the basic (survival-enhancing) affordances that are relative to each animal.

In section 3.3 I pointed to the importance of Dewey's notion of situation, where situation is not equivalent to the objective environment, but includes the agent or experiencing subject in such a way that there is no way for the agent to gain an objective perspective on the situation. This is reflected in the idea that by perception alone the organism doesn't know or control its own viability conditions. It discovers them and can control them only by taking action.[2]

So within the free-energy framework, it is *action* that does the work of actually minimizing surprisal. Actions change an organism's relation to the environment, thereby changing the sensory states of the organism, a process that Friston calls active inference (2012). Free energy, as we understand it, is a measure of the dis-attunement of the internal dynamics and the environmental dynamics [= sur-prise = increasing entropy]: it is low when the sensory states are anticipated, by the animal, and high when they are not. The free energy principle says that minimizing free-energy is a necessary and sufficient condition for living systems to maintain their organization in their econiche.

(Bruineberg, Kiverstein, and Rietveld 2016, 9)

The enactivist interpretation places the emphasis on action; the PC interpretation places the emphasis on perception (Friston endorses both, noting that by perception we can also minimize surprise by adjust-ing our priors). Note, however, that action is not something happening in the brain, and is not just providing new sensory input for the brain; it's what the whole organism does in its interactions with the environment or, under a different description, what a person does in the world (see section 7.4), and this changes the world as much as it changes the brain. On this view, the priors that inform action are not assumptions or beliefs that inform inferences (as in PC); they're embodied skills and patterns of action-readiness that mesh with an affordance space (Brincker 2014; Gallagher 2015; see section 9.4). Perception is not isolated from such action; 'perception is an inevitable consequence of active exchange with the environment' (Friston 2009, 293). Perception and action involve dynamical adjustments to physical, social, and cultural affordances defined in terms of organism–environment, frequently involving nor-mative practices that sometimes include science itself.

If nature cannot be understood apart from the finite cognitive capaci-ties and action affordances that humans have to investigate it (and this is not only the enactivist view but a hermeneutical principle), this makes the scientific enterprise—which is itself a form of active engagement and exploration—more complicated. An enactivist philosophy of nature supports a kind of holism in which a plurality of factors are understood

---

[2] Friston (2010; 2013b) expresses this by saying that an agent does not *have* a model of its world, but rather *is* a model of its world.

to contribute to the full conception of mind. This is still a practical complication for experimental science, although it is certainly not necessary that in every case we must include absolutely everything when dealing with a particular concrete question. At the same time, practically speaking, it's a matter of deciding what factors are crucial, on the supposition that it may be easier to include than to ignore them. Including embodied interactions in explanations of social cognition, for example, might actually involve less complexity if keeping them out of the picture requires the elaboration of more convoluted explanations in terms of representations, inferences, or other concepts that may hold no other status than that of dominant metaphors. Likewise, including action, embodied processes, and environmental factors in explanations of perception and cognition more generally should lead us to a more comprehensive picture that is only as complex as it needs to be to account for the actual complexity of cognition.

7

Action and the Problem of Free Will

Enactivism rejects representationalist and inferentialist explanations of the mind. For this reason some philosophers have suggested that enactivism is a version of behaviorism. Ned Block argues that the enactivist model, as found in Noë (2004), is a form of neo-behaviorism since it fails to provide any account of the internal processes that mediate between sensorimotor inputs and outputs (2005; see Block 2001; also see e.g., Aizawa 2014; Carruthers 2015; Shapiro 2011, 28; and discussion in Hutto and Myin 2013, 17ff.). Given the phenomenological roots of enactivism, equating it with behaviorism seems a strange idea. Phenomenologists emphasize the importance of consciousness and defend the idea that the intentionality of action involves some form of autonomy and the possibility of free choice. In at least one small part, the distinction between behaviorism and a phenomenologially inspired enactivism concerns the traditional question of free will and the role of consciousness. To address these issues, I'll start with a brief historical review.

7.1 The Question of Free Will as Commonly Understood

Some philosophers have argued that Descartes was wrong when he characterized non-human animals as purely physical automata—robots devoid of consciousness. It seemed to them obvious that some animals are conscious. Other philosophers have argued that it is not beyond the realm of possibilities that robots and other artificial agents may someday be conscious—and it seems both appropriate and practical to take the intentional stance toward them (the philosophers as well as the robots) even now. I'm not sure that there are philosophers or scientists who would deny consciousness to animals but affirm the possibility of consciousness in robots. In any case, and in whatever way these thinkers define consciousness, the majority of them do attribute consciousness to humans. Amongst this group, however, there are some who want to reaffirm the idea, explicated by Shadworth Holloway Hodgson in 1870, that in regard to action the presence of consciousness doesn't matter since it plays no causal role. Hodgson's brain generated the following thought: neural events form an autonomous causal chain that is independent of any accompanying conscious mental states. Consciousness is epiphenomenal, incapable of having any effect on the nervous system. James (1890, 130) summarizes the situation:

To Descartes belongs the credit of having first been bold enough to conceive of a completely self-sufficing nervous mechanism which should be able to perform complicated and apparently intelligent acts. By a singularly arbitrary restriction, however, Descartes stopped short at man, and while contending that in beasts the nervous machinery was all, he held that the higher acts of man were the result of the agency of his rational soul. The opinion that beasts have no consciousness at all was of course too paradoxical to maintain itself long as anything more than a curious item in the history of philosophy. And with its abandonment the very notion that the nervous system *per se* might work the work of intelligence, which was an integral, though detachable part of the whole theory, seemed also to slip out of men's conception, until, in this century, the elaboration of the doctrine of reflex action made it possible and natural that it should again arise. But it was not till 1870, I believe, that Mr. Hodgson made the decisive step, by saying that feelings, no matter how intensely they may be present, can have no causal efficacy whatever, and comparing them to the colors laid on the surface of a mosaic, of which the events in the nervous system are represented by the stones. Obviously the stones are held in place by each other and not by the several colors which they support.[1]

As it is commonly understood, when we ask whether consciousness causes behavior we are asking whether consciousness plays a role in the initiation of bodily movement and motor control. This way of understanding the question characterizes a large part of the thinking that goes on in the ongoing debate about free will. I'll try to present

---

[1] The idea that even if the animal were conscious nothing would be added to the production of behavior, even in animals of the human type, was first voiced by La Mettrie (1745), and then by Cabanis (1802), and was further explicated by Hodgson (1870) and Huxley (1874).

134 ACTION AND THE PROBLEM OF FREE WILL

evidence and examples for how pervasive this understanding is, at least in this one small corner of philosophical discussion.

The common understanding of the question can be seen in the epiphenomenalist answer where causal efficacy is attributed to neural mechanisms but not to consciousness. Neural events cause bodily movement and consciousness, but consciousness cannot cause neural events or bodily movement. The understanding of the question itself, however, had already been set by Descartes and involves the Cartesian concept of mind as a mental space in which I control my own thoughts and actions. The roots of this modern idea go back at least as far as the Stoics. They helped to relocate certain important aspects of action. For Ancient Greek thinkers like Aristotle action was something that happened publicly, in the world, as a display of moral character (Arendt 1958). In Stoic philosophy, the better parts of action are moved into the interior of the person. It no longer matters whether the external expression of action is even possible—and it can be made impossible by the constraints of the situation, e.g., being chained up in prison. What matters is the integrity and intentions of one's interior life. What one does, even in one's public behavior, one does primarily within the space of one's own mental realm. As we then find this thought developed in Augustine (395), one is to be judged not simply by external behavior, but by one's internal intentions, which define the significance of one's actions. As is well known, Descartes' concept of the mind as an interior mental space in which the exercise of will means affirming or denying ideas, derives from this tradition (see, e.g., Gaukroger 1997).

This concept of the mind, as an interior space accessible to reflection, frames the modern understanding of free will. What constitutes an action, as an action, involves certain mental processes that lead up to bodily movement. On the Cartesian view, what makes a certain behavior an action is the contribution of these mental processes. Without such processes we have mere behavior, the sort of thing possible for automata and animals. Unless the action takes place in the mind first—in some cases acted out explicitly in imagination—then the external behavior is not really an action. Action on this definition is always intentional action. If my bodily movement is not intentional, then it is mere behavior, something like reflex behavior. If my bodily movement is determined by something other than my own reflective thought, then it is involuntary movement, but not action.

The epiphenomenalist adopts the same Cartesian framework and simply answers 'no' to the question of whether consciousness causes bodily movement. Action, then, is nothing more than behavior that is determined by processes other than conscious thought. The epipheno-menalist does not deny that there is conscious thought, or even neces-sarily that conscious thought appears to be something similar to what Descartes describes. But consciousness simply does not have causal efficacy in regard to the organism's behavior.

On this reading, it is possible for a Cartesian and an epiphenomenalist to agree on the phenomenology, but disagree on the etiology of action. What is the phenomenology that they could agree on? Allegedly it is just this: when I act, I reflectively experience having a desire or intention and then experience making an effort that generates bodily movement. My action appears to be formed in these mental processes, and insofar as I am conscious of these mental processes along with my bodily move-ments, my actions appear to be under my conscious control. The Carte-sian will then say that what appears to be the case is the case; the epiphenomenalist will say that what appears to be the case is not the case. Both are answering the same question. Do these mental processes cause the bodily movements that constitute my behavior? The idea of free action emerges if the answer is yes. The effort that we feel and the movement that follows is the result of our willing to do the action. If the answer is no, then the feeling of effort is nothing more than a feeling produced by brain processes that really control the action. My sense of agency is simply a by-product of neural happenings, and it lacks veracity.

The concept of free will, then, commonly gets understood in terms of this question. Does the mental event operate as a cause that moves the body? Is there some kind of direct transformation from conscious willing to moving muscles? Descartes suggested that the mental events somehow interact with the brain, which then activates the muscles.[2] Carpenter

---

[2] 'Now the action of the soul consists entirely in this, that simply by willing it makes the small [pineal] gland to which it is closely united move in the way requisite for producing the effect aimed at in the volition ... when we will to walk or to move the body in any manner, this volition causes the gland to impel the spirits toward the muscles which bring about this effect' (Descartes 1649, §§ xli, xliii). Concerning the will he also writes: 'Our volitions, in turn, are also of two kinds. Some actions of the soul terminate in the soul itself, as when we will to love God, or in general apply our thought to some non-material object. Our other actions terminate in our body, as when from our merely willing to walk, it follows that our legs are moved and that we walk' (1649, § xviii).

(1874) describes the mental state as closing a physical circuit in the 'nerve-force' or as a translation between the psychical and the physical. For the epiphenomenalist, however, there is no interaction, no circuit to be closed, no translation. To say there is, is to say that physical causality is insufficient to explain physical events.

7.2 Reflective and Perceptual Theories

Within this debate different views of how consciousness relates to action are sometimes cast in terms of a reflective theory of how movements are under conscious control. On this kind of theory, consciousness enters into the explanation of action just in so far as my action is controlled by my introspectively reflective choice-making, together with a self-monitoring of movement. The reflective theory, as Naomi Eilan characterizes it, 'holds that it is some form of reflection on some aspect of the intention or the action that makes the action conscious' (2003, 189), and that puts me in control. That is, attentional consciousness is directed at my inner intention, and at how that intention is translated into bodily movement.[3] Perceptual theories, in contrast, state that 'it is some form of consciousness of the environment that makes the action conscious' (189). Eilan specifies this by explaining that perception plays two knowledge-yielding roles in regard to action. First, it delivers knowledge of the environmental objects or events that we target with the action. Second, perceptual feedback provides knowledge of whether the action was properly accomplished (see Eilan 2003, 190).

We can clarify the difference between the reflective and perceptual theories by considering a simple case of normal action such as getting a

---

[3] A recent example of this view can be found in Metzinger (2003, 422): 'Conscious volition is generated by integrating abstract goal representations or concrete self-simulations into the current model of the phenomenal intentionality relations as object components, in a process of decision or selection.' The self-simulation, which forms the object component of this process, is in fact a conscious 'opaque simulation' of 'a possible motor pattern' (p. 423), i.e., a possible movement of my own body. An opaque simulation is one of which we are explicitly conscious. 'A *volitional first-person* perspective—the phenomenal experience of practical intentionality—emerges if two conditions are satisfied. First, the object component must be constituted by a particular self-simulatum, by a mental simulation of a concrete behavioral pattern, for example, like getting up and walking toward the refrigerator. Second, the relationship depicted on the level of conscious experience is one of *currently selecting* this particular behavioral pattern, as simulated' (422).

drink. I'm thirsty and decide to get a drink. I get up from my desk and walk to the fridge, open it, and reach in for a drink. On the reflective theory, my action originates in (is caused by) my conscious decision to get a drink, and this conscious decision is usually described in terms of becoming aware of my desire for a drink motivated by thirst sensations, having a belief that there is something to drink in the fridge, and then, for just these reasons, consciously moving my body in the direction of the drink. This may be an oversimplified version of the story, but it provides a clear indication of the kinds of conscious processes required to effect the action according to this theory. The basic idea is that I initiate and control my action by consciously deciding on what I want, and consciously moving my body to accomplish the goal. Consciousness, on this view, is self-attending or self-monitoring. On the perceptual theory, in contrast, consciousness is primarily directed towards the world. I'm conscious of the thing that I want to get, where I'm moving, and what I'm looking for—the fridge, the drink. This perception-for-action is complemented by sensory–motor feedback—proprioceptive and visual—that tells me that I've accomplished (or failed to accomplish) my goal. Perceptual consciousness seems important for making the action successful, and so plays a necessary and causal role in moving the action along.

The perceptual theory of how consciousness causes behavior, however, fares no better than the reflective theory from the point of view of epiphenomenalism. All of the perceptual aspects described above can be causally explained in terms of third-person physical mechanisms. The perceptual information required is precisely the kind of perceptual input that is required for motor control. Indeed, most perceptual information of this sort is unconsciously processed, and, according to epiphenomenalism, it is that information processing that is running the show (see, e.g., Jeannerod 2003 for a summary of such accounts). Clearly, we can build a non-conscious robot that could retrieve a drink from the fridge, and it is also quite clear that the initial motivation—our thirst—is itself reducible to non-conscious processes that launch the larger action process. Consciousness may keep us informed about what is going on in broad and general terms, it can act as a 'dormant monitor' (Jeannerod 2003, 162), and so, as Eilan would have it, allow us to know what we are doing, but it plays no role in the causal processes that move us. We, as conscious animals, are seemingly just along for the ride.

Differences between reflective and perceptual theories aside, what becomes clear about the way the question gets asked (and, as I will argue, what is problematic about this discourse when it is applied to the issue of free will) is summarized nicely by Joëlle Proust (2003, 202). 'Standard philosophical approaches [to] action define action in terms of a particular psychological state causing a relevant bodily movement'. She indicates that there is 'now widespread convergence on this causal approach', even if there is some disagreement about the kind of psychological state involved. The familiar candidates, at least on the reflective approach, are desire and belief (Davidson 1980; Goldman 1970) or intentions (Searle 1983; Mele 1992), providing conceptual reasons for acting. The best arguments for giving causal efficacy to consciousness are posed in these terms, and these terms are precisely the ones rejected by epiphenomenalism. According to Proust, there is no necessary connection between the justification of action and the cause of action, since animals are capable of purposeful actions without having a worked-out conceptual understanding of why they acted that way (2003, 203–4). And we know that even humans who have well-thought-out reasons for acting in a particular way, may in fact be acting in that way due to different and unconscious reasons.

On some analyses, even 'minimal' actions (Bach 1978), e.g., postural shifts, pre-attentive movements such as the scratching of an itch or avoiding an object in the environment, or the detailed movements associated with 'intention in action' (Searle 1983), which specifies the details of how intentions are to be realized, even if not a matter of control by large or complex psychological states, still rely on perceptual models, and retain the focus on causal control of relevant bodily movements (Proust 2003, 206). Such perceptual processes, however, as Proust notes, may be fully unconscious. For Proust, 'what is pertinent is whether or not the bodily movements tend to be under the agent's guidance . . . Whatever the causal antecedents of a specific goal-directed movement may be, what makes it an action is the contribution of the corresponding agent to actively maintain the orientation of his bodily effort towards achieving a target event' (207).

On such views, i.e., on 'standard philosophical approaches', or on what I am calling the 'common understanding of the question', including the epiphenomenal view, the agent performs its action by keeping its body under control, either by an implicit (pre-reflective) perceptual consciousness, or by non-conscious processes. Indeed, in general terms, a good understanding of motor control and the performance of action can be worked out in terms of perceptual non-conscious processes. The problem, however, is that this way of thinking about action gets carried over into questions about whether action is free or not, and more generally into debates about free will, and this is where things start to go wrong.

7.3 Libetarian Experiments

A good example of how things can go wrong can be found in the debates that surround the experiments conducted by Benjamin Libet (1985; 1992; 1996; Libet et al. 1983). As he indicates, 'The operational definition of free will in these experiments was in accord with common views' (1999, 47). Libet's experiments show that motor action and the sense of agency depend on neurological events that we do not consciously control, and that happen before our conscious awareness of deciding or moving. In one of Libet's experiments, subjects with their hands on a tabletop are asked to flick their wrists whenever they want to or when they have an urge to do so. Their brain activity is monitored with special attention given to the time course of brain activity leading up to the movement, between 500 and 1000 milliseconds prior to the movement. Just before the flick, there are 50 milliseconds of activity in the motor nerves descending from motor cortex to the wrist. But this is preceded by several hundred (up to 800) milliseconds of brain activity known as the readiness potential (RP). Subjects report when they were first aware of their decision (or urge or intention) to move their wrists by referencing a large clock that allows them to report fractions of a second. It turns out that, on average, 350 milliseconds before they are conscious of deciding (or of having an urge) to move, their brains are already working on the motor processes that will result in the movement. Thus, Libet concludes, before there is a conscious decision to move, unconscious cerebral processes initiate the process (Libet 1985; see Schultze-Kraft et al. 2015). The brain seemingly decides and then initiates its decisions in a non-conscious fashion, on a subpersonal level, within a tight elementary timescale, but then, on one interpretation, also inventively tricks us into thinking that we consciously decide matters.

These results motivate a question, which Libet poses in precise terms: 'The initiation of the freely voluntary act appears to begin in the brain unconsciously, well before the person consciously knows he wants to act. Is there, then, any role for conscious will in the performance of a voluntary act?' (Libet 1999, 51). The epiphenomenalist interpretation of these results is that what we call free will is nothing more than a false sense or impression, an illusion (e.g., Wegner 2002). Libet himself answers in the positive: consciousness can have an effect on our action, and free will is possible, because there are still approximately 150 milliseconds remaining after we become conscious of our intent to move, and before we move. So, he suggests, we have time to consciously veto the movement (1985, 2003).[4]

Do these experiments decide, or even address, the question of free will? Only on the supposition that the question is correctly framed in terms of initiation and control of bodily movement, which is, as I indicated, the common understanding of the question. Patrick Haggard, who extends Libet's experiments with a series of his own, clearly indicates this supposition: 'The central philosophical question about action has been whether conscious free will exits. That is, how can "I" control my body?' (2003, 113).[5] Haggard does not make a clear distinction between the question of motor control and the question of free will; indeed, for him, apparently, the question of free will is a question about motor control. His concern is to dismiss reflective theories of free will and to focus on the more specific details of motor control, and the notion of intention-in-action rather than prior intention. The question becomes, 'how does my will or intention become associated with the actions [i.e., the bodily movements] that it causes'? (113). Will or intention-in-action is captured, for Haggard, in the milliseconds of physiological signals of the lateralized RP, which is a more specific part of the RP. Approximately 500 milliseconds prior to the onset of movement,

---

[4] At least part of the most recent controversy about these experiments is whether the RP is indeed specific to the (non-conscious) planning of a particular movement, or isn't rather a more general activation, part of a background neuronal noise that is not directly related to a particular movement. See Schurger, Sitt, and Dehaene (2012); Schurger, Mylopoulos, and Rosenthal (2015).

[5] Haggard and Libet (2001) frame the question in the same way, referring to it as the traditional concept of free will: 'how can a mental state (my conscious intention) initiate the neural events in the motor areas of the brain that lead to my body movement?' (47).

the bilateral RP activity begins to lateralize to the motor cortex contra-lateral to the hand that will move. It is this lateralized signal that generates not only the movement, but our awareness of initiating the movement. 'This view places consciousness of intention much closer to the detailed pattern of motor execution than some other accounts. [Awareness of willing] thus looks rather like intention in action, and much less like prior intention' (118). Thus, consciousness of an action is 'intertwined with the internal models thought to underlie movement control' (119).

The common understanding in the standard reflective, perceptual, or epiphenomenal theories, as well as in the recent debates richly informed by neuroscience, is that free will is either explained or explained away by what we have learned about motor control—that is, about how 'I' control my body. I propose, however, that these are two different questions, in the same way that 'Where shall we drive?' is different from 'How does this car work?' You should think it strange if in response to your question, 'Where do you want to drive today?' I start to tell you in precise terms how the internal combustion engine in my car turns the wheels. Developing a good answer to one of these questions is not the same as answering the other.

The best answers we have to the question of motor control indicate that most control processes happen at a subpersonal, unconscious level in the elementary timescale. As we move through the world we do not normally monitor the specifics of our motor action in any explicitly conscious way. As I walk out to the beach I am not normally conscious of how I am activating my leg muscles. The object of my awareness is the beach, the ocean, the anticipated enjoyment of sitting in the sun and reading the latest volume on the science of voluntary action, etc. Body-schematic processes that involve proprioception, efference copy, forward comparators, ecological information, etc., keep me moving in the right direction. Both phenomenology and neuropsychology support a combination of perceptual and non-conscious explanations of how we control bodily movements, and they rule out reflective theory in the normal case. That is, in the normal situation, we do not require a second-order consciousness of bodily movement; we do not have to be reflectively conscious of the onset of the action or the course of the movement as we execute it. Rather, in moving, input from our percep-tual experience of the objects that we target and perceptual-ecological feedback about our bodily performance contribute to motor control. In this context, some of this feedback is consciously generated, as when I decide to reach and grasp this particular object rather than another, or when I have a general idea which way the beach is located. In addition, however, much of the feedback is generated non-consciously—for example, by the non-conscious visual processes that shape my grasp (Jeannerod 2003). In regard to these latter aspects, conscious awareness adds nothing to motor control, and may even interfere with the timing or smoothness of action.

We should expect that answers to *how* I control my body, or *how* I make my body move, will be of this sort. If, as in the case of deafferentation (which involves loss of proprioceptive feedback), we had to control our movement consciously or reflectively (Gallagher and Cole 1995), or if we were normally required to consciously represent our movements in a Cartesian mental space before we effected them in worldly space, we would have to exert great cognitive effort and slow things down to a significant degree.[6] Libet's results, then, are of no surprise unless we think that we control our bodily movements in a conscious and primarily reflective way. The Libetarian experiments are precisely about the control of bodily movement, although even in this regard they are limited insofar as they effect an atypical involution of the question of motor control. In the experimental situation we are asked to pay attention to all of the processes that we normally do *not* attend to, and to move our body in a way that we do not usually move it (in a rough sense, we are asked to act in a way that is similar to the way that the deafferented subject is required to act).

These experiments, however, and more generally the broader discussions of motor control, have nothing to tell us about free will per se. If they contribute to a justification of perceptual or epiphenomenal theories of how we control our movement, these are not theories that address the question of free will. The question of free will is a different question.

---

[6] Jeannerod (2003, 159) notes: 'The shift from automatic to [consciously monitored] controlled execution involves a change in the kinematics of the whole [grasping] movement; movement time increases, maximim grip aperture is larger, and the general accuracy degrades.' Also see Gallagher (2005a).

7.4 Motor Control and Free Will

As in the experiments, something similar happens in standard philo-sophical contexts when philosophers try to find examples of free action. There is a long tradition of appealing to examples of bodily movements in discussions of free will, e.g., 'Look how I can freely raise my arm' (see, for instance, Chisholm 1964; Searle 1984; Mohrhoff 1999).[7] Jonathan Lowe (1999, 235–6), for example, claimed that:

[i]n the case of normal voluntary action, movements of the agent's body have amongst their causes intentional states of that agent which are 'about' just such movements. For instance, when I try to raise my arm and succeed in doing so, my arm goes up—and amongst the causes of its going up are such items as a desire of mine *that my arm should go up*. The intentional causes of physical events are always 'directed' upon the occurrence of just such events, at least where normal voluntary action is concerned.

Philosophers often think of motor control as the 'prototype' of free action (Zhu 2003, 64). Such philosophical reflections, which are often cast in terms of mind–body or brain–body interaction, may be what sends the neuroscientists looking in the wrong place for free will, namely in the realm of subpersonal processes that control movement.

The attempt to frame the question of free will in terms of these subpersonal processes—either to dismiss it or to save it—is misguided for at least two reasons. First, free will cannot be squeezed into the elementary timescale of 150–350 milliseconds; free will is a longer-term phenomenon and, I will argue, it involves consciousness. Second, the notion of free will does not apply primarily to abstract motor processes or even to bodily movements that make up intentional actions—rather it applies to intentional actions themselves, described at the most appro-priate pragmatic level of description.

First, in regard to timescale, the kinds of processes associated with free actions are not made at the spur of the moment—they are not elemen-tary or momentary and cannot fit within the thin phenomenology of the milliseconds between RP and movement. The following example reflects the distinction between fast movement under automatic control on the

---

[7] Even Aristotle offers an example like this: 'an agent acts voluntarily because the initiative in moving the parts of the body which act as instruments rests with the agent himself' (*Nicomachean Ethics* 1110a, 15).

elementary timescale, and slower voluntary action on integrative and narrative timescales.[8]

1. At time T something moves in the grass next to my feet.
2. At $T+150$ milliseconds the amygdala in my brain is activated, and before I know why, at $T+200$ milliseconds I jump and move several yards away. Here, the entire set of movements can be explained purely in terms of non-conscious perceptual processes, neuronal firing, and muscles contracting, together with an evolutionary account of why our system is designed in this way, etc.
3. My behavior motivates my awareness of what is happening and by $T+1000$ milliseconds I see that what moved in the grass was a small harmless lizard. My next move is not of the same sort.
4. At $T+5000$ milliseconds, after observing the kind of lizard it is, I decide to catch it for my lizard collection.
5. At $T+5150$ milliseconds I take a step back and *voluntarily* make a quick reach for the lizard.

My choice to catch the lizard is quite different from the reflex behavior. What goes into this decision involves awareness of what has just happened (I would not have decided to catch the lizard if I had not become conscious that there was a lizard there) plus recognition of the lizard as something I could appreciate. At $T+5150$ milliseconds I take a step back and reach for it. One could focus on this movement and say: at $T+4650$ milliseconds, without my awareness, processes in my brain were already underway to prepare for my reaching action, before I had even decided to catch the snake—therefore, what seemed to be my free decision was actually predetermined by my brain. But this ignores the context defined by the larger timeframe—which involves previous movement and a conscious recognition of the lizard. Furthermore, it could easily happen that things don't proceed as fast as I've portrayed, and perhaps, waiting for the strategic moment, I don't actually reach for the lizard until 10 seconds after I made the decision that it would be a good addition to my collection. Now Libet and some philosophers might insist that an extra decision would have to be made to initiate my bodily

---

[8] Automatic movement is not the opposite of voluntary movement. Fast automatic movement may be purely reflex, or it may be voluntary in the sense that it may fit into and serve an intentional action.

movement precisely at that time. But it is clear that any such decision about moving is already under the influence of the initial conscious decision to catch the lizard. My action, in this case, is not well described in terms of making bodily movements, but rather of attempting to catch the lizard for my collection, and this is spread out over a larger timeframe (involving integrative and possibly narrative timescales) than the experimental framework of milliseconds.[9]

This leads to the second point, namely about the proper level of description relevant to free will. As I have been suggesting, and in contrast to the common understanding, the question of free will is not about bodily movements, but about intentional actions. The kinds of actions that we freely decide are not the sort of involuted bodily movements described by Libet's experiments. If I am reaching to catch the lizard and you stop and ask what I'm doing, I am very unlikely to say any of the following: 'I am activating my neurons.' 'I am flexing my muscles.' 'I am moving my arm.' 'I am reaching and grasping.' These are descriptions appropriate for a discussion of motor control and bodily movement, but not for the action in which I am engaged. Rather, I would probably say 'I am trying to catch this lizard for my collection.' This latter statement is the most appropriate description of what I freely decided to do—both practically and normatively, in terms of what one would expect as an appropriate answer.

I suggest that the temporal framework for the exercise of free will is, at a minimum, the temporal framework that allows for the process to be informed by a specific type of consciousness. This consciousness is not the sort described by the reflective theory, according to which my reflective regard would be focused on how to move my body in order to achieve a goal. I am not at all thinking about how to move my body— I'm thinking about catching the lizard. My decision to catch the lizard is the result of a consciousness that is *embedded* or *situated* in the particular context defined by the present circumstance of encountering the lizard, and the fact that I have a lizard collection. This is an embedded or situated reflection (Gallagher and Marcel 1999), neither introspective nor focused on my body. It is 'a first-person reflective consciousness that is embedded in a pragmatically or socially contextualized situation. It

---

[9] For an interesting discussion of the role of consciousness in addiction, see Clune (2013, 85–6) who explores the difference between this lizard example and an addictive behavior.

involves the type of activity that I engage in when someone asks me what I am doing or what I plan to do' (Gallagher and Marcel 1999, 25). To answer that kind of question, I tend to look outward to my circumstances and to what I may be able to make of them. This is an affordance-based reflection. I do not reflect on my beliefs and desires as states within a mental space; nor do I reflectively consider how I ought to move my arm or shape my grasp. Nor is it a matter of forming a prior intention; it is rather something closer to the formation of an intention-in-action as I am about to engage the affordances that present themselves. I start to think matters through in terms of the object that I am attending to (the lizard), the collection that I have, and the possible actions that I can take (leave it or catch it) just here in this situation. When I decide to catch the lizard, I make what, in contrast to a reflex action, must be described as a conscious choice that reflects some degree of autonomy, and this choice shapes my actions.

In this kind of situated reflective consciousness, certain things in the environment begin to matter to the agent. Meaning and interpretation come into the picture. The agent's memory and knowledge about lizards and such things, rather than being epiphenomenal, has a real effect on behavior. Why I reach to catch the lizard would be inexplicable without recourse to this kind of situated, affordance-based reflection.

Epiphenomenalists might object that this relegates the explanation to a 'space of reasons' rather than a 'space of causes', and at best explains the motivation, but not the cause of the action (cf. McDowell 1994). My reflective decision to catch the lizard does not *cause* me to try to do so. But this narrow definition of causality already begs the question and limits the notion of causality to the determined mechanics of motor control. That is, it frames the question of free will in precisely the wrong way. If the notion of causality at stake in this debate is narrowly construed on the traditional billiard ball model of determined mechanisms, then the question of free will is not about causality at all. Yet, it seems undeniable that the embedded reflection described here does have an effect on my action, and must play a role in the explanation of how (and not just why) that action is generated.

To the extent that consciousness enters into the ongoing production of action, and contributes to the production of further action, even if significant aspects of this action rely on automatic non-conscious motor control, our actions are intentional and voluntary. Voluntary actions are not about neurons, muscles, body parts, or even movement—all of which play some part in what is happening, and for the most part, do so non-consciously. Rather, recursively, all such processes are carried along by (and are intentional because of) my decision to catch the lizard—that is, by what is best described on a personal level, and in an integrative timescale, as my intentional action. The exercise of free will cannot be captured in or reduced to a description of neural activity or muscle activation or mere bodily movement.

I am not arguing here for a disembodied notion of free will, as something that occurs in a Cartesian mind; nor do I mean to imply that the non-conscious brain events that make up the elements of motor control are simply irrelevant to free will. Indeed, for two closely related reasons, such non-conscious embodied processes, including the kind of neurological events described by Libet, underpin and support the kind of autonomy that is specifically human. First, non-conscious body-schematic mechanisms of motor control support intentional action and are structured and regulated by relevant intentional goals. Intentionality goes all the way down into the kinematic aspects of movement, so that different action intentions entail different kinematic characteristics (Becchio et al. 2012). In line with Anscombe (1957), operations at the elemental timescale are intentional, even if they are not intentional actions. All such relevant processes are structured and regulated by my intentional goals as much as they also limit and enable my action. When I decide to reach for the lizard, all of the appropriate physical movements fall into place. These embodied mechanisms thus enable the exercise of free will.

Second, precisely to the extent that we are not required to consciously deliberate about bodily movement or such things as autonomic pro-cesses, our attention can be directed at the more meaningful level of intentional action. Affordances for action are diminished to the extent that these supporting mechanisms fail. Nonetheless, proposals that answer the question of free will just in these terms of mind–body or mind–brain interaction are looking in the wrong place. Consistent with enactivist approaches to embodied cognition, the relevant interactions to consider are in the dynamic couplings between a situated mind–body system and its physical–social environment.

Thus, the exercise of free will should not be conceived as equivalent to those processes that contribute to motor control, or as something that is generated at a *purely* subpersonal level, or as something instantaneous, an event that takes place in a knife-edge moment located between being undecided and being decided. Free will involves temporally extended consciousness on the integrative and narrative timescales.

7.5 Restructuring Behavior

In contrast to the position just outlined, Daniel Dennett (2003) maintains that the processes that constitute free will need not be conscious and need not depend on conscious decision. Indeed, he suggests that I am too Cartesian when I claim that consciousness is necessary for free will (Dennett 2003, 242n3). The notion of a situated affordance-based reflective consciousness, however, is not at all Cartesian. Understood enactively, freely willed action is not something that occurs in the head— whether that is conceived, following a long philosophical tradition, as in a mental space, or following a more recent neuroscientific conception, as in the brain. Nor is it accomplished in a mindless way. Freely willed action is something accomplished in the world, amongst the things that I reach for and the people I affect. Actions of this sort do involve (1) motor intentions that are close to motor control processes, built into the action itself, and measurable in the Libet elementary timeframe— and with Dennett we could say that these are the non-conscious aspects of intentional action. But they also involve (2) 'immediate' intentions-in-action that are conscious and context relative (Pacherie and Haggard 2010), and measurable in the integrative timeframe; they may also motivate situated affordance-based reflection. In some, but not all cases, freely willed actions may also involve (3) distal intentions that are prior to and more detached from the immediacy of action, measurable in the narrative timeframe, and that require a more developed deliberative reflection (Gallagher 2012; Pacherie 2006).

I'll return to the notion of reflection in the final chapter (see section 10.3). Let me conclude by re-addressing the question with which we started this chapter—whether enactivism is a version of behaviorism. In the same way that enactivism suggests that we rethink the notion of mind, and perhaps even the notion of nature, so also it suggests that we rethink what behavior means. The idea that action is complexly intentional—that it may involve an intentional structure of motor or operative intentions, contextualized immediate intentions-in-action, as well as distal intentions, and that in some of these aspects it involves consciousness—speaks against a reduction of intentional action to mere behavior. Mere behavior, as classic behaviorism understands it, rules out free will because it rules out the complex structure of behavior that would make it action.

In this respect, Merleau-Ponty (1964) had things right in his phenomenological critique of behaviorism. Just as he rejected the notion of nature as 'a multiplicity of events external to each other and bound together by relations of causality' (1964, 1), and the mechanistic conception of organism as *partes extra partes*, he rejected the notion of *mere* behavior and offered a richer concept of human behavior as involving a 'perpetual debate . . . with a physical and social world'—a concept that was lost or 'compromised by an impoverished philosophy' (226). That kind of philosophy considers only two options: either action is guided by an ideational intentionality of beliefs and desires, or intention reduces to neuronal processes. On the enactivist alternative we need to take into account the full system—brain–body–environment—which involves 'a directed activity that is neither blind mechanism nor intellectual behavior, and which is not accounted for by classic mechanistic accounts or intellectualism' (1964, 40, trans. revised). As Merleau-Ponty put it, 'Behavior, inasmuch as it has a structure, is not situated in either of these two orders' (45). It is not a thing reducible to elementary neuronal processes; nor is it an idea or a pure consciousness. It is rather a structure (form or Gestalt) of complex relations.

8

Making Enactivism Even More Embodied

Although I have been focused on action in the last several chapters—considering what action is and how it is involved in perception—an embodied approach to understanding the mind, in its fullest sense, is not just a matter of action-oriented processes; enactivism is about more than action. One of the most widely cited versions of enactivist-embodied cognition has been the work of O'Regan and Noë (2001; Noë 2004). Their emphasis on sensory–motor contingencies and the role of action in perception, however, builds itself on a conception of embodiment that remains too narrow. While such an emphasis is clearly an important aspect for understanding cognition, in this chapter I will argue that it is not as richly embodied as it should be, and that it leaves out important aspects of affectivity and intersubjectivity.[1]

In previous chapters I already touched on issues that have to do with affectivity and intersubjectivity. In this chapter I'll deepen the enactivist concept of embodiment by focusing further on these aspects. The goal is to make clear that these issues are important ones for continuing development of the enactivist approach. These issues also motivate, once again, a contrast between enactivist accounts and more standard conceptions of brain function in terms of B-formatted representations and predictive coding models. These models, I'll argue, fail to take affectivity and intersubjectivity into account in the right way.

---

[1] One starts to see this in some recent authors who have distinguished the O'Regan and Noë brand of enactivism as the 'sensorimotor approach' *in contrast to* the enactivist approach (e.g., Kyselo and Di Paolo 2013; also Stapleton 2013). Emphasis on affectivity and intersubjectivity is consistent with the enactivism associated with Varela, Thompson, and Di Paolo.

8.1 Affectivity

An enactivist account of perception highlights the integration of a variety of bodily factors into perceptual processes. The body, understood as what phenomenologists call the 'lived body', includes the related notion of 'body schema' (Gallagher 2005a). The role of the body schema pertains to motor control and precisely the kind of sensory–motor contingencies emphasized by O'Regan and Noë (2001) and Noë (2004); it facilitates interactions with one's surroundings, and it contrasts to the 'body image', a term that designates the ways in which the body shows up for consciousness, in certain circumstances, as its intentional referent.

The lived body in its full sense, however, involves more than the sensorimotor body schema and body image. An account that focuses only on sensorimotor contingencies falls short due to its neglect of the relevance of affective aspects of embodiment. The latter include not only mood-related and emotional factors, but bodily states such as hunger, fatigue, and pain, as well as a complex motivational dimension that animates body–world interaction (Bower and Gallagher 2013; Stapleton 2013; Colombetti 2013). Bodily affectivity thus involves a complex ensemble of factors that govern conscious life. They usually operate in a pre-noetic fashion, below the level of conscious monitoring and manipulation, although the experiencing subject can become conscious of them and they may certainly have an effect on what experience feels like (Gallagher and Aguda 2015). I may consciously experience the blues, or I may be unaware that my whole demeanor reflects the blues. Affect, in any case, is deeply embodied, involving aspects of embodiment that are not penetrated by consciousness.

The agent's meaningful encounters with the world imply some basic motivation to perceptually engage her surroundings. Schemata of sensorimotor contingencies give an agent the *how* of perception, a tacit knowledge of potential sensorimotor engagements, without giving its *why*, which depends on latent valences that push or pull for attention in one direction or another, and for potential sensory–motor engagement, reflecting, for example, a degree of desirability. Consider particular instances of the affects involved in hunger and fatigue. Somaesthetic factors such as hunger delimit our perception and action possibilities, as well as our cognitive possibilities. William James once noted that an apple appears larger and more invitingly red when one is hungry than when one is satiated. A recent study (Danziger, Levav, and Avnaim-Pesso 2011) reinforces the idea that hunger can shape, and perhaps even distort, cognitive processes. The study shows that the rational application of legal reasoning does not sufficiently explain the decisions of judges. 'Extraneous factors' such as hunger may play an important role.

> The percentage of favorable rulings [made by judges] drops gradually from ≈65% to nearly zero within each decision session [e.g., between breakfast and lunch] and returns abruptly to ≈65% after a [food] break. Our findings suggest that judicial rulings can be swayed by extraneous variables that should have no bearing on legal decisions.   (Danziger, Levav, and Avnaim-Pesso 2011, 6889)

In one sense, such affective factors, although clearly extraneous to the formal aspects of legal reasoning, are 'extraneous' to *cognition* only if we think of cognition as something disembodied. In any case, it seems reasonable to think that this embodied-affective aspect of hunger has an effect on the jurist's perception of the facts, as well as on the weighing of evidence, and doesn't appear out of nowhere just when the judicial decision is made.

At a very basic level, affective phenomena like fear, for example, are modulated by the functioning of the circulatory system and respiration. Even heartbeat influences how and whether fear-inducing stimuli (e.g., images of fearful faces, in experiments by Garfinkel et al. 2014) are processed. When the heart contracts in its systole phase, fearful stimuli are more easily recognized, and they tend to be perceived as more fearful than when presented during its diastole phase. I mentioned in *Chapter 6* that respiration also modulates sensory processes and behavioral performance (e.g., Liu, Papanicolaou, and Heck 2014; Peiffer et al. 2008), including emotion and pain perception (Iwabe, Ozaki, and Hashizume 2014; Zautra et al. 2010; Zelano et al., 2016). That is, the fact that we are breathing, flesh and blood creatures equipped with beating hearts (rather than, say, just brains suspended in vats) explains in part why we experience just the sorts of affective states we do.

Typically, however, one's embodied condition does not reflect a simple, isolated affect—rather, there is a cocktail, a mélange of aspects that make up one's affective state. After a day of trekking up a mountain, one's perception may be informed by a combination of hunger, pain, fatigue, troubled respiration, feelings of dirtiness, and the kinaesthetic difficulty involved in climbing. It's likely the mountain path looks more challenging at that point than after a good night's sleep, not because of certain objective qualities that belong to the path, but because of one's affective state. Moreover, these things are not experienced purely and simply, but are modulated by intentionality. My physical state may be felt as an overwhelming fatigue that is a barrier to any further climbing; or it may contribute to a feeling of satisfaction as I sip a glass of wine in front of the fire at the end of the day. Such affective aspects color my perception as they more generally constrain my way of being in the world. As such, affects may clearly manifest themselves in the effects they have on perception and action.

The connection between affect and perception has been noted by many enactivists (Colombetti 2007; 2013; Ellis 2005; Thompson 2007; Thompson and Stapleton 2009). Affective phenomena are pervasively integrated into perceptual experience (Pessoa 2013; Barrett and Bliss-Moreau 2009). Shifts of attention may be led in one direction or another by the affective ebb and flow of what we experience. From a phenomenological perspective Husserl (2004) describes such affective states involving tension, resolution, exertion, unease, and satisfaction/dissatisfaction as modulating our perceptual (but not only perceptual) attention. Attention, in this sense, is embodied in a variety of related ways. In visual experience, for example, attending to something may involve squinting or opening the eyes widely, it may involve a contortion of the face all the way from the scalp down to a gaping mouth or pursed lips, and so on (Bergson 2001, 27–8). A certain tension may be expressed by eyes darting about, which always involve kinaesthetic accompaniment from extra-ocular muscles.

Importantly, affect motivates a sense of interest or investment. The notion of 'perceptual interest' (Bower and Gallagher 2013) denotes the affective sense of the stakes or the costs involved in exchanges with one's environment. This is not the same as Husserl's concept of the 'I can', which signifies the effect on perception of possessing a sense of skill or competence. The *I can* captures the idea that I see objects in the environment pragmatically in terms of what I can do with them, or in terms of what they afford. Even if one is capable of accomplishing some feat in those terms, however, still one might not feel 'up to the task', or inclined to do the work it might take. The task may be boring, or it may not be worth doing. Such are the affective nuances the sense of interest is supposed to highlight. Thus, interwoven with perception and action is a sense of the affective stakes of exerting effort to do something or to make something available or present. To make something available involves definite costs in following through on transactions with environmental affordances. One's environment affords many possibilities for action, but each has its affective price tag, and they are not all equally affordable. One thus not only has a practical (sensorimotor) understanding of accessibility, but an affective take on that same accessibility, in terms of interest or inclination to follow through.

The latter may also involve a perceptual sense of the ease or difficulty of making something present. In this regard it is closely related to the phenomenon of perceptual presence elaborated by Noë (2004). Perceptual presence is the sense one has of the perceptual accessibility of non-apparent aspects or sides of a perceived object, or, more broadly, of what is not directly perceived in the present moment (e.g., the side of the object that is not visible). The sense of the presence of the other side of an object, of what is behind one, of what is in an adjoining room, and the like, touches—over and above one's generic strategies for bodily coping with the environment—one's individual condition with all of its strengths and weaknesses. In a very simple example, what Noë calls the 'grabbiness' of an object is dependent not only on one's sense of pertinent sensorimotor contingencies, whether the object is near or far, and properly shaped and weighted, etc., and not only on whether one is in a state of pain, or fatigue, or fear, etc., but on whether one is even concerned about (or inclined to) the possibility of grabbing the object.

While everyone is affected by such circumstances in one way or another, each individual lives them out in a unique way. It's true that a perceiving agent's perceptual stance is determined by a mastery of sensorimotor contingencies needed to access environmental affordances in suitable ways. Such mastery, however, once acquired, may be a relatively constant, more or less generic, or standard set of skills suitable for most transactions with the world. *Ceteris paribus*, anyone with that same skill set might perceive in the same way. In contrast, the particularities of affect will differ from one individual to another, or from one day to another, from morning to night. Taking affective phenomena into account importantly enriches one's understanding of perception, since it clarifies the nature of individual perspective in perception. A broad spectrum of individual life circumstances may, in terms of affect, be brought to bear on perception, judgment, memory, imagination, and so on. These circumstances include not only physical burdens and impediments, such as the impediment of fatigue from physical exertion, but also broader circumstances having to do with time of day, since one typically is energized at the start of the day and tired toward the end, or with longer-term life phases, since youth and old age surely shape one's perceptual interest, and by this means, one's intentionality.

Consider again the notion of erotic perception discussed in section 4.2. Something has sexual signification for me when I have a particular embodied-affective disposition towards it. Erotic intentionality is not a matter of a propositional attitude or an instrumental rationality; it is not reducible to the mere observation of behavior, or to some attributional/inferential link between behavior and belief. It is even more than an 'I can . . . ' insofar as it depends on a certain form of affective interest. It's a form of affective intentionality, which, as Merleau-Ponty (2012, 158–9) suggests, brings to view 'the vital origins of perception'.

8.2 Intersubjectivity

In a series of experiments Proffitt et al. (1995; 2003) purportedly show that the estimation of distance is influenced by anticipated effort. Subjects saddled with a heavy backpack tend to overestimate perceived distance, whereas those without backpacks do not. Proffitt et al. (1995) similarly describe how subjects overestimate the degree of incline of a slope when fatigued, and this may translate into the subject's lack of inclination (to climb), which further informs perception. The hill looks not only steeper, but also uninviting. One's judgment and perhaps perceptual experience is informed by one's present affective state. These results, however, have been challenged by Durgin et al. (2009), in a way that nicely points in a different, but equally important direction for our considerations here. They show that steeper estimates of incline while wearing a backpack 'are judgmental biases that result from the social, not physical, demands of the experimental context' (964). Without awareness of this bias, subjects who sense the aim of the experiment estimate a steeper incline than subjects who are led to believe that the backpack has some other purpose (e.g., that it contains electromyographic equipment to measure muscle tension). In other words, those subjects who had a sense of the experimenters' intentions were biased in favor of those intentions, without necessarily knowing it.

If Proffitt is right (see Proffitt 2009; 2013 for further discussion), his experimental results point clearly to the embodied-affective nature of perception. But if Durgin et al. (2009; 2012) are right, their results still point to an embodied phenomenon—namely, the significant effect of others on our perceptual experiences.

There are several ways to understand intersubjectivity as an embodied phenomenon. For example, weak EC theorists (see section 2.1) understand empathic consciousness or social cognition to be embodied in a minimal sense. That is, they understand social cognition to depend on B-formatted neural processes, specifically the activation of mirror neurons (MNs), which they interpret as a form of simulation. A more enactivist approach, however, interprets the mirror system to activate as part of response preparation, anticipating an agent's response to the other's behavior. That is, MN activation does not ordinarily involve simulation defined as matching (in one's own system), or imitating, the action of the other person (see Catmur, Walsh, and Heyes 2007; Dinstein et al. 2008; Csibra 2005 for empirical evidence against the simulation-as-matching hypothesis; also Gallagher 2008d); rather, it involves anticipatory processes for the possibilities of interaction or preparation for a complementary action in response to an observed action (Newman-Norlund et al. 2007). In other words, it is part of an agent's response to social affordances. It may involve the elementary timescale of neural processes, but it is immediately integrated into the ongoing dynamics that involve intersubjective interaction.

On the enactivist view, social cognition is characterized by, and sometimes constituted by, embodied interaction itself (Di Jaegher, Di Paolo, and Gallagher 2010). This view is usually worked out in contrast to theory of mind (ToM) approaches that emphasize mindreading by either theoretical inference or simulation (Gallagher 2001; 2005a; 2008c). On this enactivist-interactionist view, intersubjective interaction is not about mindreading the mental states of others; it involves, in some cases, directly perceiving their intentions and emotions in the kinematics of their movements, in their postures, gestures, facial expressions, vocal intonations, etc., as well as in their actions in highly contextualized situations (that include physical environment, social roles, culture, etc.) (Gallagher and Varga 2013). Interactive responses to social affordances just are ways that we enter into our understanding of others.

Charles Goodwin's (2000; 2007) work on conversation analysis provides a rich example of how speech acts are embedded in interactions and circumstances that involve posture, movement, position, environmental arrangements, affordances, other persons, and so forth. It's worth rehearsing one of his examples, even though his account is more extensive than I can outline here. Goodwin gives a detailed analysis of a dispute between two young girls over a game of hopscotch. There is an interactive organization of various factors that have to be considered to understand the full encounter. Goodwin emphasizes the 'visible, public deployment of multiple semiotic fields that mutually elaborate each other' (2000, 1494). These include:

- The temporal flow/rhythm of high *vs* low, hard *vs* soft vocal intonation of the speech—some of which has a deontic rather than descriptive force.
- A set of instituted norms (in this case, the rules of the game of hopscotch).
- Reference to a completed action (e.g., one of the girls throwing a marker down on one of the squares).
- Intentional movement and position (e.g., one girl moving her body intentionally so as to stand in the way of the other girl, interrupting the game).
- Bodily orientations (which allow for eye contact and joint attention towards the hopscotch pattern on the ground—and which also include the temporal modifications in those postures).
- Hand gestures that are dynamically integrated with the speech, but also with the body positions of both girls.

One of the girls positions 'her body to structure the local environment such that her gestures can themselves count as forms of social action ... Carla's hand is explicitly positioned in Diana's line of sight ... thrusting the gesturing hand toward Diana's face, [twisting] Carla's body into a configuration in which her hand, arm and the upper part of her torso are actually leaning toward Diana' (Goodwin 2000, 1498). How close is the gesture to the other girl's face? That proximity has affective meaning. If it were not a gesture, but a touch—how hard or soft, and where the touch occurred—would also have meaning. The gesture is meant to be attention grabbing, forcing the other to orient to the point being made in speech, or to a point of joint attention on something in the environment—a grab could do the same thing.

This encounter is not one-sided: Diana is standing on one foot, attempting to finish her jump through the hopscotch squares— attempting to ignore Carla and an accusation of cheating. At one moment joint attention is broken when one girl looks away. So the accomplishment of meaning involves two-way interaction and is not under the control of just one individual. Nor is the interaction, the conversation, confined to vocalization and gesture—reference is also made to the physical environment, with glances to the hopscotch squares under discussion. Cognition is distributed and involves material engagement. Thus at another moment, Carla stomps her foot in a gesture that hits three semiotic points: (1) where Diana is looking; (2) on the hopscotch square in question; and (3) on the object that Carla is iterating in speech.

Goodwin thus shows that meaning emerges at the intersection of social, cultural, material, and sequential structures of the environment where action and interaction occur. Meaning is accomplished not just via speech, but by drawing on different kinds of semiotic resources available in the environment and in whole-body pragmatics. In some regard, these are different kinds of affordances that enable the interaction. According to enactivist-interactive approaches, social understanding builds on pre- cisely this complex integration of primary and secondary intersubjective capacities, situated within pragmatic and social contexts, supplemented with and supporting communicative processes.

Another important aspect of social context is the effect that interacting with others has on perception and learning. Developmentally, we learn what is important or significant in the surrounding world through a process that may involve 'natural pedagogy'. In this process, how the caregiver relates to the child influences what the child learns. Natural pedagogy, which involves ostensively directing the infant's attention to some object or event,

enables fast and efficient social learning of cognitively opaque cultural knowledge that would be hard to acquire relying on purely observational learning mechan- isms alone . . . [H]uman infants are prepared to be at the receptive side of natural pedagogy (i) by being sensitive to ostensive signals that indicate that they are being addressed by communication, (ii) by developing referential expectations in ostensive contexts and (iii) by being biased to interpret ostensive-referential communication as conveying information that is kind-relevant and generalizable. (Csibra and Gergely 2009, 148)

More generally, we learn what objects are significant and valuable through our interactions with others, or even just our perception of what they are doing with objects in the environment. We learn to see the world along these lines of significance and value, and oftentimes objects that fall outside of such lines don't even register. In the same way that expert training hones the perceptual system so that experts are able to perceive things that non-experts fail to perceive, we all tend to be experts in the affairs of everyday living. We become experts in everyday life through our interactions with others.

Indeed, this intersubjective education of perception continues throughout life. Such effects show up even in cases where we are not explicitly interacting with others, although others are present. Adult subjects presented with a face looking towards (or away from) an object evaluate the object as more (or less) likeable than those objects that don't receive much attention from others. If one adds an emotional expression to the face, one gets a stronger effect (Bayliss et al. 2006; 2007). Furthermore, seeing another person act with ease (or without ease) toward an object will influence observers' feelings about the object (Hayes et al. 2008 but also see Firestone and Scholl 2015 for dissenting discussion on some of these issues). The Social Simon Effect (Sebanz, Knoblich, and Prinz, 2003) also suggests that our perception–action system is influenced when we are embedded in a social situation where the other person is doing a related task or similar action.

Social interactions, social roles, and groupings also have their influence on how one perceives and acts in the world. To modify Proffitt's scenario, imagine being exhausted, but the incline is a hill that you are climbing with friends or to meet a loved one (see, e.g., Schnall et al. 2008). Or, again, think of the affective import in situations where one would be seen by others as not up to the task, negatively impacting one's personal image. In some social circumstances one may find a particular object or setting to be of more interest and more attention-grabbing than if one were with a different group, or alone.

8.3 The Embodied and Enactive Brain

Following the 'weak' version of embodied cognition pursued by Goldman (2012; 2014) and others (section 2.1), one might object that all such affective and intersubjective effects are ultimately processed in the brain, so that even the most enactive aspects of cognition are cashed out in brain processes. Moreover, one might continue to insist that when we look at how the brain works, we need concepts like representation and inference to explain it, and these go against strong enactivist claims. After all, even if one were to accept the enactivist interpretation of MNs, their activations are nothing other than B-formatted representations. On the weak EC view, claims about enactive perception, affectivity, and intersubjectivity can still fit neatly into orthodox internalist accounts.

The issue concerning how the brain works will not be resolved simply by asking the neuroscientists to adjudicate, however. Most neuroscientists are Helmholtzian and would endorse the idea that the neural processes underlying perception are inferential and representational. Bayesian predictive coding approaches, as we've seen, treat perception and object recognition as inferential processes (Friston 2012, 248; also see Clark 2013a). Yet there continue to be significant objections to the Helmholtzian idea that perception involves subpersonal inferences (see Bennett and Hacker 2003; Hatfield 2002; Hutto and Myin 2013; Orlandi 2012; 2014). Even if the predictive coding approach were right about how brain dynamics are organized—in a hierarchical way involving synaptic inhibition based on empirical priors—it's not clear why we should think of it as a kind of inference rather than a kind of dynamic adjustment process in which the brain, *as part of and along with the larger organism*, settles into the right kind of attunement with the environment—an environment that is physical but also social and cultural. In contexts of social interaction, as Goodwin shows, not all of the action is going on just in the brain. Rather than predictive coding or predictive processing, it's a matter of predictive engagement (Gallagher and Allen 2016).

The notion of an enactive system requires conceiving of the brain in a different way. In evolutionary terms, the brain does what it does and is the way it is, across some scale of variations, because it is part of a living body that has arms that can reach, and hands that can grasp in certain limited ways, and because it has eyes structured to focus, and so on. The sensorimotor system is the way it is because of the kind of organism the human body is. The organism has autonomic and peripheral nervous systems, and not just a central system. It attains an upright posture, which, in evolutionary terms, reshapes essential features, including the brain (see section 9.2), allowing the person to cope with specific kinds of environments, and with other people. Changes to any bodily, environmental, or intersubjective conditions elicit responses from the organism as a whole. On this view, as we have seen, rather than representing or computing information, the brain is better conceived as participating in the action, enabling the system as a whole to attune to changing circumstances.

The enactivist interpretation is not simply a reinterpretation of what happens extra-neurally, out in the intersubjective world of action where we anticipate and respond to social affordances. An enactivist interpretation of the MN system, for example, points beyond the orthodox explanation of information processing to the possibility of rethinking not just the neural correlates of perception or intersubjectivity, but the very notion of neural correlate, and how the brain itself works. More than this, it suggests a different way of conceiving brain function, specifically in non-representational, integrative, and dynamical terms (Gallagher et al. 2013).

The enactivist view of how brains work is that brains are involved in worldly interactions such that they bear less of a cognitive load than assumed in the internalist and predictive coding models. Brains participate in complex worldly, affordance-oriented interactions in ways that shape perceptions and intentions, and guide actions. In this regard, a brain is not reconstructing the world with inner representations or computing inferential predictions about what's 'out there'—it is part of a system that is participating in a dynamical process that it doesn't fully control. Rather than trading in the currency of representations and inferences, brain processes are part of a dynamical Gestalt (Merleau-Ponty's notion of form or structure) and are best explained in terms of dynamical concepts such as synergy, coordination, and structural stability, ecological concepts such as affordance, and the concept of metaplasticity (Malafouris 2013).

We naturally tend to think that the best explanation of brain function will be worked out in the vocabulary of neuroscience. Indeed, since the 1990s, the assumption has been that neuroscience will at some point replace psychology and that we will adjust our philosophy of mind accordingly (see, e.g., Gazzaniga 1998). What I am suggesting is that the best explanation of brain function may be found in the vocabularies of Gestalt psychology, ecological psychology, dynamical systems theory, intersubjective interaction, embodied and situated cognition, and the anthropological insights found in discussions that extend from concepts of cultural niche to material engagement. The question is whether neuroscience can start to speak this different language and enter into the right kind of dialogue.

When the embodied agent interacts with the world or with others, that engagement doesn't generate sensory input for the brain to process; what it generates is already, on the elementary timescale, a response by the whole organism. What is typically called sensory input involves neural activations that set off a wide network of activation that is already affective, motoric, and autonomic. Here I point back to some of the empirical data reviewed in previous chapters: e.g., the fact that early visual processing in V1 anticipates reward (Shuler and Bear 2006); the fact that 'from the very moment that visual stimulation begins' muscular and hormonal changes throughout the body generate interoceptive sensations associated with prior experience that dynamically integrate with visual stimulation and help to guide ongoing and subsequent response (Barrett and Bar 2009, 1325); the fact that face recognition is not just recognition, but activates affective areas as well as the dorsal visual pathway, indicating that it is also attuned to social affordances and the possibilities of ongoing interaction; the fact that complex processes related to homeostasis impinge upon cognitive processes in a non-representational way.

With respect to affect, if hormonal changes in the body, and neurotransmitter levels in the brain, play any part in shaping cognition, attention, and experience, as the evidence indicates, it seems difficult to model such chemical modulations in terms of inference. In contrast, on the enactivist view, the explanatory unit of perception (and action, and cognition) is not the brain, or even two (or more) brains in the case of social cognition, but dynamic relations between organism and environment, or between organisms, which include brains, but also include their own structural embodied features that enable specific perception–action loops involving social and physical environments, which in turn effect statistical regularities that shape the structure and function of the nervous system.

The question is, what do brains do as part of a dynamical attunement of organism to environment in the complex mix of transactions that involve moving, gesturing, and interacting with the expressive bodies of others, with their eyes and faces and hands and voices; bodies that are gendered and raced, and dressed to attract, or to work or play; bodies that incorporate artifacts, tools, and technologies, that are situated in various physical environments, and are defined by diverse social roles and institutional practices?

The answer is that the brain participates in a system, along with eyes and face and hands and voice, and so on. And the brain would work differently if its embodiment lacked eyes, face, hands, voice, and so on. This is a fully embodied system that enactively anticipates and responds to its environment. How an agent responds and what an agent perceives will depend to a great degree on the overall dynamical state of the brain, but also on environmental factors, embodied-affective and intersubject-ive factors, the person(s) with whom she is interacting, her worldly and intentional circumstances, the bodily skills and habits she has formed, her physical condition, as well as her history of personal experiences, and what the other person may expect in terms of normative standards stemming from communal and institutional practices (Gallagher et al. 2013). Change any of these things and we can expect changes in neural processing, not because the brain represents such changes, but because the brain is part of the larger embodied system that is coping with its changing environment.

In this chapter I've argued that it's not enough to model an enactivist approach to perception and cognition on sensorimotor contingencies alone, even if they do play an important role in such matters. I've pointed to significant evidence showing that affective and intersubjective aspects of embodiment are also important contributories to perceptual and cognitive processes. This fuller sense of embodiment-environment pushes us to rethink the role played by neuronal processes in the brain. Even a neuro-science that frames brain function in terms of predictive coding needs to recognize how the brain is part of a system that attunes to and responds to its environment in a way that enacts a meaning relative to the particular-ities of that embodiment. *Who would deny this?*—an often-heard response to these enactivist claims. Very few people deny that the body and envir-onment are playing some role in cognitive processes. That's fine, but it also means that these factors have to enter into the explanation in the right way, and once they do they push in the direction of rethinking the nature of mind and brain.

9

The Upright Posture
Its Current Standing

Embodied approaches to cognition, including extended mind and enactivist approaches, emphasize not only the bodily aspects of perception and cognition, but also the importance of environment, artifacts, tools, and technologies that surround the perceiving subject and define specific cultural niches (Sterelny 2007; 2010). On these views perception and action, but also higher-order cognitive tasks, involve an integration of resources that cut across brain, body, and environment. Such views are strongly supported by evolutionary theory. In 1949 Erwin Straus published an essay titled, simply, 'The upright posture' (Straus 1966). It was an essay written in the phenomenological anthropological tradition, and informed by both speculation and science. More recent biological and evolutionary theory on the upright posture also continues to be informed by both speculation and science. In this chapter, referencing this recent literature, I update Straus's account, extending it to encompass a greater emphasis on environment, and considerations about social and cultural factors. I also deepen his analysis by introducing the notion of *affordance space* and relating it to the important role that human hands play in the attainment of rationality. These are themes that fit well into an enactivist account of cognition.

9.1 The Genesis of Upright Posture: Recent Biological and Evolutionary Theory

If one keeps a close focus on the anatomy of the human body, the upright posture seemingly provides no advantages, and introduces all kinds of problems. For example, it slows movement compared to quadrupedal arrangements (Lovejoy 1981)—quadrupeds are faster than bipeds. It generates problems for balance and increases the likelihood of falling (Skoyles 2006). Attaining the upright posture consumes energy for quadrupedal primates (Nakatsukasa et al. 2004). And for those who have already attained it, and attempt to maintain it, it increases joint stress, back pain, etc. (Niemitz 2010). All of this leads Deloison to suggest, 'Whatever one may think of it, the upright posture does not offer sufficient advantages for it to have persisted according to the classic criteria of natural selection' (2004; cited and translated in Niemitz 2010, 243).

And yet, since hominoids attained and maintained the upright posture, sufficient advantages must have existed. This poses the challenge for evolutionary theories about how the upright posture came about. Although there are, in fact, multiple theories—thirty hypotheses developed over the past century (Niemitz 2010)—so far the debate remains unresolved. Generally the most coherent theories look beyond the anatomy of the body and consider the specific kinds of environment that would motivate this kind of change in posture.

For example, the now discredited *savannah hypothesis* suggested that we started walking upright for better vision, for scavenging or hunting on open, dry terrain. The *forest hypothesis*, in contrast, emphasizes the harvesting of food, so that the upright posture was attained, assisted by support of the upper extremity, to stand up to reach for high food (Wrangham 1980; Hunt 1994). One of the more recent proposals, the *shoreline (wetlands) hypothesis* suggested that when foraging in the water, primates are forced not only to stand up but also to walk (Niemitz 2010).

The savannah hypothesis, as mentioned, has been discredited by evidence that hominoid ancestors of humans were bipedal prior to the time period of savannah (Pickford et al. 2002). Most current theories adopt the forest hypothesis (e.g., Parravicini and Pievani 2016). Niemitz (2010), who favors the shoreline hypothesis, reviews a total of twelve hypothetical benefits to the upright posture: e.g., improved visual perspective for spotting predators; freeing of hands; ability to throw; improved infant carrying; food reaching; carrying of food; enhancement of competitive display; extended posture during locomotion in trees; improved thermoregulation. The latter, closely tied to the savannah hypothesis, is the idea that the upright posture helps to reduce exposure to equatorial solar radiation and thereby to control body temperature. Taking into consideration that night time on dry, open land is freezing cold, however, and that equatorial nights last exactly as long as equatorial days, one has to wonder whether the presumed advantage of keeping cool during the day is balanced by the disadvantage of trying to keep warm at night (Vaneechoutte 2014)—although one might also think this is motivation to lie down and sleep at night.

Niemitz argues for the shoreline hypothesis, expanding on Morgan's (1990) Aquatic Ape Theory. To play with this chapter's subtitle a little more, the Niemitz hypothesis is that the upright posture derives from current standing. In water, standing with or against the current prevents drowning. And, wading in water requires bipedal walking.

In most cases, a monkey or ape assumes an upright bipedal posture as soon as it ventures into the shallow water . . . In contrast to all other hypotheses discussed above, wading behaviour, as proposed here, is the only behavioural pattern in which a primate is not only stimulated to stand up or to make one or two steps. When foraging in the water, the monkey or ape is forced not only to stand up but to walk. (Niemitz 2010, 253)

This view is consistent with several other factors: improved visuals—a steeper angle improves spotting of objects in shallow water—freeing of hands, infant carrying, and food carrying are improved. The thermo-regulation issue is reinterpreted.

In humans [in contrast to other non-upright primates] the skin of the face, neck, and shoulders as well as the ventral and dorsal upper thorax are used for heat exchange, while the lower abdomen, gluteal region, and hip, as well as the whole hind extremities are well insulated. No other functions than thermoregulation in a wading fashion are suitable to explain [this]. (Niemitz 2010, 258)

This very brief outline is just the skeleton of the ongoing theoretical discussion, but I think I've already presented enough to be able to draw some lessons from this debate. First, looking just at anatomy—or the morphological aspects of the body by itself—is insufficient for revealing the advantages that come along with the upright posture; we need to look at environments, and to think in terms of organism–environment coup-ling. Second, there may be more than one cause or motivation that justifies the struggle for upright posture. Each hypothesis tends to pro-vide only one single or main reason why an orthograde posture or locomotion might bear a positive selective favor. But the ecological and behavioral setting for the very beginning of upright posture and loco-motion was, certainly, much more complicated, and it is unlikely that there was only 'one specific reason why bipedalism was selected for' (Niemitz 2010, 250, citing Harcourt-Smith 2007).

9.2 What Upright Posture Does for Human Cognition

Erwin Straus, in his 1949 essay on the upright posture, continues Darwin's (1874) and Huxley's (1894) story of the effects of the human achievement of upright posture, a pre-eminence in the animal kingdom, closely connected with the growth of culture and civilization. According to Darwin (1874), for the human 'to stand firmly on his feet' allowed hands and arms to be free to use and manufacture tools, leading to the enlargement of the brain, etc. Straus clearly proclaims his interest 'in what man is and not in how he supposedly became what he is' (1966, 169). That is, he is not so interested in the causes or motives for attaining the upright posture; he is rather interested in what the upright posture does for human existence. He notes that the upright posture is distinctive for the human species, and that this has far-reaching consequences for perceptual abilities (enhancement of vision; decline of olfaction), and also in regard to moral values and judgments. The phrase 'to be upright' has a moral connotation and, as Straus suggests, this may signal more than just a metaphorical expression.

His more general claim is this: 'the shape and function of the human body are determined in almost every detail by, and for, the upright posture' (Straus 1966, 167). Consider the following.

1. Human anatomy and skeletal structure: this includes the shape and structure of the human foot, ankle, knee, hip, and vertebral column, as well as the proportions of limbs, demanding a specific musculature and nervous system design. Such changes enable the upright posture, but are also shaped by the attainment of the upright posture. All of this in turn permits the specifically human development of shoulders, arms, hands, skull, and face.
2. With these changes what counts as the world is redefined since such changes bring along changes in what we can see and what we can grasp.
3. Developmentally, attaining the upright posture is delayed in humans and requires the infant to learn to stand and walk in a

struggle with gravity. This has implications for how the infant relies on and relates to others.

4. In addition, maintaining the upright posture depends on a basic level of consciousness, namely wakefulness. Fall asleep and you fall down. Not only upright posture, but movement itself, including early crawling behavior, influences the development of perception and cognition (see Campos, Bertenthal, and Kermoian 1992). The change of posture that comes with standing and walking equally affects what we can see and to what we can attend.

5. Perception: With the upright posture and distance from the ground the olfactory sense declines in importance; seeing (the sense of distance) becomes primary. Distal sight grants foresight and allows for planning. Olfactory mechanisms shrink and no longer dominate facial structure, which allows for changes in brain capacity, development of jaw structure, and so forth. The transformation of the facial structure coordinates with the expansion and remodeling of brain structure and nervous system.

6. Action space: The hands are liberated for more proficient grasping, throwing, and catching. The upright posture provides some distance from things, as well as specific forms of closeness to and distance from fellow humans.

7. Language: The mouth is also liberated for purposes other than just eating. The upright posture transforms jaw structure (along with dietary possibilities)—less need for massive musculature and skeletal infrastructure. This allows for the development of the more subtle phonetic muscles. Along with language and a larger, more developed cortex comes the rationality that makes us human.

On the one hand, from the perspective of embodied cognitive science, Straus reflects an enlightenment-style dualism. We can see in the upright posture a differentiation between human and animal; between vision and the other senses; between above and below the waist—brain and handy manipulation above *versus* sexual organs and locomotion below (see Sheets-Johnstone 1990; Ingold 2004).

On the other hand, Straus's story seems much more embodied than recent emphasis on exclusively brain-based B-formatted representations—the 'sanitized' version of weak EC discussed in section 2.1. Connected evolutionary stories about neural reuse or exaptation are important but incomplete—at least to the extent that they fail to make significant reference to bodily processes and focus exclusively on 'neural niches' (Anderson 2010, 257; Iriki and Sakura 2008) rather than environmental factors and cultural niches (Sterelny 2007; 2010). But Straus's story is also incomplete. His focus is more on the body itself, and he has little to say about environmental factors. What François Jacob says of the brain, viz., that '[a]lthough our brain represents the main adaptive feature of our species, what it is adapted to is not clear at all' (1977; cited in Fitch 2012, 613), can also be said about changes in the body if we focus strictly on those changes. Indeed, if we stay with Straus's embodied, but somewhat unembedded account, we just don't have an account of how the phylogenetic advantages outstripped the anatomical problems—and what the brain and body adapted *to* remains somewhat mysterious. That is, if brain and body adapted, the full story depends on knowing what they adapted to—we need a brain–body–*environment* account.

9.3 Extending Straus's Embodied Account

Let's start with speech. For Straus, the human larynx descends for purely mechanical reasons due to the assumption of upright posture and a change in skull conformation—a byproduct (or spandrel) that then came to serve speech. Tecumseh Fitch (2012) acknowledges this possibility but suggests an alternative possibility: that 'the descended larynx evolved as an adaptation for size exaggeration, was later exapted for phonetic use, and that subsequent evolution has converted it to a true adaptation for spoken language' (626). Size exaggeration involves display in a social environment. Fitch (2012) is wary of speculation, however, and so leaves a lot of questions about language open.

> ...despite significant advances in understanding the mechanistic basis of speech, this historical adaptive question will remain challenging...no confident assertions about the adaptive value, for speech, of a descended larynx or vocal imitation in humans...can be justified by currently available data.
>
> (2012, 626)

Whether the descent of larynx in infants is an adaptation for the production of vowels; or the further descent in pubertal adult males is adaptation for body size exaggeration, no existing evidence will settle this issue, so we are left with speculation.

Mario Vaneechoutte (2014) provides a more developed and detailed evo-devo (but also more speculative) account; literally, a *song and dance* account that includes some important *hand-waving*. Let me explain that. No doubt, in agreement with Straus, there are mechanical changes in the skull and face; but to explain their functional implications, we also have to consider practical constraints tied to environmental aspects (Vaneechoutte 2014). Building on the shoreline hypothesis, not only wading, but also diving, the rhythm of swimming, and the control of breath may be pre-adaptations (naturally selected for other reasons, independent of each other) contributing to the development of language capability.

> The swimming and diving adaptations of the upper airway (and vocal) tract led to increased vocal dexterity and song [consistent with the musical origins of language], and to increased fine tuning of motoric and mimicking abilities.
>
> (Vaneechoutte 2014, 1)

That's the song and dance part.[1] There's also some important hand-waving involved—indeed, there is an ongoing debate about the role of gesture in the evolution of language. Arbib (2005) argues for the import-ance of mimesis and pantomime (the gesture first hypothesis). McNeill et al. (2008; also Deacon 1997) argue that gesture evolves along with speech. In either case, the brain evolves along with the body—Straus and Vaneechoutte emphasize changes in facial jaw structure, larynx, and hands as obviously influencing the evolution of brain structure and function.

Holekamp, Swanson, and Van Meter (2013) confirm the connection between brain plasticity and behavioral plasticity in reference to both face and hands, emphasizing, more than Straus did, the role of social relations. The shape and function of paws (in contrast to hands), for example, allow for fast locomotion, but limit social interaction. For species with paws rather than hands,

> the richness of their tactile interactions with their environments is quite limited relative to that of primates, and this in turn limits both the complexity of their

---

[1] 'Song and dance are equally intrinsically linked, supporting the idea that well-developed mimicking motoric abilities, for moving freely in 3 dimensions (in air or in water, but not in trees), developed for diving/swimming. This ability further evolved for dancing/singing, and predisposed for spoken/gestural language' (Vaneechoutte 2014, 28).

social interactions and the broader embodiment of their intelligence . . . Hands permit many novel forms of social interaction, not the least of which is the elaborate manual allogrooming behaviour typical of many primates.

(Holekamp, Swanson, and Van Meter 2013, 4)

In regard to evolutionary changes in skull and brain, the dual function of the skull as 'a protective housing for the brain . . . and a platform for the feeding apparatus' leads to a trade-off that is locked to changes in limb structure, and, importantly, what the environment affords (Holekamp, Swanson, and Van Meter 2013, 5). Paws, speed, hunting prey in particular environments, larger jaws, smaller brains—all in contrast to hands, slowness, foraging in shoreline environments, smaller jaws, larger brains.

These recent evo-devo ideas reinforce the lessons that need to be applied to Straus's analysis. Namely, we need to add (or emphasize) that physical changes may occur for more than one reason, and such reasons may not be reduced to merely mechanical or biological ones; and evolutionary change is helped along with practices tied to specific physical and social environments. 'Selection operates when animals interact with their environments, so the broader the array of interactions permitted by limb structure, the more variable the extended phenotype . . . hence the greater the evolvability of the animal's behavioural flexibility' (Holekamp, Swanson, and Van Meter 2013, 5; citing Dawkins 1982).

Finally, let's consider two complaints. The first we can call the 'head over heels' complaint lodged by Tim Ingold (2004). He acknowledges that evolution accounts for upright posture and the set of anatomical changes that come with it—brain size, remodeled hand, and so forth, as well as the claims for the advancement of rationality along with reaching and grasping and language, and so forth. But, for Ingold, the story fails in regard to locomotion and the feet. What Darwin called the loss of the foot's original grasping function, and the equation of rationality with brain and hands, is not fully an evolutionary story. The former part is a cultural story. According to Ingold, we traded prehensile feet for improved locomotion with the invention of shoes and a built environment. He cites Edward Tylor (1881), who compared images of the chimp *versus* the human foot (see Figure 9.1), but, as Taylor himself points out, and as Ingold emphasizes, the human foot is purposively a foot shaped by European boots.

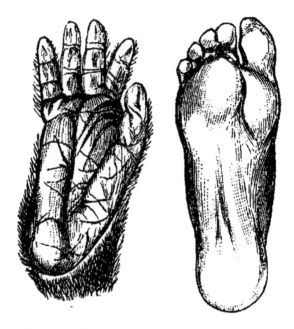

Figure 9.1. Chimpanzee foot *versus* the human foot (from Edward Tylor 1881).

The second complaint, specifically pitched against Straus, is the 'throwing like a girl' complaint raised by Iris Young in her famous 1980 essay, which targeted Straus's claim that girls throw differently from boys due to 'feminine' anatomy. Straus is puzzled because this 'amazing difference' appears very early in development (prior to breast development) and there is no obvious anatomical reason for it. He refers to a 'feminine attitude' as the likely cause. In her critique, Young follows Simone de Beauvoir: human existence is defined by its situation: historical, cultural, and social. Young goes even further in this direction than de Beauvoir, who gives some emphasis to anatomy and physiology, and not enough emphasis to 'the situatedness of the woman's actual bodily movement and orientation to its surroundings and its world' (1980, 139). The throwing difference, Young argues, is due to social formation in a particular historical epoch, and the resulting way that females live their body. Young makes no claim to universality; she allows for the possibility that women may throw differently, and more generally move differently in different time periods and different cultures. In every case, however, cultural and social practices condition a typical gender-specific style of movement (for boys and girls, men and women)—a style that 'consists of particular modalities of the structures and conditions of the body's existence in the world' (1980, 139). Most generally, while engaged in intentional physical action involving large movements, the female who is raised in contemporary advanced industrial and urban society, does not put her whole body into directed motion, but rather, concentrates movement in one body part. Her movement is not inclined to reach, extend, or follow through in the direction of her intention. This style of movement is coordinated with a certain constricted character of spatial perception that, in turn, constrains certain types of action affordances. Young provides a number of examples in the area of athletics. The reason for this difference of style, Young argues, is not anatomical; it's rather tied to cultural practices, the kinds of opportunities and activities that girls and women are (or have been) encouraged (or allowed) to pursue within particular cultures—activities that are often sedentary and enclosed. It's not just lack of practice (in activities that would develop movement differently) but the specific kinds of practices, the 'specific positive style[s] of feminine body comportment and movement, which [are] learned as the girl comes to understand that she is a girl', that shape motor performance (1980, 153).

The point of these two complaints (head over heals and throwing like a girl) is that one needs to be careful in discriminating what changes (plastic or otherwise, of brain, body, environment) belong to evolution as opposed to development and culture. At the same time, one should also take into consideration all kinds of 'looping effects' (Hacking 1995) that complicate any attempt to create strict separations between evolution, development, and culture. For example, one can argue that our hands and arms evolved in conjunction with the upright posture; but we also invented tools and armaments, which led to adopting specific gaits when carrying such armaments in battle. Bremmer (1992), for example, argued that aspects of the Western male gait are modeled on Greek classic gait, which originates in earlier practice when every man had to carry arms in order to be ready to fight. This endorses a point made by Marcel Mauss (1979): 'there is simply no such thing as a "natural" way of walking that may be prescribed independently of the diverse circumstances in which human beings grow up and live their lives' (quoted in Ingold 2004, 335).

9.4 Affordance Spaces and Enactive Hands

In sorting what evolution, development and cultural practices do to cognition, one analytic tool that may be useful is the concept of affordance space. This concept derives from Gibson's notion of affordance: it defines possibilities for action that depend on both body and environment. Such affordance spaces can be physical, but also social and cultural (see Brincker 2014).

An affordance space is the (abstract) range of possibilities provided by any change in body or environment. An individual's occurrent affordance space is defined by evolution (the fact that she has hands), development (her life-stage—infant, adult, aged), and by social and cultural practices (normative constraints). The human affordance space differs from a non-human animal's due to differences in evolution. Humans have hands and capacities for certain kinds of movement, as well as a variety of cognitive possibilities. A child's affordance space differs from an adult's due to differences in developmental factors. Humans learn to throw or to move or think in specific ways across developmental parameters. One individual's affordance space differs from another's due to differences in experience, skill level, normative constraints, etc. Humans are enabled or constrained to throw or to move or to think in particular ways due to their prior experiences and plastic changes in both brain and body.

Perhaps the clearest example of how specifics of embodiment fit into affordance spaces is in regard to the human hand, which, as Jacob Bronowski (1975, 116) puts it, 'is the cutting edge of the mind'. The upright posture, of course, is what frees the upper limbs for a different kind of movement. Hands become what they are and are able to do what they do because they are freed up to do such things by the attainment of the upright posture. The upright posture allows for doing things that we would otherwise not be able to do; hands allow for acting in ways that we otherwise would not be able to act.

The enactivist view of human cognition starts with the idea that we are action oriented. Our ability for making sense out of the world comes from an active and pragmatic engagement with the world, along with our capacities to interact with other people. In this regard Anaxagoras' observation that we humans are the wisest of all beings because we have hands better reflects an enactivist view than Aristotle's claim that

'Man has hands because he is the wisest of all beings.'[2] Still, in the Aristotelian tradition the hand is raised to the level of the rational by considering it the *organum organorum*. More generally, in the history of philosophy hands are inserted here and there to provide a firm grasp on some important philosophical notions. Thus, a statement attributed to Newton suggests that the thumb is good evidence of God's existence, and Kant (1992) used the fact that hands are incongruent counterparts, e.g. a left hand doesn't fit properly into a right-hand glove, to prove that Newton was right about space being absolute.

But this is not the main line drawn by the philosophical traditions. With respect to rationality the eyes were thought to have it more than a show of hands. At least since Plato rationality has been associated with vision: to understand is to see, and to see the highest of all things is to see that which can be seen—the *eidos*—which is not something you can touch or hold in your hand. The focus on vision leads to high church cognitivism, idealism, and the main insights of metaphysics and epistemology. Furthermore, to see someone's soul you need to look into her eyes. Hands will tell you only what kind of work the person does, while contemplation (gazing theoretically upon the *eide*), even if infrequently realized, is philosophically more celebrated than the life of action (*vita activa*), and purportedly of a higher value than the kind of work done with one's hands.

The idea that vision dominates and often trumps the hand is backed up by scientific evidence. There are many examples of this. Consider recent findings on the rubber hand illusion (RHI). One of your hands is hidden from your direct view beneath a blind; there is a rubber arm/hand on the table, in front of you, positioned so that it is close to where you would normally see your hand. The experimenter starts to stroke both your hidden hand and the rubber hand synchronously and you suddenly

---

[2] 'Standing erect, man has no need of legs in front, and in their stead has been endowed by nature with arms and hands. Now it is the opinion of Anaxagoras that the possession of these hands is the cause of man being of all animals the most intelligent. But it is more rational to suppose that his endowment with hands is the consequence rather than the cause of his superior intelligence. For the hands are instruments or organs, and the invariable plan of nature in distributing the organs is to give each to such animal as can make use of it ... We must conclude that man does not owe his superior intelligence to his hands, but his hands to his superior intelligence. For the most intelligent of animals is the one who would put the most organs to use; and the hand is not to be looked on as one organ but as many; for it is, as it were, an instrument for further instruments.' (Aristotle 350 BCE. *On the Parts of Animals* 4.10 687a7)

feel the tactile stimulus in the rubber hand as if it were your hand. You start to feel that the rubber hand is part of your body (your sense of ownership for the body part is modulated). On the one hand, the synchrony of the stroking is important for this effect; on the other hand, however, the real force is vision. Close your eyes and the illusion disappears; the sensation shifts back to your real hand (Botvinick and Cohen 1998).

Vision trumps proprioception as well. While experiencing the illusion you are asked to indicate using a ruler on the table the precise position of your hidden hand located beneath the blind. Most subjects indicate that their fingers are closer to the position of the rubber hand than they actually are. This is termed 'proprioceptive drift'. One might argue, however, that the hands themselves are not fooled. Thus Kammers et al. (2009) showed proprioceptive drift toward the rubber hand for the ruler-based perceptual judgment about the location of one's hidden hand, but no proprioceptive drift when one is asked to use the other (real) hand to point to the position of the hidden hand. The suggestion is that the motor system does not succumb to the illusion. In a follow-up study, however, Kammers et al. (2010) showed that in a grasping action the motor system can also be susceptible to the illusion. When, while experiencing the RHI with all hands shaped in a grasping posture, you are asked to use the hidden hand to reach out to take hold of a visible object, your reach is imperfectly calculated by the degree of proprioceptive drift. So the hand is fooled. Although the claim has been that the illusion disappears when the stroking is asynchronous, certain effects can be had even with vision alone and without the synchronous stroking. Rohde et al. (2011) have shown dissociation between proprioceptive drift in RHI and the sense of ownership for the rubber hand. While the feeling of ownership for the rubber hand requires synchronous stroking, proprioceptive drift occurs not only in the synchronous stroking condition but also in the two control conditions: asynchronous stroking, and vision alone. If you simply stare at the rubber hand long enough, your real hand is subject to proprioceptive drift.

What about the hand being quicker than the eye? Even if the effects of vision are quite powerful, every now and then one finds that the hands take the lead—and a corresponding line of thought (some version of which one can find in the Aristotelian tradition) leads in the direction of embodied cognition and practical (not just contemplative) wisdom—even if it does not fully reach an enactivist view.

In a book entitled *Hands*, advertised as 'intended for all readers—including magicians, detectives, musicians, orthopedic surgeons, and anthropologists', John Russell Napier states: 'The hand is the mirror of the brain, there can be no such combination as dextrous hands and clumsy brains' (1980, 25). One can confirm this in experiments where the hands do seem to outsmart conscious vision, at least, and indeed where the hands seem to know something that the agent doesn't. Thus, if you are asked to reach out and grab an object placed in front of you, and then, after you have started reaching, the object is moved slightly and quickly to the right or left, your arm and hand will adjust its trajectory and precision grip to the new position of the target, although you remain unaware that the target moved or that your hand made the adjustment (Pélisson et al. 1986). The movement doesn't register in conscious vision (the ventral stream), although it must do so in unconscious vision (the dorsal stream). This is Goodale and Milner's (1992) well-known distinction between two visual pathways in the brain: one, the ventral, serving recognition, and the other, faster dorsal pathway, serving motor control. The hand is faster than conscious vision, but not faster than unconscious vision. As an agent reaches to grasp something, the hand automatically shapes itself into just the right posture to form the most appropriate grip for that object and for the agent's purpose. If an agent reaches to grab an apple in order to take a bite, the shape of her grasp is different from when she reaches to grab a banana, but also different from when she reaches to grab the apple to throw it (Ansuini et al. 2006; 2008; Jeannerod 1997; Marteniuk et al. 1987; Sartori, Becchio, and Castiello 2011). This happens without the agent monitoring or being aware of (or consciously seeing) the difference in the shape of the grasp. Still the hand does not do this blindly; it requires the cooperation of the dorsal visual stream to provide visual information about the shape of the apple and where in the near environment it is located.

Evidence for this can be found in visual agnosia patients, as in one of Milner and Goodale's patients, DF, who has lesions in both temporal lobes which prevent her from seeing which way an object is oriented. When presented with a disk she is unable to say whether it is presented vertically or horizontally. But when she is handed the disk and asked to put it into a slot (similar to a mailbox), she has no problem orienting the disk to the proper angle (Milner and Goodale 1995). Likewise Robertson and Treisman (2010, 308) report on a patient of Rafal with visual agnosia who was unable to recognize objects. 'When the patient was shown a picture of a clarinet, he hesitated in naming it, suggested it was a "pencil," but meanwhile his fingers began to play an imaginary clarinet.' There is much to say about gesture in this regard as well. As Andy Clark points out, and as Susan Goldin-Meadow shows experimentally, one may unconsciously express something in gesture that one is unable to articulate in conscious speech (Clark 2013b; Goldin-Meadow 1999; Goldin-Meadow et al. 2001; also see Gallagher 2005a, ch. 6).

These examples tell us something again important about how we should understand brain function. On the enactivist view, the brain is not composed of computational machinery locked away inside the head, representing the external world to provide knowledge upon which we can act. Rather, in action—whether reaching and grasping or pointing, or gesturing—the brain partners with the hand and forms a functional unit that properly engages with the agent's environment and exploits the affordance space that is defined in relation to all of these elements. For example, one can show experimentally that in basic actions (e.g. reaching and grasping), in contrast to passive perception (e.g. estimating the distance between two sensations on one's skin), the felt differentiation between hand and arm across the wrist is reduced (Vignemont et al. 2009). That is, in action, the hand is not experienced as a body part differentiated from the arm, but as continuous with the arm. Likewise the arm with the shoulder. In action, the body schema functions in a holistic way (in contrast to the perceptual and articulated aspects of body image) (Gallagher 2005a). In the same way, it seems right to say that the brain is part of this holistic functioning. It's not a top-down regulation of movement, brain to hand; nor a bottom-up emergence of rationality, hand to brain. Rather, neural processes coordinate with and can be entrained by the hand movements, forming a single integrated cognitive system (Iverson and Thelen 1999). This implies a reciprocal unity of feed-forward-feed-back processes in which the hand and the brain form a dynamical system that reaches into the world.

And perhaps beyond! Horst Bredekamp (2007), in his art-historical study of Galileo, comments on the fact that Galileo's drawings of Jupiter were more accurate than the images he could see through his telescope. In some sense—in its own motoric sense—his drawing hand was smarter than his eye. Bredekamp suggests that this was a kind of manual thinking (*manuelles Denken*). Again, however, we should think of this as a holistic thinking involving eye, brain, and hand. It may be that Galileo inter-polated detail between what vision told him, and certain of his assumptions about smoothness and continuity. But this could not account for his accuracy, which can be verified by more sophisticated telescopes today. Might it be that Galileo received more information through the slight movements of the telescope, since, in some cases, more details may be discerned in perceptions across moving images? The detail may not appear in a single view from the telescope but may emerge across multiple views. Galileo's friend, the artist Cigoli, suggested something closer to the enactivist story of an interaction between visual perception and the motor ability that comes with practiced drawing.

For Cigoli, Galileo could see better, because he was better prepared by his artistic training and knew how to draw. In an autodidactic process taking place between hand and eye, Galileo was better able to attain knowledge, both because he had learned to perceive the unusual and because he could demonstrate it in the medium of drawing.   (Bredekamp 2001, 180)

Practicing one's drawing, of course, will result in plastic changes in the brain. It seems that these plasticity effects accompany whatever habits one forms with one's hands. The famous experiments by Merzenich et al. (1983) demonstrate this. The experimenters tied down certain fingers of monkeys so that they were forced to use only select fingers in habitual movement of the hand. This habitual movement altered the details of the brain's functional maps of the hand. Patterns of hand use physically shape those sensory and motor parts of the brain that register and control hand movement in monkeys, as well as in humans (see Rossini et al. 1994). This brain reorganization also happens as we train our hands to play piano or other musical instruments (Pascual-Leone et al. 1995). Since the general rule is high intermodal connectivity in the brain it is easy to think that such plastic changes in multiple (motor and sensory) maps related to hand, affecting touch and proprioception, will also modulate visual modalities. Even if one is not clinically synaesthetic, haptic touch communicates with vision and vice versa.

9.5 Manipulatory Areas

The hands lead us towards things. As Handy et al. (2003) show, grasp-able objects grab our attention. When we see different hand postures, they automatically direct our attention towards congruent target objects (Fischer, Prinz, and Lotz 2008). The position of one's hands, for example, has an effect on visual attention. Objects located near one's hands receive enhanced visual attention. In a study of several classic visual attention tasks (visual search, inhibition of return, and attentional blink)—participants held their hands either near the stimulus display, or far from the display. The position of the hands altered visual processing so that subjects shifted their attention more slowly between items when their hands were located near the display (Abrams et al. 2008). The results suggest that the hands facilitate the evaluation of objects for potential manipulation.

The basic principle of 'active vision', i.e., vision in the service of motor control, is summarized by Cagli et al.: 'eye movements depend on the task at hand, and if the task is a sensorimotor one, it is reasonable to expect a dependence on body movements as well' (2007, 1016). In effect, the hands help to define a pragmatic area or affordance space around the body that has significance for movement, action, attention, and accomplishing tasks. George Herbert Mead called this reachable peripersonal space around the body the 'manipulatory area' and suggested that what is present in perception is not a copy of the perceived, but 'the readiness to grasp' what is seen (1938, 103). The perception of objects outside of the manipulatory area is always relative to 'the readiness of the organism to act toward them as they will be if they come within the manipulatory area ... We see the objects as we will handle them ... We are only "conscious of" that in the perceptual world which suggests confirmation, direct or indirect, in fulfilled manipulation' (104–5). On this enactivist account of perception, the manipulatory area, defined in part by the hands, and the extent of our reach (but also, as Young points out, in part by cultural practices [see section 9.3]), is the index of how something pragmatically counts as a percept. Perceptual consciousness arises in specific contexts, already defined by the possibilities of action in relation to objects located in one's manipulatory area and outside of it.

Pragmatic engagement with the world is primary and priming for more explicitly cognitive graspings. Heidegger (1962) is famous for (among other things) making this point. Primarily and for the most part, things are ready-to-hand (*Zuhanden*). That is, they are things that we pick up and use, or integrate into our practical projects. In this regard the world presents us with specifiable affordances (Gibson 1977). Only when the affordance is blocked, or when a tool breaks, or something disrupts our action do we shift gears and start to consider things in more theoretical ways. Things then become, as Heidegger puts it, 'present-at-hand' (*Vorhanden*). On this view, it's not so much that we carve out an affordance space from the surrounding world, as that we find ourselves in a world and within an already established (pre-personal) affordance space that opens up through the dynamic relation between body and world.

The very first affordance space may be the mouth. One of the earliest coordinated and systematic movements to be found in the fetus is the movement of hand to mouth (deVries, Visser, and Prechtl 1984; Nillsson and Hamberger 1990). The very same synergetic movement is found in early infancy where the mouth opens to anticipate the hand and where the hand, especially the thumb (Newton's proof for the existence of God) finds a place to link up with the gustatory sense (Butterworth and Hopkins 1988; Lew and Butterworth 1997; Rochat 1993; Rochat and Senders 1991). If you allow an infant to grasp your finger, it too will likely end up in the infant's mouth, as do many other things that you put into the infant's hands; it's well known that the infant explores the world orally, but usually with the hand involved. As the child learns to reach and grab for itself, and the fine motor skills of the hand are improved, the manipulation becomes more haptic and the infant's exploratory skills become finer (Needham, Barrett, and Peterman 2002; Rochat 1989). Hand–mouth coordination then gives way to hand–eye coordination.

Tools and technologies allow us to expand our affordance space (e.g. Farnè, Iriki, and Làdavas 2005; Iriki, Tanaka and Iwamura, 1996; Witt, Proffitt, and Epstein 2005), and this is reflected in our use of demonstratives ('this', 'that') (Coventry et al. 2008). Generally, 'this' comes to signify anything reachable; 'that' indicates something outside of periper-sonal space. We can grasp *this*, or at least touch it; we can only point to *that*, although we can also point (in a different way) to *this*. Goldstein (1971) distinguishes between these two manual capacities: grasping (which is 'concrete') and pointing (which is 'abstract'/categorical). These distinctions are not strict, however, and they remain somewhat ambiguous so that even normal grasping capacity may sometimes require the categorical attitude (Goldstein 1971, 279–80).

Although the normal person's behaviour is prevailingly concrete, this concrete-ness can be considered normal only as long as it is embedded in and codetermined by the abstract attitude. For instance, in the normal person both attitudes are always present in a definite figure-ground relation.

(Goldstein and Scheerer 1964, 8)

Notice that this is not a scaling-up problem—we don't move from a concrete attitude to an abstract one by going 'up' to higher-order thinking; we shift perspective within a figure–ground relation, without leaving our hands behind (see section 10.1 for more on this issue).

Despite the ambiguity in the distinction between grasping and pointing, it has been taken by some phenomenologists to mean that concrete behavior (e.g. grasping) is more basic (with the evidence being that it survives certain pathologies where pointing does not), and that it characterizes our normal motor intentionality in its non-representational, non-conceptual form (e.g. Kelly 2000, 2004). In pathological cases, for example, these two capacities can come apart, as in the very complex case of Schneider who was diagnosed with visual agnosia and a form of apraxia after suffering brain damage from a wound (Goldstein and Gelb 1920; Merleau-Ponty 2012). Schneider could find his nose in concrete situations, e.g., when he wanted to scratch it; but he could not point to his nose on command, or in abstract situations. There are several important qualifications to be made here, however. The extent of Schneider's brain damage is unclear, and as Tony Marcel (2003) notes, we need to carefully distinguish between normal functions that manifest themselves more clearly in pathological cases, and functions that emerge as compensatory within the pathology. Kelly's assumption that Schneider's intact concrete capacities are normal may be unwarranted. Also, one should clarify what kind of pointing is at stake. There are various forms of non-communicative pointing (e.g., touching X in an experimental situation) which contrast with communicative (deictic) pointing. In addition one can distinguish between imperative pointing (to something I want), and declarative pointing (for calling another's attention to something). Moreover, in different pathologies communicative pointing and gestures may be intact when concrete grasping and non-communicative pointing are impaired (see, e.g., Cole, Gallagher, and McNeill 2002).

Likewise, in optic ataxia, which involves impairment in bodily actions guided by vision, subjects are unable to grasp visual objects even though their motor capacities are unimpaired, and yet their abilities to perceive and recognize shape, orientation, and size are intact (Jeannerod, Decety, and Michel 1994). This doesn't mean that reaching and grasping are somehow 'higher' functions than geometrical recognition, any more than is grasping more 'basic' than visual recognition *vis-à-vis* Milner and Goodale's patient with visual agnosia. It means simply that they are different functions that depend on different components of the system—dorsal *versus* ventral visual pathways, for example.

Hand actions—grasping, pointing in various ways, gesturing—shape our cognitive processes. There is a reflective reiteration of hand aspects in language—but also concurrent hand action can interfere with judgment. In a study by Glenberg and Kaschak (2002), subjects respond faster in judging whether a sentence makes sense when the direction of their hand movement for responding (away *vs.* toward their body) matches the movement implied by the sentence compared to when there is a mismatch. This is the case for both abstract and concrete meanings (also see Chen and Bargh 1999). Many priming studies, when the prime is a picture of a hand, for example, show specific effects on perception and cognition (see, e.g., Setti, Borghi, and Tessari 2009).

9.6 Handling Others

The hand's capacities for pointing and grasping depend not only on the brain, and not only on motoric function, but on the situation, which may be abstract, instrumentally concrete, or social and communicative. Gallagher and Marcel (1999) distinguished between these three characterizations of situations. Situations may be:

- Non-contextualized (e.g. relatively abstract, experimental situations)
- Instrumentally contextualized (e.g. practical or concrete situations)
- Socially contextualized

Consider, for example, an apraxic patient who, in the clinic or testing room, is unable to lift a small block of wood to her cheek (a relatively meaningless and abstract action). In her home, however, she is able to make similar movements (drinking tea) in a close to fluid manner when she is entertaining guests (a socially contextualized situation), and to a lesser extent when she is clearing up dishes (an instrumentally contextualized situation). Her hands behave differently in these different contexts because these different contexts define different types of affordance spaces.

Social forces also shape the development of how we use our hands. Imperative pointing is not only a social signal; it depends on other people for its development.

> [T]he child may attempt to grasp an object that is out of reach and leave the hand hanging in the air. At this point the mother comes to aid and interprets the gesture. A motor act becomes a gesture for another person, who reacts to the child's attempt and ascribes a specific meaning to the grasping movement.
>
> (Sparaci 2008, 210)

Accordingly, as Vygotsky (1986) contends, as the child learns that this gesture motivates that particular response in the other person, the failed reach for grasping is transformed into communicative pointing—something that would not happen without the other person there to interpret it as such.

The presence of another person also modulates the extent of one's affordance space, and, similar to the effect mentioned above in regard to the use of tools and technologies, this is reflected in use of demonstratives. Whether any particular object on a table is referred to as 'this' or 'that' will depend on whether I or another person puts it there, regardless of how close it is to me (Coventry et al. 2008).

Merleau-Ponty points to a certain reversibility associated with hands touching. We can approach this idea by thinking about what happens when we touch some object. We not only feel the surface and shape of the object but we can feel the surface and shape of our own fingers. Tactile perception is ecological in the sense that it tells us something about our own body as well as about the object. Merleau-Ponty borrows an example from Husserl who thinks about the phenomenon of my one hand touching my other hand and the ambiguity that emerges as the touched hand can easily become the touching hand. Merleau-Ponty tries this experiment while one hand is touching an object.

> We spoke summarily of a reversibility . . . of the touching and the touched. It is time to emphasize that it is a reversibility always imminent and never realized in fact. My left hand is always on the verge of touching my right hand touching the things, but I never reach coincidence; the coincidence eclipses at the moment of realization, and one of two things always occurs: either my right hand really passes over to the rank of the touched [i.e., becomes an object], but then its hold on the world is interrupted [it is no longer an aspect of the perceiving agent]; or it retains its hold on the world, but then I do not really touch it—my right hand touching; I palpate with my left hand only its outer covering.   (1968, 147–8)

This reversibility becomes a principle that is also applicable to our relations with others—relations that never reach complete coincidence (see Merleau-Ponty's concept of 'intercorporeity'—discussed in section 4.4). The completion remains imperfect, not only in our hands, but also in our relations with others—it remains always imminent and never fully realized, since we either continue to interact or cease to do so, and even in the former case the other person experiences something completely different than I do. He experiences *me* (whereas, I experience *him*) in this reversibility. We are two, differentiated and inexchangeable embodied perspectives who gaze back at each other, or join our gazes as we look towards something else, ecologically touching and being touched, or creating a joint affordance space between us. Such interactions have room to develop as long as they do not reach a coincidence of the absurd sort that one finds in the fascinating experiment conducted by Petkova and Ehrsson (2008) where, through the magic of virtual reality, the eye is quicker than the hand. The subject wears virtual reality goggles in which he sees the live video feed generated by a camera worn on the head of another person who is standing directly in front of him, a camera directed at him (the subject). In effect, he sees himself. When he reaches and shakes hands with the other person it feels as if he is shaking hands with himself. In this experiment, the hand that I see myself shaking is visually mine, but tactilely (and really) belongs to someone else. So while normally we could agree with Donn Welton (2000, 97) that when 'the hand touching our hand is not ours but that of another, when our hand is grasped by a hand not my own, the circuit of reversibility encompasses others and corporeality becomes intercorporeal', in the touch of these hands the reversibility is short-circuited; it collapses into an ecological involution, it fails to open any kind of joint affordance space.

It is also the case that the other person's hands are important for our ability to see their intentions. Six-month-old infants react differently to observed grasping actions of human hands *versus* an artificial (mechanical) claw. Only the former are perceived as goal directed (Woodward, Sommerville, and Guajardo 2001)—defined by what we called (in *Chapter 4*) operational intentionality. The infant's early propensity to attend to goals seems to be tied to the specific human aspect of the hand. Infants see meaning in the reaching, grasping, pointing, and gesturing of the other's hands, just as they see their own possibilities for action in the actions of and with others.

Such detailed interactions with others are reflected in our hand movements, actions, and gestures, and in our handed signs and vocabulary: we not only shake hands, we sometimes 'lend a hand'. Often, also, we don't know what to do with our hands in the presence of others, unless they are taken up in gesture. That's because we sometimes do want to reach out and touch them—either to push them further away, or to share our feelings. Imagine the normative chaos that would be entailed if we let our hands do what they were inclined to do. Anarchic Hand Syndrome (AHS) presents a good example of this. The result of brain lesions, in AHS the hand seems to have a mind of its own. It's often the case that the anarchic hand ends up doing things that the owner of the hand would never dream of doing. In one case, for example, it was reported that the subject's anarchic hand reached over and grabbed food off the plate of a fellow diner (see Della Sala 2000; Della Sala, Marchetti, and Spinnler 1994).

The concept of affordance space reflects several lessons learned from our previous considerations. First, we need to look at more than just anatomy and at more than just the body, in order to see the advantages of the upright posture. Once we recognize that human hands are what they are, and do what they do because they are freed up to do such things by the attainment of the upright posture, then we need to look at environments and manipulatory areas, and to think in terms of organism–environment couplings. Second, there may be more than one cause or motivation that explains complex human behavior. Discriminating what changes (of brain, body, environment) belong to evolution as opposed to development or culture, or individual experience is difficult, especially if we take into consideration the various looping effects that complicate any attempt to create strict separations between evolution, development, and experience. An affordance space is constituted in any particular place by a system of dynamic looping effects that integrate brain, body, and the physical, social, and cultural environments. Neither hands nor brains work by themselves, but are always part of a larger system; the system defines the affordance space within which we find and also constitute meaning. This reinforces the idea that rationality and meaning are primarily enactive.

10

The Practice of Thinking

In this chapter I want to address what has been called the 'scaling-up' problem. Specifically, the claim is often made that enactivist approaches to cognition can deal well with lower-order or basic types of processes involving perception and action, but they have not been able to explain higher-order cognitive capabilities, such as memory, imagination, reflective judgment, and so on (e.g., Shapiro 2014b; Clowes and Mendonça 2016 Foglia and Grush 2011). These are regarded as 'representation-hungry' capacities (Clark and Toribio 1994). Thus, Chemero (2009) suggests that it will be important to 'scale up' dynamic systems approaches from the analysis of action and perception to higher cognitive performance. 'It is still an open-question how far beyond minimally cognitive behaviors radical embodied cognitive science can get' (Chemero 2009, 43).

10.1 Simulating Solutions

One response to the scaling-up problem among enactivists has been to appeal to a kind of simulation, where scaling up to cognitive states such as imagining or remembering means that the system re-enacts some aspects of original perceptual processes—processes that are not representational to begin with, and are therefore not representational as they are re-enacted. On some accounts, these non-representational processes would be coupled to a new cognitive action that constitutes memory or imagination. In remembering, for example, there may be reactivation of perceptual areas that had been activated during the original experience. There may be other non-neural bodily factors that, just as in perception, are activated to some degree in cases of remembering, imagining, reflecting, etc.—involving subliminal tensing of muscles, facial expressions, gestures, hormonal flows, etc.

Thompson (2007), for example, returns to a phenomenological account, appealing to Husserl's distinction between the kind of presenting (*Gegenwärtigung*) found in perception and the kind of reactivated presenting (*Vergegenwärtigung*, sometimes translated as 're-presentation') found in memory and imagination. For Husserl memory literally reactivates previous perceptions to bring something that is not present (a past event) to presence, or a kind of 'quasi-presence'. Likewise, imagination activates perceptual processes to bring something that has never been (and may never be) perceptually present to presence. Contemporary neuroscience confirms that perceptual areas are activated during memory and imagination tasks (e.g., Schacter et al. 1996; Slotnick, Thompson, and Kosslyn 2005). To be clear, this is not an appeal to representation in the classic sense of an inner state that mediates between a self-enclosed mind and the outside world. Rather, on the enactivist view, memory or imagination involves a (re-)activated presentational activity that evokes or brings to presence something that is absent (Thompson 2007). If the product or result of this process is in some sense a representation, representation is not something involved in the production process itself. Imagination, on this account, involves a visualization of something by mentally enacting a possible visual experience of it. Memory and imagination thus involve:

'offline', simulated or emulated sensory experience. An emulation represents an activity by reenacting it in a circumscribed and modified way—for example, as an internal process that models but does not loop through the peripheral sensory and motor systems (Grush 2004). Remembering could involve emulating earlier sensory experiences and thus reenacting them in a modified way.

(Thompson 2007, 290–1)

In effect, when one imagines, remembers, or visualizes something, one is 'subjectively simulating or emulating a neutralized perceptual experience' of it (2007, 292; see p. 154).

Whereas Thompson evokes the notion of a Grush emulator, although rejecting any standard reading of representation in this context, Daniel Hutto seems more suspicious of the emulator concept since it is too frequently conceived in terms of representational content. For Hutto, it would be a defeat for enactivist accounts 'if emulators are part of the best explanation of mental imagery and the detailed account of how they work turns out to involve the manipulation of representational contents'

(Hutto 2015, 72), or if an enactivist approach to mental imagery 'is unworkable unless it makes appeal to representations' (Foglia and Grush 2011, 36). Moreover, if Clark (2013a, 198) were right to think of the emulator theory of representation as a coherent part of the predictive coding story, then this would have to mark another distinction between PC and enactivist accounts (Hutto 2015, 72–3).

Hutto's solution to the scaling-up problem is to first of all scale down the cognitive processes under consideration. We can ask how very basic memory and imaginative capacities contribute to perception and action tasks. He appeals to the example of Middle Paleolithic hominin tool-making capacities in working with stone flakes to form instruments (the Levallois technique). A similar example can be seen in traditional stone-masons. In the part of Ireland that my parents came from, for example, walls that separate fields are built by the precision placement of irregularly shaped stones—no cement necessary. The expertise of the stonemason involves looking at a pile of stones, grabbing the one that precisely fits the place in the wall that is currently in need of the next stone, and placing it in just the right way. His perception of the stone seems to be integrated with working memory and imaginative features. He looks away from the wall but retains some sense of what is needed; he sees a stone and must in some sense imagine how it will (or will not) fit in place. In these processes, seeing, remembering, and imagining are all tightly integrated, much like the stones in the completed wall. Much like hominin tool making, there is not much one can provide in terms of descriptions of how to do it; there is nothing like content or a set of rules that can be explicated discursively. Nor is there need for something like an internal representation of the stone—the mason simply sees the stone in terms of where it can be placed and the work it will do in holding up other stones—he sees this in the stone, its size, shape; he feels it in the weight. The mental processes involved in building the wall—the perception, the imagination, the memory—are integrated with the reaching and grabbing and are insep-arable from that embodied activity. Hutto, making reference to Material Engagement Theory (Malafouris 2013), reminds us, in reference to his tool-making example, that not only are the hands not isolated from the brain, they are not isolated from the objects that they manipulate.

Of course that's not all that goes into building a wall. One must also consider that there is a prior intention to build a wall at a certain place and of a certain dimension, and that to confirm such an intention one might have to imagine what that wall would look like—and that seems to be a kind of imagination that is not directly tied to any stones that have been (or have not yet been) gathered up for the task. What precisely is that sort of imagination if not representational? Hutto suggests that the way someone imagines the wall 'is likely to be strongly constrained by the ways they engage with the kinds of things that are modeled and vice versa' (2015, 87). Clearly, such imaginings may differ if the one imagining the possible wall is me, or the person who commissions the wall, rather than the skilled stonemason. My engagement with the wall may be purely aesthetic or purely instrumental in terms of what a wall can do (e.g., make good neighbors, or *not*, as Robert Frost suggests). The stonemason's imagining in the service of forming a prior intention may be much closer to the very activities that are implicated in building the wall. My imagining the wall may involve the formation of a model; the stonemason's imagining the wall may be something akin to a simulation, or simulated enactment of building the wall.

Hutto's argument is that whether it is a model or a simulation (and he seems to favor the latter),[1] there is no necessity for thinking that these cognitive accomplishments require representational content. If remembering and imagining are re-enactments or creative enactments, respectively, of perceptual activities, and there is no representational content in the perceptual activity involved in building or in aesthetically/pragmatically appreciating the wall, then there need be no representational content in higher-order cognitive activities. A re-enactment of a non-representational process is a non-representational process, although it may *result* in a proper (contentful) representation of some possible, or past or future event—in a way that is scaffolded by language and narrative—and constrained by pre-established schemas (see Hutto, in press).

---

[1] He suggests that there is an 'initial plausibility to the simulation of perception hypothesis of imagining, which holds that basic imaginings are, or centrally involve, perceptual reenactments...This simulation theory of re-creative imagining is attractive because it holds out hope of explaining why imaginings are in many ways similar to perceivings and yet still different from them in others (e.g. vivacity). The best explanation of these facts may well be because imaginings only simulate perceivings but do not replicate them exactly. This hypothesis is plausible because of the considerable, but still only partial, overlap in neural processing paths exploited by both perceiving and imagining. The simulationist idea gains support from its fit with the general finding that the brain often re-uses its neural apparatus to do various distinct kinds of cognitive work' (Hutto 2015, 76); he cites Michael Anderson's work on reuse.

Rather than pursuing the idea that remembering or imagining may involve an internal simulation or model (representational or not), however, in this chapter I want to argue that an enactivist account of such cognitive activities should focus on the fact that in the kind of activities that we are considering, these activities are just that—activities, or *doings*. When I am remembering or imagining something, I am doing something. I am engaged in some kind of action, whether for purposes of solving a problem or of putting myself in a situation of aesthetic enjoyment, gathering some information, constructing some account, or constructing a wall. To think in this way is to focus on the continuity that exists between different cognitive activities—perception, action, memory, imagination, and the more specialized cognitive activities of which we are capable.

In this regard I want to return to a proposal made by Goldstein and Scheerer, cited in section 9.5, about how we should think of very basic concrete versus abstract attitudes.

Although the normal person's behaviour is prevailingly concrete, this concreteness can be considered normal only as long as it is embedded in and codetermined by the abstract attitude. For instance, in the normal person both attitudes are always present in a definite figure-ground relation.
(Goldstein and Scheerer 1964, 8)

The idea is to think of specialized and more abstract cognitive activities, not as higher-order accomplishments, located at the higher points on a hierarchy of cognitive acts, but as integrated with perception and action in an ongoing dynamical pattern, *Gestalt* or figure–ground relation.

To gain some traction on this idea, I propose three different interventions. *First*, I want to pick up on the discussion of imagination and suggest a different way of thinking about the role of simulation. In this respect I'll go back to some considerations introduced by Gilbert Ryle in *The Concept of Mind*, and offer an updated enactivist account of affordance-based imagining that is more genuinely enactivist than the (simulation-based) ones offered by either Thompson or Hutto. *Second*, I will generalize this account by reference to a recent debate between Hubert Dreyfus and John McDowell. Dreyfus, invoking phenomenologies of action and perception as found in Heidegger and Merleau-Ponty, famously argues that most of our everyday practices are mindless. This doesn't mean they are dumb or irrational. It means that they tend to happen without thought about the specifics of practice. Our attention is not directed to the specifics of what we are doing; it is rather intentionally directed outward and forward to the environment and to our goals. There is some truth to this, but I'll argue that Dreyfus, in his debate with McDowell, takes this idea to an extreme that is unwarranted. I'll then present the enactivist solution for thinking about reflective thinking—namely, thinking of it as a skillful practice much in the same way that walking and playing tennis are skillful practices. *Finally*, I'll apply this conception of thinking as practice to the example of mathematical reasoning, which involves memory and imagination and is usually considered to be *higher-order* reasoning if anything is.

10.2 Affordance-Based Imagining

I want to draw upon the chapter on imagination in Gilbert Ryle's *The Concept of Mind*. Ryle begins by criticizing Hume for thinking that imagination is just a variant of actual seeing (or witnessing), or for thinking that impressions (or perceptions) are more lively or vivid than ideas (or imaginative visualizations), rather than understanding imagination as something different from perception. Ryle then goes on to offer his own positive account of imagination. I note that Ryle later (in 1958) admitted his dissatisfaction with this account. He indicated that after he had offered his critique of Hume, 'I was obliged to try to give the correct positive account, and in this conceptual search I got lost' (1971, 201). I think, however, that he makes some important suggestions that can be further developed by taking an enactivist approach.

What is imagining? Ryle's answer is that there is no one thing that the imagination is, in the same way that there is no one thing that farming is. One can't say that it is only when you are feeding the chickens that you are farming; or only when you are milking the cow. Farming means doing all kinds of different things. If imagining does involve a number of different things, Ryle indicates only two in *The Concept of Mind*: pretending and simulating.

He suggests, first, that instead of thinking of pretense as dependent on imagination, think of imagination as a form of pretense—a kind of playacting. Second, with respect to simulation, take the example of imagining how a tune goes—it requires the person to produce the tune—'using this knowledge; he must be actually thinking how it goes;

and he must be thinking how it goes without the tune being actually played aloud to him or hummed aloud by him. He must be thinking how it goes, in its absence' (Ryle 1971, 201). In other words, we do what we would do if we were going to hum the tune, but simply stop short of actual humming. In this respect, we engage in a form of simulation.

Now there are two ways to think about this sort of simulation. One way is to think of it as repeating or re-enacting the tune as if we were hearing it. This would be a re-enactment of perception, along the lines suggested by Thompson and Hutto. The other way to think of it is that we engage in a kind of active pretense, which seems to me to be what Ryle is suggesting. We engage in a kind of imagining action.

In both cases—imagination as a kind of simulative action and imagination as pretense or playacting—Ryle is making the same point. We should think of imagination first as a kind of active engagement with possibilities. This idea is reflected in an enactivist account of pretending, for example, worked out in terms of pretend play (Rucińska 2014; 2016). In the case of children's pretend play, it's not that the child first imagines X, and then playacts it out: rather, the imagination is accomplished in the playacting. Ryle's example: the child can pretend to be a bear. In this case the child 'roars, he pads around the floor, he gnashes his teeth, and he pretends to sleep in what he pretends is a cave' (1949, 243). The child might also pretend that his teddy bear is his friend, and he may do this by hugging the bear and feeding it, etc. Or he may pretend that the same bear is his sworn enemy, and that the bear is attacking him. In none of this does he have some kind of sensory image in his head. Rather, the imagining just is the playacting. It's literally enacting something in bodily movement that may include the use of props.

In such cases, imagination is not something that happens first in the head; it's rather something that involves embodied action, using toys, props, artifacts, instruments, and so on.[2] One does not need to generate ideas in one's head about these possibilities if one can 'see' them in the process of interacting with objects and others. Playacting, as a practice of

---

[2] Hutto makes this clear when he links his radical enactivism with material engagement theory (MET) and the work of Lambros Malafouris (2013). I think this needs to be the starting point for the analysis of imagination. Engagement in pretend play, or in working with material things, such as stone tool making, is where the imagination starts. 'Stone tools are not an accomplishment of the hominin brain, they are an opportunity for the hominin brain—that is an opportunity for active material engagement' (Malafouris 2013, 169).

imagination, allows for expansion on a set of affordances (Gibson 1977)—an expansion of the affordance space (Brincker 2014) or the landscape of affordances that belong to a form of life (Rietveld and Kiverstein 2014). This applies equally to two of Ryle's further examples: the actor imagines by acting out; the author imagines by writing. If we follow this path—imagination as pretend play, or embodied doing— we get a better, and more enactivist, affordance-based conception of imagination.

Starting from pretend play, then, we can work towards a fuller conception of imagination. Pretend play involves acting on affordances. These affordances, as in the above examples, can be physical, where objects and props in the environment offer possibilities for manipulation. They can also be social, where others occasion joint actions. In almost all cases, they are also cultural, involving instituted practices that we have learned from others. Object-substitution play (Sainsbury 2009) is a good example: 'young children's ability to pretend that one thing stands for another (playing that a banana is a phone) is explained not by an individual, offline "symbolic" thinking process, but by direct engagement with the banana in a shared context of "play"' (Rucińska 2014, 175). Eighteen-month-old infants, with presumably limited linguistic and conceptual capacities relative to adult cognition, are capable of basic object-substitution pre-tense. In such pretend play, the infant literally manipulates the banana— grasps it and puts it to her ear. In doing so, specifically, in the doing itself, she treats the banana metaphorically. The metaphor at stake, however, is not sitting someplace in her head. It seems unlikely that the infant needs to work things out ideationally first to effect the pretense—the pretense, the imagination, is in her hand and in the movement that she makes with the banana. The child, in effect, enacts the metaphor (see Gallagher and Lindgren 2015 for the notion of enactive metaphor). This can happen, 'within any medium—including bodily actions, gestures and sounds, and has considerable consequence, in that it allows organisms to experience something as something else—a doll as a baby, a stick as a horse . . . which is essential for pretence' (Mitchell 2002, 8).

Just as language, and specifically engaged speech, accomplishes thought, as Merleau-Ponty suggests (1964, 183), and just as gesture too accomplishes thought (Gallagher 2005a, 121), so also action and social interaction, as well as pretense, including pretend play, accomplishes thought, and in this case, imaginative thought.

On an overly intellectualist view, imaginative transformation is simply to 'substitute one thought content for another', thus, 'accessing and controlling inputs (beliefs and desires) to the acts of imaginative projection that underpin pretence' (Currie and Ravenscroft 2002, 140). The intellectualist interpretation relies heavily on belief-like states and thinking processes to underpin such abilities.

> In pretence one acts under a supposition, for example, that the box I am sitting in is a car; in suppositional mode one can also consider an idea, draw consequences from it, consider the evidence for it, and compare it with other ideas.
>
> (Currie 2004, 233)

It's not clear, however, that the infant is doing any of this when she literally grasps the banana as a phone, or drives the box as a car.

Affordances are relational—defined by the relations of body, skill level, cultural practices—to items or events in the environment. On this view, imagination as a practice or action depends on action possibilities and meanings that can also emerge through interaction with others. But engagement in play practice or play action also allows for a derivation. Just as, developmentally, engagement with others from the very beginning allows for the emergence of observational abilities that enable prediction and explanation of another's behavior (so-called theory of mind), engagement in pretend play enables a more abstract seeing-as. Or, to follow Goldstein and Scheerer (1964), the more abstract form of imagination may form a *Gestalt* with concrete pretense.

Imagining involves a variety of different practices—some of them actively embodied, some of them involving the manipulation of bits of the environment, some of them sitting still and picturing something by manipulating concepts or thoughts or images (re-enacted perceptions)—which in any case may still involve affective and kinaesthetic aspects of embodiment. All of these practices may be accomplished at different skill levels. Even in the case of more abstract practices of imagining, we are still dealing with affordances. Pragmatically considered, concepts or thoughts can be regarded as nothing other than affordances that offer (or solicit us to) possibilities to follow one path or another as we engage in thinking. Once again, this is consistent with Ryle's view, where thinking can be a kind of pretending.

One variety of pretending is worthy of mention at this point. A person engaged in a planning or theorizing task may find it useful or amusing to go through the

motions of thinking thoughts which are not, or are not yet, what he is disposed
ingenuously to think. Assuming, supposing, entertaining, toying with ideas, and
considering suggestions are all ways of pretending to adopt schemes or theories.
(1949, 249)

In this respect, the imaginative practice is to manipulate concepts,
thoughts, images—take them up and play with them, move them around,
in order to solve a problem, or map them onto novel affordance spaces.
This is a process that is most frequently scaffolded by language—most
clearly in Ryle's example of the author who imagines by writing. In this
regard, an author may be manipulating words, in a literally pretentious
way, in the same way she manipulates things in pretense, since humans
'think through concrete things, with words being a special case' (Roepstorff
2008, 2051; see Elias and Gallagher 2014; Overmann 2016).[3] This is a
process that clearly involves more than automatic neural simulations—
even the kind of simulation associated with language (e.g. Pulvermüller
2005), discussed in *Chapter 2*.

Although Ryle thinks of the imagination as active—involving the
manipulation of various materials—in contrast to the enactivists he
thinks of perception as passive. But on the enactivist idea of perception
as active or action-oriented, i.e., the idea that we see things in terms of
what we *can do* with them, we should think that there is an aspect of
imagination in perception itself, as a number of phenomenologists have

---

[3] Some people doodle as they listen to lectures expressing a variety of abstract ideas, and
this practice seemingly helps them to keep track of those ideas. My dissertation advisor, José
Ferrater-Mora, took this one step further. He was teaching himself Arabic and he used to
practice the formation of Arabic script (*abjadiyah*) as he listened to lectures. In this regard,
it is important to consider the role of materiality in defining physical affordances (found in
paper and pencil, and the formation of doodles, images, or script) even in thinking about
how we get from physical practices with our hands to abstractions in the mode of thought.
In the context of writing on clay tablets, for example, as Karenleigh Overmann (2016, 292;
also see Malafouris 2013) points out, straight lines are more easily made than curved ones.
This facilitated the development of picto-/ideographs into more and more abstract forms,
and this, in turn, promoted simplicity and speed of production. These kinds of material
(and cultural) affordances have an effect not only on the neural plasticity that accompanies
such practices, the dexterity, hand–eye coordination, the fine-tuning of vision and the
cognitive processes involved in such practices, but also on the further development of our
manual, visual, and cognitive abilities. A socio-political dimension is also relevant since the
development of literacy in these practices, which depends on significant repetition for such
effects to take place, 'appears to happen only when the repetition involved is that of a state-
level bureaucracy (e.g. Mesopotamia, Egypt, China, Mesoamerica)' (Overmann 2016, 293;
also see Gallagher 2013a).

suggested (see, e.g., Casey 2000; Lohmar 2005). In visual perception, for example, I see possibilities in things involving actions that have not yet happened—which is, in part, what affordance means. Likewise, in audition, the musician may hear things that afford improvisations that have not yet happened. So imagination is primarily this basic projection/ enactment of possibilities in perception and in the action of pretend play, and it is only derivatively the seeing of, and the playing with, such possibilities in imagistic or conceptual format.

10.3 Debating Minds

In San Francisco in 2005 Dreyfus delivered his American Philosophical Association Presidential Address. In his presentation, with McDowell in mind, Dreyfus rejected the idea that perception is conceptual and defended his long-held views on non-conceptual embodied coping—we are, according to him, in the world primarily in terms of embodied skills. Dreyfus rejects what he calls the 'myth of the mental', and holds that perception and action most often occur without mental intervention. This address initiated what has become known as the McDowell–Dreyfus debate. In the following paragraphs I'll summarize relevant bits of the debate, but will not try to set out all of the rich details.

McDowell (2007a; 2007b), in response to Dreyfus' Presidential Address, argues that perception (and agency) and embodied coping are conceptual and rational, and therefore not as 'mindless' as Dreyfus contends. Dreyfus (2007a; 2007b) takes McDowell's response to mean perception is 'upper floor' (that is, it involves higher-order, abstract concepts that are detached from the specifics of the situation) 'all the way down', and that McDowell ignores non-conceptual, situated embodied coping, and therefore buys into the myth of the mental. McDowell explains, however, that rationality does not have to be situation independent, and this can be seen in the Aristotelian notion of *phronesis* (practical wisdom) as a model for situated rationality—one that Dreyfus himself takes as a model for embodied coping. For McDowell, *phronesis* involves an initiation into conceptual capacities.

Dreyfus (2005, 51), in contrast, following Heidegger's interpretation of Aristotle, understands *phronesis* to be 'a kind of understanding that makes possible an immediate response to the full concrete situation'. McDowell, for his part, accepts Heidegger's characterization of *phronesis*, but, on his view, it doesn't decide the issue of whether we should consider perception/action rational or conceptual. Indeed, for McDowell, influenced by Gadamer on this point, 'the practical rationality of the *phronimos* is displayed in what he does even if he does not decide to do that as a result of reasoning' (2007a, 341). Rationality is built into action insofar as we can think of reasoning as the ability to differentiate which affordances to respond to and how to go about responding to them. McDowell calls this our 'means-end rationality', which involves a 'stepping back'. Here he appeals to the idea of deliberation.

[The] structure of what Aristotle offers as an account of deliberation should be relevant more widely than where action issues from reasoning. There is no implication that the reconstruction I envisage, for displaying actions that do not issue from prior deliberation as nevertheless cases of a properly formed practical intellect at work, involves rational structures in which the concrete details of the situation figure only in specifying what some situation-independent conception of how to act is implicitly applied to.   (2007a, 341–2)

In other words, the fact that we are able to give reasons for our action, even if we did not form deliberative reasons prior to the action, suggests that our actions and embodied copings have an implicit structure that is rational and amenable to conceptuality.[4]

For Dreyfus, however, the concept of rationality does not mean something inherent in life or action. Rather, he thinks of rationality in terms of giving reasons for our actions, which involves detached, reflective thoughtful processes associated with language—propositional discourse, the space of reasons, conceptual articulation. For McDowell, however, language use is closely tied to the situation in which it occurs. Our openness to the world involves a situated categorial aspect—this allows us to register it linguistically (even if we don't always do so). In other words, we are not 'ready in advance' to put a word to every

---

[4] We can find some pointers in phenomenology for this view. For example, Heidegger (1994, 88) writes: 'The categories are nothing invented, no "framework" or independent society of logical schemata; they are rather in an originary fashion in life itself; of life, in order to "cultivate" it. They have their own mode of access which, however, is not such as would be foreign to life itself, imposed upon it arbitrarily from without, rather it is just the eminent way in which life comes to itself' (translated in Zahavi 2013, 333). Zahavi (2013, 333) reiterates: 'Rather than simply distorting lived experience, our articulation of it might, at best, simply be accentuating structures already inherent in it.'

aspect of experience, but following Gadamer and Heidegger, we have a pre-ontological understanding that shapes our experience—and McDowell would interpret this as a conceptual understanding. Moreover, language ability makes a difference in what counts as perceptual affordances for the human *versus* the animal. So for McDowell, a cat merely 'inhabits' an environment and perceives it differently from a human who is open to a world. Likewise, both humans and dogs are able to catch Frisbees, but the human's behavior involves having a concept of what she is doing so that she can give reasons for her behavior (even if she is not called upon to do so); in contrast to the dog, who has no concept of what he is doing, according to McDowell.

One question of importance pertains to how we should think of the 'stepping back' involved in reflection.

I agree with McDowell that we have a freedom to step back and reflect that nonhuman animals lack, but I don't think this is our most pervasive and important kind of freedom. Such stepping back is intermittent in our lives and, in so far as we take up such a 'free, distanced orientation', we are no longer able to act in the world. I grant that, when we are absorbed in everyday skillful coping, we have the capacity to step back and reflect but I think it should be obvious that we cannot exercise that capacity without disrupting our coping.

(Dreyfus 2007a, 354)

Dreyfus goes on to distinguish affordances as facts from affordances as solicitations. 'Although when we step back and contemplate them affordances can be experienced as features of the world, when we respond to their solicitations they aren't figuring for a subject as features of the world [in McDowell's sense]' (2007a, 358). McDowell, according to Dreyfus, assumes that the world is already a set of facts that are determinate and that can then be named and thought and fit into concepts. In contrast, for Dreyfus, the world is indeterminate, 'not implicitly conceptual and simply waiting to be named. Our relation to the world is more basic than our mind's being open to apperceiving categorially unified facts' (2007a, 359). Specifically, he points to Merleau-Ponty's notion of operative intentionality as a more basic, non-conceptual way of relating to the world (see section 4.4).

On one interpretation of this debate, we reach an impasse. On another interpretation it seems that the two philosophers are on different pages with respect to how they define rationality. In this respect, I think there is room for an alternative view that would allow us to think of rationality as an embodied-enactive practice. In short, I think it's better to push McDowell down than to pull Dreyfus up.

McDowell argues that our actions/embodied copings have a structure that is already rational and amenable to conceptuality. We can push this thought more into Dreyfus' territory by suggesting that we should think of this rationality as, in the first place, an embodied pragmatic rationality. The world is laid out in perception, not in terms of a conceptual, or proto-conceptual meaning, but first of all, in terms of differentiations that concern my action possibilities—the object is something I can reach, or not; something I can lift, or not; something I can move or not. Our ability for making sense of the world comes, *in part*, from an active and pragmatic engagement with the world. If we can then turn around and discover that our world or our experience has an inherent rational or proto-conceptual structure, that's because that structure has already been put there by our pre-predicative embodied engagements. I take this to be consistent with some things that Dreyfus says even if he rejects the idea that this is a form of rationality.

As indicated in *Chapter 9*, there is a rationality that is implicit in the hand. Hands (as part of a complete system) are action oriented and smart. As an agent reaches to grasp something, the hand automatically (and without the agent's conscious awareness) shapes itself into just the right posture to form the most appropriate grip for that object and for the agent's purpose. If I reach to grab a banana in order to take a bite, the shape of my grasp is different from when I reach to grab a banana in order to pretend it's a phone. Differences in my grasp reflect my intention (the operative intentionality that is implicit in my bodily movement) so that if I grasp the fruit to eat it, the kinematics of my movement are different from when I grasp it to offer it to you, and different again from when I grasp it to throw at you (Ansuini et al. 2006; 2008; Jeannerod 1997; Marteniuk et al. 1987; Sartori, Becchio, and Castiello 2011). Hands are integrated with visual perception (via the dorsal visual pathway), so that I see the fruit as graspable for specific purposes. The brain evolved to do what it does in this regard only because it had hands to work with— hands that evolved with the brain in a holistic relation with other bodily aspects of (upright) posture (*Chapter 9*).

Sometimes (perhaps often) very smart hand–brain dynamics take the lead over a more conceptual, ideational intelligence. Recall the example of the patient with visual agnosia who was unable to recognize objects.

When shown a picture of a clarinet, he called it a 'pencil' at the same time that his fingers began to play an imaginary clarinet (Robertson and Treisman 2010, 308). The body and its movement in this regard are rational and perform a kind of manual thinking (Bredekamp 2007). The manual thinking of the hand has the potential to integrate its action across all perceptual modalities. We can think of touch and haptic exploration, hand–mouth coordination, hand–eye coordination, shading the eyes; cupping the ears, holding one's nose, or waving away a bad smell.

The hand not only facilitates perception and action; it transforms its movements into language (via gesture) and into thinking. Evidence from gesture studies suggests that there are close relationships between gesture, speech, and thinking—they are part of the same system, which David McNeill calls the hand–language–thought system (Cole, Gallagher, and McNeill 2002; McNeill et al. 2008; Quaeghebeur et al. 2014). Gesture adds to cognitive ability. In this regard, however, there is no break, no discontinuity, no 'stepping back' that comes between this kind of movement (gesture) and spoken language—nor between manual thinking and thinking proper—they are part of the same system, the same *Gestalt*.

Bodily coping is rational in this same basic sense, and there is con-tinuity between the rational movement of the body and reflective think-ing. Reflective thinking, in so far as it is an *embedded* or *situated* reflection (Gallagher and Marcel 1999), *contra* Dreyfus, is a *skill* as much as the physical coping involved in skiing is, for example.[5] Indeed, reflective thinking can be a form of embodied coping. Reflection in the expert downhill skier is not disconnected from the skier's performance,

---

[5] In Oslo at the Norwegian School of Sports Sciences in 2006, at a daylong workshop that included an audience of Olympic trainers, Dreyfus defended his well-known model of expertise, where the expert is mindlessly in the flow. One of the Olympic trainers offered a description based on her interaction with one of the top Norwegian Olympic downhill skiers. The downhill skier, she suggested, may be in the flow, but also has to reflectively consider potential changes in the texture of the snow as he descends the hill in order to anticipate possible adjustments to his skiing style. Dreyfus's response was that when the skier is in the flow he is not thinking; and when he begins to reflect in the way described, he is no longer in the flow, and in that sense is no longer the expert skier. The presence of a reflective (thoughtful) element necessarily disturbs the expert performance. At that meeting I offered my own response to this, which was that I thought expertise would include knowing when to reflect, and how to reflect, and what to think about in terms of anticipating changes in snow texture. Dreyfus, however, resisted this idea.

but is part of it—a dimension of the flow rather than something different from it. The expert skier should know when to reflect and when not to; and what to reflect about—such reflection is a skill, and a way of coping with her environment. Neither the knowing of when, and when not, to reflect, nor the reflection itself is discontinuous with action in a way that would interrupt the flow of action. Rather, situated reflection is continuous with, or part of, the performance. It's the type of reflection found in a teacher who is able to demonstrate an action as she reflectively describes what she is doing, or the type of reflection that can occur during musical performance even as the musician stays in the flow (Høffding 2015; Salice, Høffding, and Gallagher 2017). In some circumstances the expertise of the teacher or the musician is just this ability to do both at once, and it would be odd to claim that this kind of performance is not expert performance because one is able to reflect as one is engaged in the performance. The reflections of the downhill skier, the teacher, and the musician are likely different in each case, but nonetheless nuanced and integrated with their different physical actions.

McDowell seemingly makes this point when he accuses Dreyfus of treating minded/mental processes as disconnected from the body—which McDowell (2007a) calls 'the myth of the disembodied intellect'. But as Zahavi (2013) points out, both Dreyfus and McDowell continue to retain and share an overly intellectualized (conceptualized, languaged) conception of the mind—a mind that is not in the hand, or ready-to-hand, but one that is in the head. In contrast to this traditional, conceptualist, internalist conception of mind (which is the concept of mind that Dreyfus rejects and McDowell accepts), the alternative is to think of mental skills such as reflection, problem solving, decision making, and so on, as enactive, non-representational forms of embodied coping that emerge from a pre-predicative perceptual ordering of differentiations and similarities.

The formulation of a different conception of the mind (more embodied, more enactive) than either Dreyfus or McDowell proposes, is not the final word on the McDowell–Dreyfus debate. That would be to ignore social or intersubjective factors—and indeed, hand gestures point us in a direction that suggests that something more is involved—namely, that meaningful action, and gesture, and language, and thinking are not things that happen without other people. We need to note that the differences and value distinctions between things in the environment that count as, and that we perceive as, salient or significant affordances (*versus* those that we don't) are laid out along affective, hedonic lines that are tied to other agents and what I see them do. Our perception of objects is shaped not simply by bodily pragmatic or enactive possibilities, but also by a certain intersubjective saliency that derives from the behavior and emotional attitude of others toward such objects (see section 8.2). More generally, I learn about things and the world in my interactions with others and by way of processes of natural pedagogy (Csibra and Gergely 2009). Developmental studies provide evidence for such socially modulated perceptual and action-related differentiations in very young infants—and such evidence counters all myths: the myth of the given, the myth of the mental, and the myth of the disembodied intellect.

Both Dreyfus and McDowell want to make use of the concept of *phronesis*—a certain kind of practiced excellence in pragmatically (action-oriented) knowing what to do. *Phronesis* is closely tied to the particularities of each contextualized situation (it's a virtue practiced case-by-case). It can be either/both intuitive/automatic (Dreyfus) *and/ or* reflective/deliberative (McDowell), but in the latter case we should consider reflective deliberation a skill continuous with embodied coping, which itself may be intuitive/automatic *or*, if necessary, metacognitive and strategic, and which can also be expertly skillful if it has been practiced sufficiently.

Most importantly, however, *phronesis* is intersubjective. *Phronesis*, as Aristotle tells us, is something that we learn from hanging around with others. In developmental terms, we need to consider the importance of our pervasive interaction with others. Our worldly knowledge, and our ability to think, are gained in very basic, intersubjective interactions— seeing things as others see them, imitating, doing what others do, valuing what others value—in processes that involve embodied rationality, nat- ural pedagogy, social norms, situated reflection, etc. To the extent that *phronesis* involves situated reflective thinking, and to the extent that it can be taken as a model of rationality, it is a thinking-*without-thinking- about-it*, continuous with and cut from the same fabric as embodied coping—which is both action and interaction. Thinking-without-thinking- about-it means that even if our reflection becomes a deliberation, it is, like an embodied coping skill, something we do without consulting rules, without a reflective stepping back that would remove it from its embeddedness in action. This kind of reflection may also be accomplished as a form of interaction with others, as part of a communicative action, as a comment or directive that may take the form of a gesture or facial expression that is part of the ongoing action.

Even in cases where we are able to *step back*, to detach ourselves from the demands of the immediate environment, and to engage in a second-order, conceptual deliberation, this stepping back does not make thinking any less of an embodied/intersubjective skill. Most of us are able to step back without tripping over ourselves. Thinking, like movement, is an embodied performance, in some cases requiring a thinking posture or a pacing that facilitates the process. It can be an explicit intersubjective process where we reflect together on a problem to be solved. In this regard, as in perception and action, there are affordances that allow us to do things, to solve problems, to communicate with others, to construct institutions, and so on. Pragmatically considered, concepts can be regarded as nothing other than affordances that offer (or solicit us to) possibilities to go one way or another as we engage in thinking. On this view, as I'll now suggest, even doing mathematics is an embodied skill, an enactive performance; even doing it in one's head (rather than with one's hands, or with pencil and paper, or with hand-held calculator or abacus or computer graphics) may involve activation of motoric and spatial brain–body systems.[6]

10.4 Doing the Math

There are good, obvious examples of how aspects of body and environment can enter into the type of cognitive processes involved in seemingly the most abstract of cognitive accomplishments, mathematics. Perhaps the most obvious example is the use of fingers to count, but also, of course, the use of abacus, hand-held calculator, or other types of apparatus that allow for calculation beyond what we can do in our heads. Hands also figure into our mathematical abilities in other ways. Gesture, for example, is sometimes thought to be an instance of extended

---

[6] Merleau-Ponty indicates something similar: 'pure ideality already streams forth along the articulations of the aesthesiological body, along the contours of the sensible things' (Merleau-Ponty 1968, 152). As Husserl puts it, 'Judging too is acting' (1969, 149/167). 'Every act, every intention in the specific sense...is a *modus* of the "I am actively [*tuend*] directed," we could even say: a *modus* of *egoic praxis*' (2008, 366).

cognition (Clark 2008a; 2013b) that allows us to offload some of the cognitive load. Gesture, like language (or considered a part of language), not only scaffolds our thinking processes, but adds or supplements meaningful information, both for the gesturing subject (actually supporting her thinking) and for the communicating partner (McNeill 1992). Gesture, formatted in visuo-spatial modalities, provides extra information that is not found in the verbal-representational format of speech alone.

With respect to mathematical thinking, as well, gesture may add or supplement the process. Thus studies by Susan Goldin-Meadow and others show that children perform better (faster and more accurately) on math problems when they are allowed to use gestures, in comparison with when they are asked to sit on their hands (Alibali and DiRusso 1999; Goldin-Meadow, Kim, and Singer 1999; Goldin-Meadow et al. 2001).

Gesture helps speakers retrieve words from memory. Gesture reduces cognitive burden, thereby freeing up effort that can be allocated to other tasks. For example, pointing improves young children's performance on counting tasks particularly if the pointing is done by the children themselves. As another example, gesturing while explaining a math task improves performance on a simultaneously performed word recall task. Gesturing thus appears to increase resources available to the speaker, perhaps by shifting the burden from verbal to spatial memory... Gesture may also provide a route through which learners can access new thoughts. For example, children participating in science lessons frequently use gesture to foreshadow the ideas they themselves eventually articulate in speech, perhaps needing to express those ideas in a manual medium before articulating them in words. (Goldin-Meadow 1999, 427)

These effects also generalize to bodily movements and environmental situations that go beyond hand gestures. Thus sensory feedback from actually pronouncing words improves verbal memory; talking the words to someone else enhances this effect (Lafleur and Boucher 2015). Whole body movement within properly designed virtual environments enhances the learning of scientific concepts in physics and astronomy (Gallagher and Lindgren 2015).

Besides these live embodied performances involved in learning, thinking, and doing math, others have argued that even the conceptual content of higher-order thinking and mathematics is grounded on embodied-environmental processes. This approach is generally associated with the work of Lakoff and Johnson (2003) who argue that, by means of image-schemata and metaphoric transformations, one's basic bodily movements and experiences are translated into higher-order, abstract thought. The concept of justice, for example, derives, metaphorically, from basic experiences of balance. Likewise, basic bodily experiences of moving in and out of spaces generate a plethora of more abstract conceptions of *in* and *out*, e.g., 'I don't want to leave anything out of my argument' or 'She is coming out of her depression.'

Lakoff and Nuñez (2000) argue that these same metaphorical transformations contribute to one's mathematical conceptions. Such transformations build on innate abilities for discriminating, at a glance, between there being one, or two, or three objects in one's visual field (an ability termed 'subitizing')—something even young infants, and some non-human animals, can do (Antell and Keating 1983; Church and Meck 1984; Strauss and Curtis 1981; Woodruff and Premack 1981)—and on basic body-related aspects, including 'basic spatial relations, groupings, small quantities, motions, distributions of things in space, changes, bodily orientations, basic manipulations of objects (e.g., rotating and stretching), iterated actions, and so on' (Lakoff and Nuñez 2000, 28). Motor control programs that allow us to move in certain ways, for example, figure into our ability to reason or infer about events and actions (2000, 34–5, citing the work of Narayanan 1997). Likewise, most sophisticated mathematical ideas are grounded in everyday bodily activities and experience. For example, the notion of a set derives from our perception of a collection of objects in a spatial area; recursion builds upon repeated action; derivatives (in calculus) make use of concepts of motion, boundary, etc. (Lakoff and Nuñez 2000, 28–9).

Saunders Mac Lane (1981) had pointed in a similar direction, acknowledging that advances in mathematics have been partly inspired by bodily and socially embedded practices, which ultimately lead to a complex of mutually supporting concepts and formal structures.

Mathematics begins with puzzles and problems dealing with combinatoric and symbolic aspects of the general human experience. Some of these aspects turn out to be systematic and intrinsic, rather than arbitrary and tied to one context. They become the stuff of elementary mathematics. From this starting point, the subject has developed to be a deductive analysis of a large number of very different but interlocking formal structures. These structures have been derived from experience in many successive stages; by abstractions from various observations of the world, its problems, and the interconnections of these problems. These

observations can be described as starting with a variety of human activities, each one of which leads more or less directly to a corresponding portion of mathematics.
(Mac Lane 1981, 463)

He provides a number of examples: counting leading to arithmetic and number theory; measuring to calculus; shaping to geometry; architectural formation to symmetry; estimating to probability; moving to mechanics and dynamics; grouping to set theory and combinatorics, and so forth. As Mac Lane suggests, 'mathematics is not the study of intangible Platonic worlds, but of tangible formal systems, which have arisen from real human activities' (470).

Clearly, according to this analysis, what starts as innate capabilities, and basic perceptual and bodily abilities, gradually builds into more sophisticated concepts that require cultural processes for their continued existence. Lakoff and Nuñez thus claim that 'much of the "abstraction" of higher mathematics is a consequence of the systematic layering of metaphor upon metaphor, often over the course of centuries' (2000, 47).

I've already indicated (in section 9.4) that the notion of affordance space can help in sorting out what evolution, development and cultural practices contribute to cognition. It can also help make sense of the Gestalt formed by the integration of basic movements, gestures, metaphors, thoughts, and even abstract mathematical conceptions. In this regard, the phenomenological tradition offers some resources. Husserl, who trained first as a mathematician and began his philosophical career with works on the philosophy of arithmetic (e.g., Husserl 2003), entitled one of his last essays the 'Origin of Geometry' (1982b). He was well aware of the pragmatic roots of geometry and mathematics: 'From the art of surveying develops geometry; from counting, arithmetic; from everyday mechanics, mathematical mechanics; etc' (Husserl 1965, 183). He is quick to consider the consequences of moving beyond pragmatic considerations, however, to more abstract conceptual realms, since he thinks this is precisely where mathematics leads. The mathematization of the world leads to our modern scientific conception of a complete objective world distinguished strictly from human spirit. Moreover, according to Husserl, the idea that natural science can also bring strict, objective, mathematical principles to bear on the explanation of the psyche threatens that spirit. He is wary of the naturalization of the mind, which he takes to be a form of reification, and he complains of those who would naturalize the mind that 'regarding the question of how formulas or mathematical objectification in general are given a sense based on life and the intuitive environing world, of this we hear nothing' (1965, 186). I think we can hear more about this from enactivist approaches.

Husserl's worry motivates an important question: whether mathematical conceptions, derived from living practices, can loop around to explain those living practices in any complete way. On the one hand, and at least on one view, given the advances and complexity of modern mathematics, including developments in dynamical systems theory, we may have the tools that can support the naturalization of phenomenology in a way that Husserl never would have suspected (Roy et al. 1999). On the other hand, we may have good reason to doubt this optimistic view, or to remain with Husserl's worry about the naturalization or mathematization of the mind. As Mac Lane (1981) points out, it is not the purely formal aspects of mathematics that determine their development or application; they are rather determined 'by aspects of the world under study or by portions of the mathematician's insight or fancy'. For Mac Lane, this turns out to be a general metaphysical issue, and in this regard, his Pythagorean question prefigures McDowell: 'How does it happen that some important facets of the real world can in fact be accurately analyzed by austere deductions from axioms? In other words, how does it happen that logic fits the world; how can one account for the extraordinary and unexpected effectiveness of formal mathematics?' (466). He suggests further that in the application of mathematics, the mathematician is guided by 'the breadth and depth of his subject' (466). The notion of *breadth* refers to those contingencies of situations in which mathematics is to apply, raising issues about the intent and relevance of the chosen abstraction. *Depth* refers to constraints on our judgment in choosing the appropriate abstractions for getting to the fundamental structures and concepts of the problem at issue (Mac Lane 1981, 471).

Such considerations set at least one direction of inquiry—a focus on how, from 'life and the intuitive environing world', we gain the realm of abstract conceptual thought, and specifically mathematics. To be sure, for Husserl, the truths of mathematics and geometry have an 'ideal objectivity' and are discovered through the 'spiritual' efforts of humans (1982b, 160). At the same time he is willing to think of geometry and mathematics as cultural accomplishments; Husserl calls them 'cultural traditions' that have their ultimate beginnings in 'materials at hand' (158)—cultural productions of our hands and brains, passed on by learning and training. In this he is in general agreement with more recent research. The cultural accomplishments of geometry and mathematics are not biological adaptations, although they are grounded on such adaptations—the evolution of the upright posture, human hands, and brains. As Richard Menary points out, 'The cortical circuits with which we are endowed through evolution are transformed to perform these new culturally specified cognitive functions, even though they evolved to perform different functions' (2013, 354; see Ansari 2008; Dehaene 1997; 2009). This is the developmental conception of neural reuse, discussed in *Chapter 2*. Neural plasticity allows for the redeployment of neural circuitry for functions not originally specified by evolution (Dehaene 1997; Dehaene and Cohen 2007). This redeployment, however, is driven by pragmatic concerns and by manipulatory possibilities that define new affordance spaces. In this regard, as we have already indicated in earlier chapters, it is not just brain plasticity, but what Malafouris (2013, 80) calls 'metaplasticity'—that is, a brain–body–environment plasticity—that allows for a reconfiguration of bodily and cultural practices in changing environments that are dynamically interlinked with brain plasticity.

On the one hand, Husserl's analysis focuses on the problem of explaining how the 'ideal objects' or idealizations of geometry came to exist in the intra-subjective consciousness of the originator, and how, by means of language—spoken and written—these objects were communicated. It's the problem of how spiritual insights become words (1982b, 164). From this perspective, the use of drawn figures is secondary; part of the teaching process that attempts (or sometimes fails) to give insight into the original idealizations (165). On the other hand, Husserl is led back to the embodied nature of the origin of geometry. We know that geometry started in construction, involving what Husserl calls 'prescientific materials'—literally Euclid used his hands and some tools (compass and straightedge) to work out and demonstrate geometrical principles. Geometry is not originally a way that the mind imposes organization on space, but an organization of the mind that derives from specific ways in which we can move our hands to manipulate objects in particular environments.

It continues to be so in the way that we learn geometry (as well as mathematics). This is something we learn to do on the page and in the context of a learning environment, in public space, before we do it in our heads. Our capacities to think have been transformed, but in this instance they are capacities to manipulate inscriptions in public space. This is a way of showing that the transformation of our cognitive capacities has publicly recognizable features.   (Menary 2013, 357)

The constructions of geometry go in two directions—outward, historically into the straight lines of agricultural fields and smooth surfaces of architecture, as well as into the lines and circles of astronomy and navigation; and inward, spiritually, as Husserl would say, but also biologically, into new neural connections that both enable and are enabled by these restructurings of affordance spaces. As Menary notes, however, arguing for the idea of cognitive integration, 'The "outside" and the "inside" are not so functionally different after this process of enculturation, because culture gets under the skin during development' (2013, 359; see Menary 2015). Indeed, whatever we can do in our head has its origins in what we can do with our hands.

If mathematics begins pragmatically by asking how we can measure up the environment or count up our exchanges, it leads directly to the manipulation of symbols. Menary points to two important aspects of this process. First, physical manipulation (describable in terms of body schemas and the movements of hands) directly moves or causes movement of symbols. We can think of such manipulations in terms of finger counting, the abacus, or more modern counting machines, and in terms of scratching lines on tablets or paper, media that eventually become manipulable, capable of expressing spatially arranged formulas with specific shapes—taking up space on a page or blackboard or computer monitor or in other physical spaces. Second, the manipulations are not arbitrary; they follow a normative pattern that can be taught and passed on from one generation to the next (Menary 2015). In this respect, spatial manipulations become rules. 'Mathematical notations, as well as letters, words, and sentences, can be arbitrarily complex, according to a recursive rule system. Recursivity allows for a potentially infinite variety of strings and allows for a potentially infinite variety of meaningful expressions' (Menary 2013, 360–1; Menary and Kirchhoff 2013). This means not simply that we end up following rules, but that we can recursively manipulate the rules—and to be able to do that is a skill that derives in some respects from original manipulation abilities.

These are the complicated functions that lead from simple counting to higher mathematics. Simple counting may have its phylogenetic roots in a basic capacity to recognize quantity and number (numerosity or sub-itizing), a capacity that allows humans (as well as some non-human animals [Uller et al. 2003; Nieder, Diester, and Tudusciuc 2006; De Cruz 2008]) to discriminate cardinality: that is, to perceive simple quan-tities of very small sets—a capacity that would benefit activities of foraging, hunting, and so on. This capacity gets enhanced with upright posture and free hands, plus certain cultural practices that follow, with the result that we are able to construct more complicated functions. In contrast to basic numerosity,

discrete mathematical operations exhibit cultural and individual variation; there is a big difference between Roman numerals and Arabic numerals. The discrete operations are subject to verbal instruction (they actually depend on language); one must learn to count, whereas one does not learn to subitize. Mathematics depends on cultural norms of how to reason (mathematical norms). The ability to perform exact calculations of mathematics depends on the public system of representation and its governing norms.   (Menary 2013, 363)

Husserl brings us back to this point. His question is: how do invariable geometrical principles and rules apply 'with unconditioned generality for all men' (1982b, 179)? From his perspective, the rules transcend the material conditions and practical applications, and it is this process that generates the rationality of the human animal. From a different perspec-tive, however, we can say that although rules inform practice, practice in some cases may transcend the rules. A well-practiced expert may perform mathematical computations not by thinking of the rules or reflectively deciding what step to take next, but by allowing her hand to move in its habitual way across the paper, or chalk board, or keyboard—moving hands to express a mathematical symbol in the same way that the stone-mason can reach and grab just the right stone. A problem-solving strategy may appear in a certain gesture or stroke—much in the same way that children may signal the correct answer to a mathematical problem in their gesture while failing to utter the correct answer vocally (Goldin-Meadow 1999). In contrast to the child who is still learning, the expert simply allows her hand to take the lead. Again, reason lives, not just in the head, but in the hands, and more generally in the body.

We can find assistance in sorting out what evolution provides from what culture contributes by looking at comparative anatomy, not only of the brain (Dehaene 2009, 191) but also of the body as a whole. Whereas Dehaene (1997; 2004) emphasizes that cultural learning can involve 'neuronal recycling' which transforms an initial use function tied to our evolutionary past into a new function tied to current cultural contexts, cultural learning equally transforms bodily practices, skills, and environmental scaffolds, creating new affordance spaces. This type of metaplasticity underpins the possibility of metaphoric transformation (as we find in Lakoff, Johnson, and Núñez), which can provide a way to understand *how* basic bodily movements and experiences can transition into more abstract conceptual patterns. Our basic bodily, egocentric experiences of space and spatial distinctions ('to my left' versus 'to my right') may indeed provide the material for more abstract conceptual distinctions on a logical or political landscape. To explain *why* we are motivated to make such distinctions, rather than to remain existentially literal, one can appeal to the notion of affordance.

Abstract concepts provide us with epistemic possibilities—possibilities for organizing our thought, for accomplishing a next step in argumentation, for designing a model, for solving a problem. This applies equally to geometry and mathematics. Just as we can understand the movement possibilities of our bodies as tracing out the physical affordances to be found in particular environments, the principles and rules and operations of geometry and mathematics can be understood as cultural affordances that allow us to solve problems, to communicate at abstract levels, to model knowledge, to construct stone walls and skyscrapers, and thereby to transform our environments; all of which also loop back into bodily processes and reshape our lives and our minds.

References

Abrams, R. A., Davoli, C. C., Du, F., Knapp, W. J., and Paull, D. 2008. Altered vision near the hands. *Cognition* 107: 1035–47.

Adams, F. and Aizawa, K. 2001. The bounds of cognition. *Philosophical Psychology* 14 (1): 43–64.

Adams, F. and Aizawa, K. 2008. *The Bounds of Cognition*. Malden, MA: Blackwell.

Adams, F. and Aizawa, K. 2009. Why the mind is still in the head. In P. Robbins and M. Aydede (eds.), *The Cambridge Handbook for Situated Cognition* (78–95). New York: Cambridge University Press.

Adams, F. and Aizawa, K. 2010. The value of cognitivism in thinking about extended cognition. *Phenomenology and the Cognitive Sciences* 9 (4): 579–603.

Aizawa, K. 2014. The enactivist revolution. *Avant* 5 (2): 1–24. DOI: 10.12849/50202014.0109.0002.

Aizawa, K. 2010. The coupling-constitution fallacy revisited. *Cognitive Systems Research* 11: 332–42.

Alibali, M. W. and DiRusso, A. A. 1999. The function of gesture in learning to count: More than keeping track. *Cognitive Development* 14 (1): 37–56.

Alsmith, A. J. T. and Vignemont, de F. 2012. Embodying the mind and representing the body. *Review of Philosophy and Psychology* 3 (1): 1–13.

Anderson, M. L. 2010. Neural reuse: A fundamental reorganizing principle of the brain. *Behavioral and Brain Sciences* 33: 245–66.

Anderson, M. L. 2014. *After Phrenology: Neural Reuse and the Interactive Brain.* Cambridge, MA: MIT Press.

Andres, M., Seron, X., and Oliver, E. 2007. Contribution of hand motor circuits to counting. *Journal of Cognitive Neuroscience* 19: 563–76.

Ansari, D. 2008. Effects of development and enculturation on number representation in the brain. *Nature Reviews: Neuroscience* 9 (4): 278–91.

Anscombe, G. E. M. 1957. *Intention*. Oxford: Blackwell.

Ansuini, C., Giosa, L., Turella, L., Altoè, G. M., and Castiello, U. 2008. An object for an action, the same object for other actions: Effects on hand shaping. *Experimental Brain Research* 185: 111–19.

Ansuini, C., Santello, M., Massaccesi, S., and Castiello, U. 2006. Effects of end-goal on hand shaping. *Journal of Neurophysiology* 95: 2456–65.

Antell, S. E. and Keating, D. P. 1983. Perception of numerical invariance in neonates. *Child Development* 54 (3): 695–701.

Apperly, I. A. and Butterfill, S. A. 2009. Do humans have two systems to track beliefs and belief-like states? *Psychological Review* 116 (4): 953–70.

Aranyosi, I. 2013. *The Peripheral Mind: Philosophy of Mind and the Peripheral Nervous System.* Oxford: Oxford University Press.

Arbib, M. A. 2005. From monkey-like action recognition to human language: An evolutionary framework for neurolinguistics. *Behavioral and Brain Sciences* 28: 105–24.

Arendt, H. 1958. *The Human Condition.* Chicago: University of Chicago Press.

Aristotle. 350 BCE. *On the Parts of Animals.* Trans. W. Ogle (http://classics.mit.edu/Aristotle/parts_animals.html).

Augustine. 395. *De libero arbitrio voluntatis/On the Free Choice of the Will.* Trans. A. S. Benjamin and L. H. Hackstaff. Indianapolis: Bobbs-Merrill.

Aydin, C. 2013. The artifactual mind: Overcoming the 'inside–outside' dualism in the extended mind thesis and recognizing the technological dimension of cognition. *Phenomenology and the Cognitive Sciences* 14 (1): 73–94.

Bach, K. 1978. A representational theory of action. *Philosophical Studies* 34: 361–79.

Bakker, F. C., Boschker, M., and Chung, T. 1996. Changes in muscular activity while imagining weight lifting using stimulus or response propositions. *Journal of Sport Exercise Psychology* 18: 313–24.

Ballard, D. H., Hayhoe, M. M., Pook, P. K., and Rao, R. P. N. 1997. Deictic codes for the embodiment of cognition. *Behavioral and Brain Sciences* 20 (4): 723–67.

Barrett, L. F. and Bar, M. 2009. See it with feeling: Affective predictions during object perception. *Philosophical Transactions of the Royal Society of London. Series B, Biological Sciences,* 364 (1521): 1325–34.

Barrett, L. F. and Bliss-Moreau, E. 2009. Affect as a psychological primitive. *Advances in Experimental Social Psychology* 41: 167–218.

Barsalou, L. W. 1999. Perceptual symbol systems. *Behavioral and Brain Sciences* 22: 577–660.

Barsalou, L. W. 2008. Grounded cognition. *Annual Review Psychology* 59: 617–45.

Bauermeister, M. 1964. The effect of body tilt on apparent verticality, apparent body position and their relation. *Journal of Experimental Psychology* 67: 142–7.

Bayliss, A. P., Frischen, A., Fenske, M. J., and Tipper, S. P. 2007. Affective evaluations of objects are influenced by observed gaze direction and emotional expression. *Cognition* 104 (3): 644–53.

Bayliss, A. P., Paul, M. A., Cannon, P. R., and Tipper, S. P. 2006. Gaze cueing and affective judgments of objects: I like what you look at. *Psychonomic Bulletin and Review* 13 (6): 1061–6.

Becchio, C., Manera, V., Sartori, L., Cavallo, A., and Castiello, U. 2012. Grasping intentions: From thought experiments to empirical evidence. *Frontiers in Human Neuroscience* 6: 1–6.

Bechara, A., Damasio, H., Tranel, D., and Damasio, A. R. 1997. Deciding advantageously before knowing the advantageous strategy. *Science* 275 (5304): 1293–5.

Bedny, M. and Caramazza, A. 2011. Perception, action, and word meanings in the human brain: The case from action verbs. *Annals of the New York Academy of Sciences* 1224: 81–95.

Beer, R. D. 2000. Dynamical approaches to cognitive science. *Trends in Cognitive Sciences* 4 (3): 91–9.

Bennett, K. 2004. Spatio-temporal coincidence and the grounding problem. *Philosophical Studies* 118 (3): 339–71.

Bennett, K. 2011. Construction area (no hard hat required). *Philosophical Studies* 154: 79–104.

Bennett, M. R. and Hacker, P. M. S. 2003. *Philosophical Foundations of Neuroscience*. Oxford: Blackwell.

Bergson, H. 2001. *Time and Free Will*. Trans. F. L. Pogson. Mineola, NY: Dover Publications.

Berthoz, A. 2000. *The Brain's Sense of Movement*. Cambridge, MA: Harvard University Press.

Berthoz, A. and Petit, J-L. 2006. *Phénoménologie et physiologie de l'action*. Paris: Odile Jacob.

Block, N. 2001. Behaviorism revisited. *Behavioral and Brain Sciences* 24 (5): 977–8.

Block, N. 2005. Book review: *Action in Perception* by Alva Noë. *Journal of Philosophy* 102 (5): 259–72.

Botvinick, M. and Cohen, J. 1998. Rubber hands 'feel' touch that eyes see. *Nature* 391: 756.

Bower, M. and Gallagher, S. 2013. Bodily affectivity: Prenoetic elements in enactive perception. *Phenomenology and Mind* 2: 108–31.

Brandom, R. B. 1994. *Making It Explicit: Reasoning, Representing, and Discursive Commitment*. Cambridge, MA: Harvard University Press.

Brandom, R. B. 2000. *Articulating Reasons: An Introduction to Inferentialism*. Cambridge, MA: Harvard University Press.

Brandom, R. B. 2008. *Between Saying and Doing: Towards an Analytic Pragmatism*. Oxford: Oxford University Press.

Bredekamp, H. 2001. Gazing hands and blind spots: Galileo as draftsman. In J. Renn (ed.), *Galileo in Context* (153–92). Cambridge: Cambridge University Press.

Bredekamp, H. 2007. *Galilei der Künstler. Die Zeichnung, der Mond, die Sonne*. Berlin: Akademie-Verlag.

Bremmer, J. 1992. Walking, standing and sitting in ancient Greek culture. In J. Bremmer and H. Roodenburg (eds.), *A Cultural History of Gesture* (15–35). Oxford: Polity Press.

Brentano, F. 2008. *Psychologie vom empirischen Standpunkte. Von der Klassifikation der psychischen Phänomene* [1862]. Ed. Mauro Antonelli. Heusenstamm: Ontos.

Brincker, M. 2014. Navigating beyond 'here & now' affordances—on sensorimotor maturation and 'false belief' performance. *Frontiers in Psychology* 5: 1433. DOI: 10.3389/fpsyg.2014.01433.

Bronowski, J. 1975. *The Ascent of Man*. New York: Little, Brown, and Co.

Brooks, R. 1991. Intelligence without representation. *Artificial Intelligence* 47: 139–59.

Bruineberg, J. and Rietveld, E. 2014. Self-organization, free energy minimization, and optimal grip on a field of affordances. *Frontiers in Human Neuroscience*, 8. DOI: 10.3389/fnhum.2014.00599.

Bruineberg, J., Kiverstein, J., and Rietveld, E. 2016. The anticipating brain is not a scientist: The free-energy principle from an enactive perspective. *Synthese*. DOI: 10.1007/s11229-016-1239-1.

Bruner, J. 1966. *Toward a Theory of Instruction*. Cambridge, MA: Harvard University Press.

Bruner, J. S. 1961. *After John Dewey, What?* New York: Bank Street College of Education.

Buccino, G., Lui, F., Canessa, N., Patteri, I., Lagravinese, G., Benuzzi, F., Porro, C. A., and Rizzolatti, G. 2004. Neural circuits involved in the recognition of actions performed by non-conspecifics: An fMRI study. *Journal of Cognitive Neuroscience* 16 (1): 114–26.

Burge, T. 2010. Origins of perception. Paper presented as the *First 2010 Jean Nicod Prize Lecture*. Paris, 14 June.

Burke, F. T. 2013. *What Pragmatism Was*. Bloomington: Indiana University Press.

Burke, F. T. 2014. Extended mind and representation. In J. R. Shook and T. Solymosi (eds.), *Pragmatist Neurophilosophy: American Philosophy and the Brain* (177–203). London: Bloomsbury Academic.

Butterworth, G. and Hopkins, B. 1988. Hand–mouth coordination in the newborn baby. *British Journal of Developmental Psychology* 6: 303–14.

Cabanis, P. 1802. *Rapports du physique et du moral de l'homme*, 2 vols. Paris: Crapart, Caille, et Ravier.

Cagli, R. C., Coraggio, P., Napoletano, P., and Boccignone, G. 2007. What the draughtsman's hand tells the draughtsman's eye: A sensorimotor account of drawing. *International Journal of Pattern Recognition and Artificial Intelligence* 22 (5): 1015–29.

Campos, J. J., Bertenthal, B. I., and Kermoian, R. 1992. Early experience and emotional development: The emergence of wariness of heights. *Psychological Science* 3: 61–4.

Carpenter, W. B. 1874. *Principles of Mental Physiology, with their Applications to the Training and Discipline of the Mind, and the Study of its Morbid Conditions*. London: Henry S. King & Co.

Carruthers, P. 2015. Perceiving mental states. *Consciousness and Cognition* 36: 498–507.

Casasanto, D. and Dijkstra, K. 2010. Motor action and emotional memory. *Cognition* 115 (1): 179–85.

Casey, E. S. 2000. *Imagining: A Phenomenological Study*. Bloomington: Indiana University Press.

Cash, M. 2008. Thoughts and oughts. *Philosophical Explorations* 11 (2): 93–119.

Cash, M. 2009. Normativity is the mother of intentionality: Wittgenstein, normative practices and neurological representations. *New Ideas in Psychology* 27: 133–47.

Cash, M. 2010. Extended cognition, personal responsibility, and relational autonomy. *Phenomenology and the Cognitive Sciences* 9 (4): 645–71.

Catmur, C., Walsh, V., and Heyes, C. 2007. Sensorimotor learning configures the human mirror system. *Current Biology* 17: 1527–31.

Chemero, A. 2000. Anti-representationalism and the dynamical stance. *Philosophy of Science* 67 (4): 625–47.

Chemero, A. 2009. *Radical Embodied Cognitive Science*. Cambridge, MA: MIT Press.

Chen, S. and Bargh, J. A. 1999. Consequences of automatic evaluation: Immediate behavior predispositions to approach or avoid the stimulus. *Personality and Social Psychology Bulletin* 25: 215–24.

Chiel, H. and Beer, R. 1997. The brain has a body: Adaptive behavior emerges from interactions of nervous system, body and environment. *Trends in Neuroscience* 20: 553–7.

Chisholm, R. 1964. Human freedom and the self. The Langley Lecture, 1964. University of Kansas. Reprinted in J. Feinberg and R. Shafer-Landau (eds.), *Reason and Responsibility: Readings in Some Basic Problems of Philosophy*, 11th ed. (492–9). New York: Wadsworth, 2002.

Church, R. M. and Meck, W. H. 1984. The numerical attribute of stimuli. In H. L. Roitblat, T. G. Beaver, and H. S. Terrace (eds.), *Animal Cognition* (445–64). Hillsdale, NJ: Erlbaum.

Churchland, P. S., Ramachandran, V. S., and Sejnowski, T. J. 1994. A critique of pure vision. In C. Koch and J. L. Davis (eds.), *Large-Scale Neuronal Theories of the Brain*. Cambridge, MA: MIT Press.

Clark, A. 1997. *Being There: Putting Brain, Body, and World Together Again*. Cambridge, MA: MIT Press.

Clark, A. 1999. An embodied cognitive science? *Trends in Cognitive Sciences* 3 (9): 345–51.

Clark, A. 2008a. *Supersizing the Mind: Reflections on Embodiment, Action, and Cognitive Extension.* Oxford: Oxford University Press.

Clark, A. 2008b. Pressing the flesh: A tension on the study of the embodied, embedded mind. *Philosophy and Phenomenological Research* 76: 37–59.

Clark, A. 2013a. Whatever next? Predictive brains, situated agents, and the future of cognitive science. *Behavioral and Brain Sciences* 36 (3): 181–204.

Clark, A. 2013b. Gesture as thought? In Z. Radman (ed.), *The Hand, an Organ of the Mind: What the Manual Tells the Mental* (255–68). Cambridge: MIT Press.

Clark, A. 2015. Radical predictive processing. *Southern Journal of Philosophy*, 53 (S1): 3–27.

Clark, A. 2016a. *Surfing Uncertainty: Prediction, Action, and the Embodied Mind.* Oxford: Oxford University Press.

Clark, A. 2016b. Busting out: Predictive brains, embodied minds, and the puzzle of the evidentiary veil. *Noûs.* Published online. DOI: 10.1111/nous.12140.

Clark, A. and Chalmers, D. 1998. The extended mind. *Analysis* 58 (1): 7–19.

Clark, A. and Grush, R. 1999. Towards a cognitive robotics. *Adaptive Behavior* 7 (1): 5–16.

Clark, A. and Toribio, J. 1994. Doing without representing? *Synthese* 101: 401–31.

Clowes, R. and Mendonça, D. 2016. Representation redux: Is there still a useful role for representation to play in the context of embodied, dynamicist and situated theories of mind? *New Ideas in Psychology* 40: 26–47.

Clune, M. 2013. *Writing Against Time.* Stanford: Stanford University Press.

Cole, J., Gallagher, S., and McNeill, D. 2002. Gesture following deafferentation: A phenomenologically informed experimental study. *Phenomenology and the Cognitive Sciences* 1 (1): 49–67.

Colombetti, G. 2007. Enactive appraisal. *Phenomenology and the Cognitive Sciences* 6: 527–46.

Colombetti, G. 2013. *The Feeling Body: Affective Science Meets the Enactive Mind.* Cambridge, MA: MIT Press.

Cosmelli, D. and Thompson, E. 2010. Embodiment or envatment? Reflections on the bodily basis of consciousness. In J. Stewart, O. Gapenne, and E. A. Di Paolo (eds.), *Enaction: Toward a New Paradigm for Cognitive Science* (361–85). Cambridge, MA: MIT Press.

Coventry, K. R., Valdés, B., Castillo, A., and Guijarro-Fuentes, P. 2008. Language within your reach: Near–far perceptual space and spatial demonstratives. *Cognition* 108: 889–95.

Craig, A. D. 2002. How do you feel? Interoception: The sense of the physiological condition of the body. *Nature Reviews Neuroscience* 3: 655–66.

Crane, T. 1998. Intentionality as the mark of the mental. In A. O'Hear (ed.), *Contemporary Issues in the Philosophy of Mind.* Royal Institute of Philosophy Supplement 43 (229–51). Cambridge: Cambridge University Press.

Crane, T. 2009. Is perception a propositional attitude? *Philosophical Quarterly* 59 (236): 452–69.

Csibra, G. 2005. Mirror neurons and action observation. Is simulation involved? *ESF Interdisciplines*. https://pdfs.semanticscholar.org/f1ec/4f02190061b90ca531d900 c22e413bc66015.pdf (accessed April 6, 2017).

Csibra, G. and Gergely, G. 2009. Natural pedagogy. *Trends in Cognitive Sciences* 13: 148–53.

Currie, G. 2004. *Arts and Minds*. Cambridge: Cambridge University Press.

Currie, G. and Ravenscroft, I. 2002. *Recreative Minds: Imagination in Philosophy and Psychology*. Oxford: Oxford University Press.

Damasio, A. 1994. *Descartes Error: Emotion, Reason, and the Human Brain*. New York: G. P. Putnam.

Danziger, S., Levav, J., and Avnaim-Pesso, L. 2011. Extraneous factors in judicial decisions. *Proceedings of the National Academy of Sciences* 108 (17): 6889–92.

Darwin, C. 1874. *The Descent of Man, and Selection in Relation to Sex*, 2nd ed. London: John Murray.

Davidson, D. 1980. *Essays on Actions and Events*. Oxford: Clarendon Press.

Dawkins, R. 1982. *The Extended Phenotype*. Oxford: Oxford University Press.

De Cruz, H. 2008. An extended mind perspective on natural number representation. *Philosophical Psychology* 21 (4): 475–90.

De Jaegher, H. and Di Paolo, E. 2007. Participatory sense-making: An enactive approach to social cognition. *Phenomenology and the Cognitive Sciences* 6: 485–507.

De Jaegher, H., Di Paolo, E., and Gallagher, S. 2010. Does social interaction constitute social cognition? *Trends in Cognitive Sciences* 14 (10): 441–7.

Deacon, T. W. 1997. *The Symbolic Species: The Co-evolution of Language and the Brain*. New York: W.W. Norton.

Debruille, J. B., Brodeur, M. B., and Porras, C. F. 2012. N300 and social affordances: A study with a real person and a dummy as stimuli. PLoS ONE 7 (10): e47922.

Dehaene, S. 1997. *The Number Sense: How the Mind Creates Mathematics*. London: Penguin.

Dehaene, S. 2004. Evolution of human cortical circuits for reading and arithmetic: The 'neuronal recycling' hypothesis. In S. Dehaene, J. R. Duhamel, M. Hauser, and G. Rizzolatti (eds.), *From Monkey Brain to Human Brain* (133–57). Cambridge, MA: MIT Press.

Dehaene, S. 2009. *Reading in the Brain: The Science and Evolution of a Human Invention*. New York: Viking.

Dehaene, S. and Cohen, L. 2007. Cultural recycling of cortical maps. *Neuron* 56 (2): 384–98.

Della Sala, S. 2000. Anarchic hand: The syndrome of disowned actions. Paper presented at *The BA Festival of Science*.

Della Sala, S., Marchetti, C., and Spinnler, H. 1994. The anarchic hand: A fronto-mesial sign. In G. Boller and J. Grafman (eds.), *Handbook of Neuropsychology*, Vol. 9 (233–55). Amsterdam: Elsevier.

Deloison, Y. 2004. *Préhistoire du piéton. Essai sur les nouvelles origines de l'homme*. Paris: Plon.

Dennett, D. 1971. Intentional systems. *Journal of Philosophy* 68 (4): 87–106.

Dennett, D. 1987. *The Intentional Stance*. Cambridge, MA: MIT Press.

Dennett, D. 1991. *Consciousness Explained*. Boston: Little, Brown, & Co.

Dennett, D. 2003. *Freedom Evolves*. New York: Viking.

Descartes, R. 1649. *The Passions of the Soul*. Indianapolis: Hackett, 1989.

deVries, J. I. P., Visser, G. H. A., and Prechtl, H. F. R. 1984. Fetal motility in the first half of pregnancy. In H. F. R. Prechtl (ed.), *Continuity of Neural Functions from Prenatal to Postnatal Life* (46–64). London: Spastics International Medical Publications.

Dewey, J. 1894. The theory of emotion: I: Emotional attitudes. *Psychological Review* 1 (6): 553.

Dewey, J. 1895. The theory of emotion: II: The significance of emotions. *Psychological Review* 2 (1): 13.

Dewey, J. 1896. The reflex arc concept in psychology. *Psychological Review* 3 (4): 357–70.

Dewey, J. 1916. *Essays in Experimental Logic*. Chicago: University of Chicago Press.

Dewey, J. 1934. *Art as Experience*. New York: Perigee/Berkley.

Dewey, J. 1938a. *Logic: The Theory of Inquiry*. New York: Holt, Rinehart, & Winston.

Dewey, J. 1938b. *Experience and Education*. New York: Macmillan.

Dinstein, I., Thomas, C., Behrmann, M., and Heeger, D. J. 2008. A mirror up to nature. *Current Biology* 18 (1): R13–R18.

Di Paolo, E. A. 2005. Autopoiesis, adaptivity, teleology, agency. *Phenomenology and the Cognitive Sciences* 4 (4): 429–52.

Di Paolo, E. A., Buhrmann, T., and Barandiaran, X. E. 2017. *Sensorimotor Life: An Enactive Proposal*. Oxford: Oxford University Press.

Di Paolo, E. A., Rohde, M., and De Jaegher, H. 2010. Horizons for the enactive mind: Values, social interaction, and play. In J. Stewart, O. Gapenne, and E. A. Di Paolo (eds.), *Enaction: Toward a New Paradigm for Cognitive Science* (33–87). Cambridge, MA: MIT Press.

Dominey, P. F., Prescott, T., Bohg, J., Engel, A. K., Gallagher, S., Heed, T., Hoffmann, M., Knoblich, G., Prinz, W., and Schwartz, A. 2016. Implications of action-oriented paradigm shifts in cognitive science. In *Where's the Action? The Pragmatic Turn in Cognitive Science* (333–56). Cambridge, MA: MIT Press.

Domínguez, J. F., Lewis, E. D., Turner, R., and Egan, G. F. 2009. The brain in culture and culture in the brain: A review of core issues in neuroanthropology. *Progress in Brain Research* 178: 43–64.

Dreyfus, H. 2002. Intelligence without representation: Merleau-Ponty's critique of mental representation. *Phenomenology and the Cognitive Sciences* 1 (4): 367–83.

Dreyfus, H. L. 1992. *What Computers Still Can't Do: A Critique of Artificial Reason*. Cambridge, MA: MIT Press.

Dreyfus, H. L. 2005. Overcoming the myth of the mental: How philosophers can profit from the phenomenology of everyday expertise. In *Proceedings and Addresses of the American Philosophical Association* (47–65). Newark, DE: American Philosophical Association.

Dreyfus, H. L. 2007a. Why Heideggerian AI failed and how fixing it would require making it more Heideggerian. *Philosophical Psychology* 20 (2): 247–68.

Dreyfus, H. L. 2007b. The return of the myth of the mental. *Inquiry: An Interdisciplinary Journal of Philosophy* 50 (4): 352–65.

Durgin, F. H., Baird, J. A., Greenburg, M., Russell, R., Shaughnessy, K., and Waymouth, S. 2009. Who is being deceived? The experimental demands of wearing a backpack. *Psychonomic Bulletin and Review* 16: 964–9.

Durgin F. H., Klein, B., Spiegel, A., Strawser, C. J., and Williams, M. 2012. The social psychology of perception experiments: Hills, backpacks, glucose and the problem of generalizability. *Journal of Experimental Psychology: Human Perception and Performance* 38: 1582–95.

Eilan, N. 2003. The explanatory role of consciousness in action. In S. Maasen, W. Prinz, and G. Roth (eds.), *Voluntary Action: Brains, Minds, and Society* (188–201). Oxford: Oxford University Press.

Elfenbein, H. A. and Ambady, N. 2002a. Is there an in-group advantage in emotion recognition? *Psychological Bulletin* 128: 243–9.

Elfenbein, H. A. and Ambady, N. 2002b. On the universality and cultural specificity of emotion recognition: A meta-analysis. *Psychological Bulletin* 128: 203–35.

Elfenbein, H. A. and Ambady, N. 2003. When familiarity breeds accuracy: Cultural exposure and facial emotion recognition. *Journal of Personal and Social Psychology* 85: 276–90.

Elfenbein, H. A., Beaupré, M., Lévesque, M., and Hess, U. 2007. Toward a dialect theory: Cultural differences in the expression and recognition of posed facial expressions. *Emotion* 7: 131–46.

Elias, J. and Gallagher, S. 2014. Word as object: A view of language at hand. *Journal of Cognition and Culture* 14 (5): 373–84.

Ellis, R. 2005. *Curious Emotions: Roots of Consciousness and Personality in Motivated Action*. Philadelphia: John Benjamins.

Engel, A. K. 2010. Directive minds: How dynamics shapes cognition. In J. Stewart, O. Gapenne, and E. Di Paolo (eds.), *Enaction: Towards a New Paradigm for Cognitive Science* (219–43). Cambridge: MIT Press.

Engel, A. K., Maye, A., Kurthen, M., and König, P. 2013. Where's the action? The pragmatic turn in cognitive science. *Trends in Cognitive Sciences* 17 (5): 202–9.

Farnè, A., Iriki, A., and Làdavas, E. 2005. Shaping multisensory action-space with tools: Evidence from patients with cross-modal extinction. *Neuropsychologia* 43: 238–48.

Fink, P. W., Foo, P. S., and Warren, W. H. 2009. Catching fly balls in virtual reality: A critical test of the outfielder problem. *Journal of Vision* 9 (13): 1–8.

Firestone, C. and Scholl, B. J. 2015. Cognition does not affect perception: Evaluating the evidence for 'top-down' effects. *Behavioral and Brain Sciences* 39, 1–77.

Fischer, M. H., Prinz, J., and Lotz, K. 2008. Grasp cueing shows obligatory attention to action goals. *Quarterly Journal of Experimental Psychology* 61 (6): 860–8.

Fitch, W. T. 2012. Evolutionary developmental biology and human language evolution: Constraints on adaptation. *Evolutionary Biology* 39 (4): 613–37.

Flexman, J. E., Demaree, R. G., and Simpson, D. D. 1974. Respiratory phase and visual signal detection. *Perception and Psychophysics* 16 (2): 337–9.

Fodor, J. A. and Pylyshyn, Z. W. 1981. How direct is visual perception? Some reflections on Gibson's 'ecological approach'. *Cognition* 9 (2): 139–96.

Foglia, L. and Grush, R. 2011. The limitations of a purely enactive (non-representational) account of imagery. *Journal of Consciousness Studies* 18 (5–6): 35–43.

Freund, P., Friston, K., Thompson, A. J., Stephan, K. E., Ashburner, J., Bach, D. R., . . . and Weiskopf, N. 2016. Embodied neurology: An integrative framework for neurological disorders. *Brain*. Published online. DOI: 10.1093/brain/aww076 1855–1861.

Frijda, N. H. 1986. *The Emotions: Studies in Emotions and Social Interactions.* New York: Cambridge University Press.

Friston, K. 2005. A theory of cortical responses. *Philosophical Transactions of the Royal Society of London.* Series B, Biological Sciences, 360 (1456): 815–36.

Friston, K. 2009. The free-energy principle: A rough guide to the brain? *Trends in Cognitive Sciences* 13 (7): 293–301.

Friston, K. 2010. The free-energy principle: A unified brain theory? *Nature Reviews Neuroscience* 11 (2): 127–38.

Friston, K. 2011. Embodied inference: Or 'I think therefore I am, if I am what I think'. In W. Tschacher and C. Bergomi (eds.), *The Implications of Embodiment (Cognition and Communication)* (89–125). Exeter: Imprint Academic.

Friston, K. 2012. Prediction, perception and agency. *International Journal of Psychophysiology* 83 (2): 248–52.

Friston, K. 2013a. Life as we know it. *Journal of the Royal Society Interface* 10 (86). DOI: 10.1098/rsif.2013.0475.

Friston, K. 2013b. Active inference and free energy. *Behavioral and Brain Sciences* 36: 212–13.

Friston, K. and Frith, C. 2015. A duet for one. *Consciousness and Cognition* 36: 390–405.

Friston, K., Adams, R. A., Perrinet, L., and Breakspear, M. 2012. Perceptions as hypotheses: Saccades as experiments. *Frontiers in Psychology*, 3. DOI: 10.3389/fpsyg.2012.00151.

Friston, K., Kilner, J., and Harrison, L. 2006. A free energy principle for the brain. *Journal of Physiology* (Paris) 100: 70–87.

Friston, K., Mattout, J., and Kilner, J. 2011. Action understanding and active inference. *Biological Cybernetics* 104 (1–2): 137–60.

Froese, T. and Gallagher, S. 2012. Getting IT together: Integrating developmental, phenomenological, enactive and dynamical approaches to social interaction. *Interaction Studies* 13 (3): 434–66.

Gallagher, S. 2001. The practice of mind: Theory, simulation, or primary inter-action? *Journal of Consciousness Studies* 8 (5–7): 83–107.

Gallagher, S. 2005a. *How the Body Shapes the Mind*. Oxford: Oxford University Press.

Gallagher, S. 2005b. Metzinger's matrix: Living the virtual life with a real body. *Psyche* 11 (5): 1–9.

Gallagher, S. 2007. Simulation trouble. *Social Neuroscience* 2 (3–4): 353–65.

Gallagher, S. 2008a. Are minimal representations still representations? *International Journal of Philosophical Studies* 16 (3): 351–69.

Gallagher, S. 2008b. Direct perception in the intersubjective context. *Consciousness and Cognition* 17: 535–43.

Gallagher, S. 2008c. Inference or interaction: Social cognition without precursors. *Philosophical Explorations* 11 (3): 163–73.

Gallagher, S. 2008d. Neural simulation and social cognition. In J. A. Pineda (ed.), *Mirror Neuron Systems: The Role of Mirroring Processes in Social Cognition* (355–71). Totowa, NJ: Humana Press.

Gallagher, S. 2009. Two problems of intersubjectivity. *Journal of Consciousness Studies* 16 (6–8): 289–308.

Gallagher, S. 2011. Time in action. *Oxford Handbook on Time* (419–37). Ed. C. Callender. Oxford: Oxford University Press.

Gallagher, S. 2012. Multiple aspects of agency. *New Ideas in Psychology* 30: 15–31.

Gallagher, S. 2013a. The socially extended mind. *Cognitive Systems Research* 25–6: 4–12.

Gallagher, S. 2013b. A pattern theory of self. *Frontiers in Human Neuroscience* 7 (443): 1–7. DOI: 10.3389/fnhum.2013.00443.

Gallagher, S. 2015. Doing the math: Calculating the role of evolution and enculturation in the origins of mathematical reasoning. *Progress in Biophysics and Molecular Biology* 119: 341–6.

Gallagher, S. 2016. Timing is not everything: The intrinsic temporality of action. In R. Altshuler (ed.), *Time and the Philosophy of Action* (203–21). London: Routledge.

Gallagher, S. and Aguda, B. 2015. The embodied Phenomenology of phenomenology. *Journal of Consciousness Studies* 22 (3–4): 93–107.

Gallagher, S. and Allen, M. 2016. Active inference, enactivism and social cognition. *Synthese*. DOI: 10.1007/s11229-016-1269-8.

Gallagher, S. and Cole, J. 1995. Body schema and body image in a deafferented subject. *Journal of Mind and Behavior* 16: 369–90.

Gallagher, S. and Hutto, D. 2008. Understanding others through primary interaction and narrative practice. In J. Zlatev, T. P. Racine, C. Sinha, and E. Itkonen (eds.), *The Shared Mind: Perspectives on Intersubjectivity* (17–38). Amsterdam: John Benjamins.

Gallagher, S., Hutto, D. D., Slaby, J., and Cole, J. 2013. The brain as part of an enactive system. *Behavioral and Brain Sciences* 36 (4): 421–2.

Gallagher, S. and Lindgren, R. 2015. Enactive metaphors: Learning through full-body engagement. *Educational Psychology Review* 27 (3): 391–404.

Gallagher, S. and Marcel, A. J. 1999. The self in contextualized action. *Journal of Consciousness Studies* 6 (4): 4–30.

Gallagher, S. and Meltzoff, A. 1996. The earliest sense of self and others: Merleau-Ponty and recent developmental studies. *Philosophical Psychology* 9: 213–36.

Gallagher, S. and Varela, F. 2003. Redrawing the map and resetting the time: Phenomenology and the cognitive sciences. *Canadian Journal of Philosophy.* Supplementary Volume 29: 93–132.

Gallagher, S. and Varga, S. 2014. Social constraints on the direct perception of emotions and intentions. *Topoi* 33 (1): 185–99.

Gallagher, S. and Zahavi, D. 2014. Primal impression and enactive perception. In D. Lloyd and V. Arstila (eds.), *Subjective Time: The Philosophy, Psychology, and Neuroscience of Temporality* (83–99). Cambridge, MA: MIT Press.

Gallagher, S., Reinerman, L., Janz, B., Bockelman, P., and Trempler, J. 2015. *A Neurophenomenology of Awe and Wonder: Towards a Non-reductionist Cognitive Science.* London: Palgrave-Macmillan.

Gallese, V. 2001. The 'shared manifold' hypothesis: From mirror neurons to empathy. *Journal of Consciousness Studies* 8: 33–50.

Gallese, V. 2007. Embodied simulation: From mirror neuron systems to interpersonal relations. In G. Bock and J. Goode (eds.), *Empathy and Fairness*, Novartis Foundation Symposium, Vol. 278 (3–19). Chichester: John Wiley & Sons.

Gallese, V. 2009. The two sides of mimesis: Girard's mimetic theory, embodied simulation and social identification. *Journal of Consciousness Studies* 16 (4): 21–44.

Gallese, V. 2014. Bodily selves in relation: Embodied simulation as second-person perspective on intersubjectivity. *Philosophical Transactions of the Royal Society of London. Series B, Biological Sciences*, 369 (177): 1–10. DOI: 10.1098/rstb.2013.0177.

Gallese, V. and Goldman, A. 1998. Mirror neurons and the simulation theory of mind-reading. *Trends in Cognitive Sciences* 2: 493–501.

Gallese, V. and Sinigaglia, C. 2011. What is so special about embodied simulation? *Trends in Cognitive Sciences* 15 (11): 512–19.

Garfinkel, S., Minati, L., Gray, M. A., Seth, A. K., Dolan, R. J. and Critchley, H. D. 2014. Fear from the heart: Sensitivity to fear stimuli depends on individual heartbeats. *Journal of Neuroscience* 34 (19): 6573–82.

Gaukroger, S. 1997. *Descartes: An Intellectual Biography.* Oxford: Clarendon.

Gazzaniga, M. 1998. *The Mind's Past.* Berkeley: University of California Press.

Gegenfurtner, K., Olkkonen, M., and Walter, S. 2006. Memory modulates color experience. *Nature Neuroscience* 9 (11): 1367–8.

Georgieff, N. and Jeannerod, M. 1998. Beyond consciousness of external events: A 'Who' system for consciousness of action and self-consciousness. *Consciousness and Cognition* 7: 465–77.

Gibbard, A. 1975. Contingent identity. *Journal of Philosophical Logic* 4: 187–221.

Gibson, J. J. 1977. The theory of affordances. In R. Shaw and J. Bransford (eds.), *Perceiving, Acting, and Knowing* (67–82). Hillsdale, NJ: Erlbaum.

Glenberg, A. M. 2010. Embodiment as a unifying perspective for psychology. *Wiley Interdisciplinary Reviews: Cognitive Science* 1 (4): 586–96.

Glenberg, A. M. and Kaschak, M. P. 2002. Grounding language in action. *Psychonomic Bulletin and Review* 9: 558–65.

Godfrey-Smith, P. 2001. On the status and explanatory structure of developmental systems theory. In P. E. Griffiths and R. D. Gray (eds.), *Cycles of Contingency: Developmental Systems and Evolution* (283–98). Cambridge, MA: MIT Press.

Goh, J., Chee, M. W., Tan, J. C., Venkatraman, V., Hebrank, A., Leshikar, E. D., et al. 2007. Age and culture modulate object processing and object–scene binding in the ventral visual area. *Cognitive, Affective, and Behavioral Neurosciences* 7 (1): 44–52.

Goh, J. O. and Park, D. C. 2009. Culture sculpts the perceptual brain. *Progress in Brain Research* 178: 95–111.

Goldie, P. 2000. *The Emotions: A Philosophical Exploration.* Oxford: Oxford University Press.

Goldin-Meadow, S. 1999. The role of gesture in communication and thinking. *Trends in Cognitive Sciences*, 3: 419–29.

Goldin-Meadow, S., Kim, S., and Singer, M. 1999. What the teacher's hands tell the student's mind about math. *Journal of Educational Psychology* 91: 720–30.

Goldin-Meadow, S., Nusbaum, H., Kelly, S. D., and Wagner, S. 2001. Explaining math: Gesturing lightens the load. *Psychological Science* 12 (6): 516–22.

Goldman, A. I. 1970. *A Theory of Human Action*. New York: Prentice Hall.

Goldman, A. I. 2006. *Simulating Minds: The Philosophy, Psychology, and Neuroscience of Mindreading*. New York: Oxford University Press.

Goldman, A. I. 2012. A moderate approach to embodied cognitive science. *Review of Philosophy and Psychology* 3 (1): 71–88.

Goldman, A. I. 2014. The bodily formats approach to embodied cognition. In U. Kriegel (ed.), *Current Controversies in Philosophy of Mind* (91–108). New York and London: Routledge.

Goldman, A. I. and Vignemont, de F. 2009. Is social cognition embodied? *Trends in Cognitive Sciences* 13 (4): 154–9.

Goldstein, K. 1971. Über Zeigen und Greifen. In A. Gurwitsch, E. M. Goldstein, and W. E. Haudek (eds.), *Selected Papers/Ausgewählte Schriften*. The Hague: Martinus Nijhoff.

Goldstein, K. and Gelb, A. 1920. Über den Einfluss des vollständigen Verlustes des optischen Vorstellungsvermögens auf das taktile Erkennen. In A. Gelb and K. Goldstein (eds.), *Psychologische Analysen hirnpathologischer Fälle II* (157–250). Leipzig: Johann Ambrosius Barth Verlag.

Goldstein, K. and Scheerer, M. 1964. *Abstract and Concrete Behavior: An Experimental Study with Special Tests*. Evanston, IL: Northwestern University. Reprint of *Psychological Monographs* 53 (2), 1941.

Goodale, M. A. and Milner, A. D. 1992. Separate visual pathways for perception and action. *Trends in Neurosciences* 15 (1): 20–5.

Goodwin, C. 2000. Action and embodiment within situated human interaction. *Journal of Pragmatics* 32: 1489–1522.

Goodwin, C. 2007. Environmentally coupled gestures. In S. D. Duncan, J. Cassell and E. T. Levy (eds.), *Gesture and the Dynamic Dimension of Language* (195–212). Amsterdam: John Benjamins.

Goodwin, C. 2013. The co-operative, transformative organization of human action and knowledge. *Journal of Pragmatics* 46: 8–23.

Grush, R. 2004. The emulation theory of representation: Motor control, imagery, and perception. *Behavioral and Brain Sciences* 27: 377–442.

Grush, R. and Mandik, P. 2002. Representational parts. *Phenomenology and the Cognitive Sciences* 1 (4): 389–94.

Gutsell, J. N. and Inzlicht, M. 2010. Empathy constrained: Prejudice predicts reduced mental simulation of actions during observation of outgroups. *Journal of Experimental Social Psychology* 46: 841–5.

Hacking, I. 1995. The looping effects of human kinds. In D. Sperber, D. Premack, and A. J. Premack (eds.), *Causal Cognition: A Multidisciplinary Approach* (351–83). New York: Oxford University Press.

Haggard, P. 2003. Conscious awareness of intention and of action. In N. Eilan and J. Roessler (eds.), *Agency and Self-Awareness* (111–27). Oxford: Clarendon Press.

Haggard, P. and Libet, B. 2001. Conscious intention and brain activity. *Journal of Consciousness Studies* 8 (11): 47–64.

Handy, T. C., Grafton, S. T., Shroff, N. M., Ketay, S., and Gazzaniga, M. S. 2003. Graspable objects grab attention when the potential for action is recognized. *Nature Neuroscience* 6: 421–7.

Harcourt-Smith, W. E. H. 2007. The origins of bipedal locomotion. In W. Henke and I. Tattersall (eds.), *Handbook of Paleoanthropology*, Vol. III: *Phylogeny of Hominids* (1483–518). Berlin: Springer.

Harris, C. S. 1965. Perceptual adaptation to inverted, reversed, and displaced vision. *Psychological Review* 72: 419–44.

Hatfield, G. 2002. Perception as unconscious inference. In D. Heyer (ed.), *Perception and the Physical World: Psychological and Philosophical Issues in Perception* (113–43). Chichester: John Wiley & Sons.

Haugeland, J. 1985. *Artificial Intelligence: The Very Idea*. Cambridge: MIT Press.

Haugeland, J. 1990. Intentionality all-stars. *Philosophical Perspectives* 4: 383–427. Reprinted in J. Haugeland, *Having Thought: Essays in the Metaphysics of Mind* (127–70). Cambridge, MA: Harvard University Press.

Hayes, A. E., Paul, M. A., Beuger, B., and Tipper, S. P. 2008. Self produced and observed actions influence emotion: The roles of action fluency and eye gaze. *Psychological Research* 72 (4): 461–72.

Head, H. 1920. *Studies in Neurology*, Vol 2. London: Oxford University Press.

Heck, D. H., McAfee, S. S., Liu, Y., Babajani-Feremi, A., Rezaie, R., Freeman, W. J., Wheless, J. W., Papanicolaou, A. C., Ruszinko, M., and Kozma, R. 2016. Cortical rhythms are modulated by respiration. *bioRxiv*. DOI: 10.1101/049007.

Heft, H. 2001. *Ecological Psychology in Context: James Gibson, Roger Barker, and the Legacy of William James's Radical Empiricism*. Mahwah, NJ: Erlbaum.

Heidegger, M. 1962. *Being and Time*. Trans. J. Macquarrie and E. Robinson. New York: Harper & Row.

Heidegger, M. 1994. *Gesamtausgabe: Phänomenologische Interpretationen zu Aristoteles: Frühe Freiburger Vorlesung Wintersemester 1921/22*. Bd. 61: Abt. 2, *Vorlesungen*. Frankfurt: Vittorio Klostermann.

Heider, F. and Simmel, M. 1944. An experimental study of apparent behavior. *American Journal of Psychology* 57 (2): 243–59.

Helmholtz, H. 1867. *Handbuch der Physiologishen Optik*. Leipzig: Leopold Voss; *Treatise on Physiological Optics*. Ed. J. Southall. Mineola, NY: Dover Publications, 2005.

Hodgson, S. 1870. *The Theory of Practice*. London: Longmans, Green, Reader, & Dyer.

Høffding, S. 2015. A phenomenology of expert musicianship. Ph.D. dissertation, Department of Philosophy, University of Copenhagen.

Hohwy, J. 2013. *The Predictive Mind*. Oxford: Oxford University Press.

Hohwy, J. 2016. The self-evidencing brain. *Noûs* 50 (2): 259–85.

Holekamp, K. E., Swanson, E. M. and Van Meter, P. E. 2013. Developmental constraints on behavioural flexibility. *Philosophical Transactions of the Royal Society of London*. Series B, Biological Sciences, 368 (1618): 1–11.

Horgan, T. E. and Kriegel, U. 2008. Phenomenal intentionality meets the extended mind. *The Monist* 91: 353–80.

Horgan, T. E. and Tienson, J. L. 2002. The intentionality of phenomenology and the phenomenology of intentionality. In D. J. Chalmers (ed.), *Philosophy of Mind: Classical and Contemporary Readings* (520–33). Oxford: Oxford University Press.

Hunt, K. D. 1994. The evolution of human bipedality: Ecology and functional morphology. *Journal of Human Evolution* 26: 183–202.

Hurley, S. 1998. *Consciousness in Action*. Cambridge, MA: Harvard University Press.

Husserl, E. 1965. *Phenomenology and the Crisis of Philosophy*. Trans. Q. Lauer. New York: Harper Torchbooks.

Husserl, E. 1969. *Formal and Transcendental Logic*. Trans. D. Cairns. The Hague: Martinus Nijhoff.

Husserl, E. 1977. *Phenomenological Psychology*. Trans. J. Scanlon. The Hague: Martinus Nijhoff.

Husserl, E. 1982a. *Ideas Pertaining to a Pure Phenomenology and to a Phenomenological Philosophy—First Book* [1913]. Trans. F. Kersten. The Hague: Martinus Nijhoff.

Husserl, E. 1982b. The origin of geometry, trans. D. Carr. In J. Derrida, *Introduction to the Origin of Geometry* (155–80). Lincoln, NE: University of Nebraska Press.

Husserl, E. 1989. *Ideas Pertaining to a Pure Phenomenology and to a Phenomenological Philosophy—Second Book: Studies in the Phenomenology of Constitution*. Trans. R. Rojcewicz and A. Schuwer. Dordrecht: Kluwer Academic.

Husserl, E. 2003. *Philosophy of Arithmetic: Psychological and Logical Investigations—with Supplementary Texts from 1887–1901*. Edmund Husserl Collected Works, Vol. X. Trans. D. Willard. Springer: Dordrecht.

Husserl, E. 2004. *Wahrnehmung und Aufmerksamkeit: Texte aus dem Nachlass (1893–1912)*. Ed. T. Vongehr and R. Giuliani. Dordrecht: Springer.

Husserl, E. 2008. *Die Lebenswelt-Auslegungen der vorgegebenen Welt und ihrer Konstitution*. Dordrecht: Springer.

Hutto, D. 2011a. Philosophy of mind's new lease on life: Autopoietic enactivism meets teleosemiotics. *Journal of Consciousness Studies* 18 (5–6): 44–64.

Hutto, D. 2011b. Enactivism: Why be radical? In H. Bredekamp and J. M. Krois (eds.), *Sehen und Handeln* (21–44). Berlin: Walter de Gruyter.

Hutto, D. 2015. Overly enactive imagination? Radically re-imagining imagining. *Southern Journal of Philosophy* 53 (S1): 68–89.

Hutto, D. (in press). Memory and narrativity. In S. Bernecker and K. Michaelian (eds.), *Handbook of Philosophy of Memory*. London: Routledge.

Hutto, D. and Myin, E. 2013. *Radicalizing Enactivism: Basic Minds Without Content*. Cambridge, MA: MIT Press.

Hutto, D. D., Kirchhoff, M. D. and Myin, E. 2014. Extensive enactivism: Why keep it all in? *Frontiers in Human Neuroscience* 8: 706. DOI: 10.3389/fnhum.2014.00706.

Huxley, T. H. 1874. On the hypothesis that animals are automata, and its history. *Fortnightly Review*, n.s.16: 555–80.

Huxley, T. H. 1894. *Man's Place in Nature, and Other Anthropological Essays*. London: Macmillan.

Ingold, T. 2004. Culture on the ground: The world perceived through the feet. *Journal of Material Culture* 9 (3): 315–40.

Iriki, A. and Sakura, O. 2008. Neuroscience of primate intellectual evolution: Natural selection and passive and intentional niche construction. *Philosophical Transactions of the Royal Society of London. Series B, Biological Sciences,* 363: 2229–41.

Iriki, A., Tanaka, M., and Iwamura, Y. 1996. Coding of modified body schema during tool use by macaque postcentral neurones. *Neuroreport* 7: 2325–30.

Iverson, J. and Thelen, E. 1999. Hand, mouth, and brain: The dynamic emergence of speech and gesture. *Journal of Consciousness Studies* 6: 19–40.

Iwabe, T., Ozaki, I., and Hashizume, A. 2014. The respiratory cycle modulates brain potentials, sympathetic activity, and subjective pain sensation induced by noxious stimulation. *Neurosci Research* 84: 47–59.

Jackendoff, R. 2002. *Foundations of Language: Brain, Meaning, Grammar, Evolution*. Oxford: Oxford University Press.

Jacob, F. 1977. Evolution and tinkering. *Science* 196: 1161–6.

James, W. 1884. What is an emotion? *Mind* 9: 188–205.

James, W. 1890. *Principles of Psychology*. New York: Dover Publications.

Jeannerod, M. 1994. The representing brain: Neural correlates of motor intention and imagery. *Behavioral and Brain Sciences* 17 (2): 187–201.

Jeannerod, M. 1997. *The Cognitive Neuroscience of Action*. Oxford: Blackwell.

Jeannerod, M. 2003. Self-generated actions. In S. Maasen, W. Prinz, and G. Roth (eds.), *Voluntary Action: Brains, Minds, and Sociality* (153–64). Oxford: Oxford University Press.

Jeannerod, M., Decety, J., and Michel, F. 1994. Impairment of grasping movements following a bilateral posterior parietal lesion. *Neuropsychoogia* 32 (4): 369–80.

Johnson, M. 1987. *The Body in the Mind: The Bodily Basis of Meaning, Imagination, and Reason*. Chicago: University of Chicago Press.

Johnson, M. 2008. *The Meaning of the Body: Aesthetics of Human Understanding*. Chicago: University of Chicago Press.

Johnson, M. 2010. Metaphors and cognition. In S. Gallagher and M. Schmicking (eds.), *Handbook of Phenomenology and Cognitive Science* (401–14). Dordrecht: Springer.

Johnson, M. 2017. *Embodied Mind, Meaning, and Reason: How Our Bodies give Rise to Understanding*. Chicago: University of Chicago Press.

Johnson, M. and Lakoff, G. 2002. Why cognitive linguistics requires embodied realism. *Cognitive Linguistics* 13 (3): 245–63.

Kammers, M. P. M., de Vignemont, F., Verhagen, L., and Dijkerman, H. C. 2009. The rubber hand illusion in action. *Neuropsychologia* 47 (1): 204–11.

Kammers, M. P., Kootker, J. A., Hogendoorn, H., and Dijkerman, H. C. 2010. How many motoric body representations can we grasp? *Experimental Brain Research* 202: 203–12.

Kant, I. 1992. Concerning the ultimate ground of the differentiation of directions in space. In D. Walford and R. Meerbote (eds.), *The Cambridge Edition of the Works of Immanuel Kant: Theoretical Philosophy, 1755–1770* (365–72). Cambridge: Cambridge University Press.

Kelly, S. D. 2000. Grasping at straws: Motor intentionality and the cognitive science of skilled behavior. In M. Wrathall and J. Malpas (eds.), *Heidegger, Coping, the Cognitive Sciences: Essays in Honor of Hubert L. Dreyfus*, Vol. 2 (161–77). Cambridge, MA: MIT Press.

Kelly, S. D. 2004. Merleau-Ponty on the body. In M. Proudfoot (ed.), *The Philosophy of the Body* (62–76). London: Blackwell.

Keysers, C. and Gazzola, V. 2006. Towards a unifying neural theory of social cognition. In S. Anders, G. Ende, M. Junghofer, and J. Kissler (eds.), *Understanding Emotions* (379–402). Amsterdam: Elsevier.

Kilner, J. M., Friston, K. J., and Frith, C. D. 2007. Predictive coding: An account of the mirror neuron system. *Cognitive Processing* 8 (3): 159–66.

Kirchhoff, M. 2015. Extended cognition and the causal-constitutive fallacy: In search for a diachronic and dynamical conception of constitution. *Philosophy and Phenomenological Research* 90 (2): 320–60.

Kirsh, D. 2005. Metacognition, distributed cognition and visual design. In P. Gardenfors and P. Johansson (eds.), *Cognition, Education, and Communication Technology* (147–80). London: Routledge.

Kitayama, S. and Park, J. 2010. Cultural neuroscience of the self: Understanding the social grounding of the brain. *Social Cognitive Affective Neuroscience* 5 (2–3): 111–29.

Kiverstein, J. 2012. The meaning of embodiment. *Topics in Cognitive Science* 4 (4): 740–58.

Kranczioch, C., Debener, S., Schwarzbach, J., Goebel, R., and Engel, A. K. 2005. Neural correlates of conscious perception in the attentional blink. *Neuroimage* 24 (3): 704–14.

Kyselo, M. and Di Paolo, E. 2013. Locked-in syndrome: A challenge for embodied cognitive science. *Phenomenology and the Cognitive Sciences* 14 (3): 517–42.

La Mettrie, de J. O. 1745. *Histoire naturelle de l'ame*. La Haye: Jean Neaulme.

Lafleur, A. and Boucher, V. J. 2015. The ecology of self-monitoring effects on memory of verbal productions: Does speaking to someone make a difference? *Consciousness and Cognition* 36: 139–46.

Lakoff, G. 2012. Explaining embodied cognition results. *Topics in Cognitive Science* 4 (4): 773–85.

Lakoff, G. and Johnson, M. 2003. *Metaphors We Live By*. Chicago: University of Chicago Press.

Lakoff, G. and Johnson, M. 1999. *Philosophy in the Flesh: The Embodied Mind and its Challenge to Western Thought*. New York: Basic Books.

Lakoff, G. and Núñez, R. 2000. *Where Mathematics Comes From*. New York: Basic Books.

Lavelle, J. S. 2012. Theory-theory and the direct perception of mental states. *Review of Philosophy and Psychology* 3 (2): 213–30.

Leslie, A. 2004. Children's understanding of the mental world. In R. L. Gregory (ed.), *The Oxford Companion to the Mind* (167–9). Oxford: Oxford University Press.

Levin, D. T. and Banaji, M. R. 2006. Distortions in the perceived lightness of faces: The role of race categories. *Journal of Experimental Psychology: General* 135 (4): 501.

Lew, A. R. and Butterworth, G. 1997. The development of hand–mouth coordination in 2- to 5-month-old infants: Similarities with reaching and grasping. *Infant Behavior and Development* 20: 59–69.

Li, S., Park, W. H., and Borg, A. 2012. Phase-dependent respiratory–motor interactions in reaction time tasks during rhythmic voluntary breathing. *Motor Control* 16 (4): 493–505.

Libet, B. 1985. Unconscious cerebral initiative and the role of conscious will in voluntary action. *Behavioral and Brain Sciences* 8: 529–66.

Libet, B. 1992. The neural time-factor in perception, volition, and free will. *Revue de Métaphysique et de Morale* 2: 255–72.

Libet, B. 1996. Neural time factors in conscious and unconscious mental functions. In S. R. Hammeroff et al. (eds.), *Toward a Science of Consciousness: The First Tucson Discussions and Debates*. Cambridge, MA: MIT Press.

Libet, B. 1999. Do we have free will? *Journal of Consciousness Studies* 6 (8–9): 47–57.

Libet, B., Gleason, C. A., Wright, E. W., and Perl, D. K. 1983. Time of conscious intention to act in relation to cerebral activities (readiness potential): The unconscious initiation of a freely voluntary act. *Brain* 106: 623–42.

Linden, D. E. J., Kallenbach, U., Heineckeô, A. Singer, W., and Goebel, R. 1999. The myth of upright vision: A psychophysical and functional imaging study of adaptation to inverting spectacles. *Perception* 28: 469–81.

Liu, L., Papanicolaou, A. C., and Heck, D. H. 2014. *Visual reaction time modulated by respiration.* Working paper. Department of Anatomy and Neurobiology, University of Tennessee Medical Center, Memphis.

Livesay, J. R. and Samras, M. R. 1998. Covert neuromuscular activity of the dominant forearm during visualization of a motor task. *Perceptual and Motor Skills* 86: 371–4.

Lohmar, D. 2005. On the function of weak phantasmata in perception: Phenomenological, psychological and neurological clues for the transcendental function of imagination in perception. *Phenomenology and the Cognitive Sciences* 4 (2): 155–67.

Lovejoy, C. O. 1981. The origin of man. *Science* 211: 341–50.

Lowe, E. J. 1999. Self, agency and mental causation. *Journal of Consciousness Studies* 6 (8–9): 225–39.

Lungarella, M. and Sporns, O. 2005. Information self-structuring: Key principle for learning and development. In *Development and Learning: Proceedings of the 4th International Conference on Development and Learning* (25–30). DOI: 10.1109/DEVLRN.2005.1490938.

Mac Lane, S. 1981. Mathematical models: A sketch for the philosophy of mathematics. *American Mathematical Monthly* 88 (7): 462–72.

McBeath, M. K., Shaffer, D. M., Kaiser, M. K. 1995. How baseball outfielders determine where to run to catch fly balls. *Science* 28 (268): 569–73.

McDowell, J. 1994. *Mind and World.* Cambridge, MA: Harvard University Press.

McDowell, J. 2007a. What myth? *Inquiry* 50 (4): 338–51.

McDowell, J. 2007b. Response to Dreyfus. *Inquiry* 50 (4): 366–70.

McNeill, D. 1992. *Hand and Mind: What Gestures Reveal about Thought.* Chicago: University of Chicago Press.

McNeill, D., Duncan, S., Cole, J., Gallagher, S., and Bertenthal, B. 2008. Neither or both: Growth points from the very beginning. *Interaction Studies* 9 (1): 117–32.

Malafouris, L. 2013. *How Things Shape the Mind.* Cambridge, MA: MIT Press.

Marcel, A. 2003. The sense of agency: Awareness and ownership of action. In J. Roessler and N. Eilan (eds.), *Agency and Self-Awareness* (48–93). Oxford: Oxford University Press.

Marteniuk, R. G., MacKenzie, C. L., Jeannerod, M., Athenes, S., and Dugas, C. 1987. Constraints on human arm movement trajectories. *Canadian Journal of Psychology* 41: 365–78.

Matsumoto, D. 2002. Methodological requirements to test a possible in-group advantage in judging emotions across cultures: Comment on Elfenbein and Ambady (2002) and evidence. *Psychological Bulletin* 128 (2): 236–42.

Mauss, M. 1979. *Sociology and Psychology: Essays.* London: Routledge & Kegan Paul.

Mead, G. H. 1938. *The Philosophy of the Act.* Chicago: University of Chicago Press.

Mead, G. H. 1964. *Selected Writings.* Ed. A. J. Reck. Chicago: University of Chicago Press.

Mele, A. R. 1992. *Springs of Action.* Oxford: Oxford University Press.

Meltzoff, A. and Moore, M. K. 1994. Imitation, memory, and the representation of persons. *Infant Behavior and Development* 17: 83–99.

Menary, R. 2007. *Cognitive Integration: Mind and Cognition Unbounded.* London: Palgrave-Macmillan.

Menary, R. 2010. The holy grail of cognitivism: A response to Adams and Aizawa. *Phenomenology and the Cognitive Sciences* 9 (4): 605–18.

Menary, R. 2011. Our glassy essence: The fallible self in pragmatist thought. In S. Gallagher (ed.), *The Oxford Handbook of the Self* (609–32). Oxford: Oxford University Press.

Menary, R. 2013. The enculturated hand. In Z. Radman. *The Hand: An Organ of the Mind* (349–68). Cambridge, MA: MIT Press.

Menary, R. 2015. Mathematical cognition: A case of enculturation. In T. Metzinger and J. M. Windt (eds.), *Open MIND* 25: 1–20. Frankfurt am Main: MIND Group. DOI: 10.15502/9783958570818.

Menary, R. and Kirchhoff, M. 2013. Cognitive transformations and extended expertise. *Educational Philosophy and Theory* 46 (6): 610–23.

Merleau-Ponty, M. 1964. *The Primacy of Perception.* Trans. J. Edie. Evanston, IL: Northwestern University Press.

Merleau-Ponty, M. 1968. *The Visible and the Invisible.* Trans. A. Lingis. Evanston, IL: Northwestern University Press.

Merleau-Ponty, M. 1983. *The Structure of Behavior.* Trans. A. L. Fisher. Boston, MA: Beacon Press.

Merleau-Ponty, M. 2012. *Phenomenology of Perception.* Trans. D. A. Landes. London: Routledge.

Merritt, M. and Varga, S. (eds.). 2013. Special issue on the Socially Extended Mind. *Cognitive Systems Theory,* vol. 25–6.

Merzenich, M. M., Kaas, J. H., Wall, J. T., Nelson, R. J., Sur, M., and Felleman, D. J. 1983. Topographic reorganization of somatosensory cortical areas 3b and 1 in adult monkeys following restricted deafferentation. *Neuroscience* 8: 33–55.

Meteyard, L., Cuadrado, S. R., Bahrami, B., and Vigliocco, G. 2012. Coming of age: A review of embodiment and the neuroscience of semantics. *Cortex* 48 (7): 788–804.

Metzinger, T. 2003. *Being No One: The Self-Model Theory of Subjectivity.* Cambridge, MA: MIT Press.

Michotte, A. 1963. *The Perception of Causality*. Trans. T. Miles and E. Miles. New York: Basic Books.

Millikan, R. 1984. *Language, Thought and Other Biological Categories*. Cambridge, MA: MIT Press.

Millikan, R. G. 1996. Pushme-pullyou representations. In L. May, M. Friedman, and A. Clark (eds.), *Mind and Morals: Essays on Ethics and Cognitive Science* (145–61). Cambridge, MA: MIT Press.

Millikan, R. G. 2005. *Language: A Biological Model*. Oxford: Oxford University Press.

Milner, D. A. and Goodale, M. A. 1995. *The Visual Brain in Action*. New York: Oxford University Press.

Mitchell, R. W. (ed.) 2002. *Pretending and Imagination in Animals and Children*. Cambridge: Cambridge University Press.

Miyahara, K. 2011. Neo-pragmatic intentionality and enactive perception: A compromise between extended and enactive minds. *Phenomenology and the Cognitive Sciences* 10 (4): 499–519.

Mohrhoff, U. 1999. The physics of interactionism. *Journal of Consciousness Studies* 6 (8–9): 165–84.

Molnar-Szakacs, I., Wu, A. D., Robles F. J., and Iacoboni, M. 2007. Do you see what I mean? Corticospinal excitability during observation of culture-specific gestures. *PLoS One* 2 (7): e626.

Morgan, E. 1990. *The Scars of Evolution: What our Body tells about Human Origins*. London: Penguin.

Nakatsukasa, M., Ogihara, N., Hamada, Y., Goto, Y., Yamada, M., Hirakawa, T., and Hirasaki. E. 2004. Energetic costs of bipedal and quadrupedal walking in Japanese macaques. *American Journal of Physical Anthropology* 124: 248–56.

Napier, J. R. 1980. *Hands*. London: Allen & Unwin.

Narayanan, S. 1997. Talking the talk is like walking the walk: A computational model of verbal aspect. In *Proceedings of the 19th Cognitive Science Society Conference* (548–53). Hillsdale, NJ: Erlbaum.

Naumann, R. 2012. Dynamics in the brain and dynamic frame theory for action verbs. *Proceedings of SMCLC*. Accessed 9 June 2016 at user.phil-fak.uni-duesseldorf.de.

Needham, A., Barrett, T., and Peterman, K. 2002. A pick-me-up for infants' exploratory skills: Early simulated experiences reaching for objects using 'sticky mittens' enhances young infants' object exploration skills. *Infant Behavior and Development* 25: 279–95.

Newen, A., Welpinghus, A., and Juckel, G. 2015. Emotion recognition as pattern recognition: The relevance of perception. *Mind and Language* 30 (2): 187–208.

Newman-Norlund, R. D., Noordzij, M. L., Meulenbroek, R. G. J., and Bekkering, H. 2007. Exploring the brain basis of joint attention: Co-ordination of actions, goals and intentions. *Social Neuroscience* 2 (1): 48–65.

Nieder, A., Diester, I., and Tudusciuc, O. 2006. Temporal and spatial enumeration processes in the primate parietal cortex. *Science* 313 (5792): 1432–5.

Niemitz, C. 2010. The evolution of the upright posture and gait—a review and a new synthesis. *Naturwissenschaften* 97 (3): 241–63.

Nillsson, L. and Hamberger, L. 1990. *A Child is Born*. New York: Delacorte.

Noë, A. 2004. *Action in Perception*. Cambridge, MA: MIT Press.

O'Regan, K. and Noë, A. 2001. A sensorimotor account of vision and visual consciousness. *Behavioral and Brain Sciences* 23: 939–73.

O'Shaughnessy, B. 1980. *The Will*, 2 vols. Cambridge: Cambridge University Press.

Oberman, L. M. and Ramachandran, V. S. 2007. The simulating social mind: The role of the mirror neuron system and simulation in the social and communicative deficits of autism spectrum disorders. *Psychological Bulletin* 133 (2): 310–27.

Orlandi, N. 2012. Embedded seeing-as: Multi-stable visual perception without interpretation. *Philosophical Psychology* 25 (4): 555–73.

Orlandi, N. 2013. Embedded seeing: Vision in the natural world. *Noûs* 47 (4): 727–47.

Orlandi, N. 2014. *The Innocent Eye: Why Vision is not a Cognitive Process*. Oxford: Oxford University Press.

Overmann, K. A. 2016. Beyond writing: The development of literacy in the Ancient Near East. *Cambridge Archaeological Journal* 26 (2): 285–303.

Pacherie, E. 2006. Towards a dynamic theory of intentions. In S. Pockett, W. P. Banks, and S. Gallagher (eds.), *Does Consciousness Cause Behavior? An Investigation of the Nature of Volition* (145–68). Cambridge, MA: MIT Press.

Pacherie, E. and Haggard, P. 2010. What are intentions? In W. Sinnott-Armstrong and L. Nadel (eds.), *Conscious Will and Responsibility: A Tribute to Benjamin Libet* (70–84). Oxford: Oxford University Press.

Palermos, S. O. 2012. Extending cognition in epistemology: Towards an individualistic social epistemology. Ph.D. thesis, Department of Philosophy, University of Edinburgh.

Palermos, S. O. 2014. Loops, constitution, and cognitive extension. *Cognitive Systems Research* 27: 25–41.

Palmer, S. E. 1999. *Vision Science: Photons to Phenomenology*. Cambridge, MA: MIT Press.

Paolucci, C. 2011. The 'external mind': semiotics, pragmatism, extended mind and distributed cognition. *Versus: quaderni di studi semiotici* 112: 69–96.

Park, J. and Kitayama, S. 2014. Interdependent selves show face-induced facilitation of error processing: Cultural neuroscience of self-threat. *Social Cognitive and Affective Neuroscience* 9 (2): 201–8.

Parravicini, A. and Pievani, T. 2016. Multi-level human evolution: Ecological patterns in hominin phylogeny. *Journal of Anthropological Sciences* 94: 1–16.

Pascual-Leone, A., Nguyet, D., Cohen, L. G., et al. 1995. Modulation of muscle responses evoked by transcranial magnetic stimulation during the acquisition of new fine motor skills. *Journal of Neurophysiology* 74: 1037–45.

Peiffer, C., Costes, N., Hervé, P., and Garcia-Larrea, L. 2008. Relief of dyspnea involves a characteristic brain activation and a specific quality of sensation. *American Journal of Respiratory and Critical Care Medicine* 177 (4): 440–9.

Peirce, C. S. 1887. Logical machines. *American Journal of Psychology* 1 (1): 165–70.

Peirce, C. S. 1931–1935, 1958. *Collected Papers of C. S. Peirce.* Ed. C. Hartshorne, P. Weiss, and A. Burks. Cambridge, MA: Harvard University Press (abbreviated: CP followed by the conventional '[volume].[page]'-notation).

Pélisson, D., Prablanc, C., Goodale, M. A., and Jeannerod, M. 1986. Visual control of reaching movements without vision of the limb. *Experimental Brain Research* 62 (2): 303–11.

Perner, J. and Ogden, J. E. 1988. Knowledge for hunger: Children's problem with representation in imputing mental states. *Cognition* 29 (1): 47–61.

Pessoa, L. 2013. *The Cognitive-Emotional Brain: From Interactions to Integration.* Cambridge, MA: MIT Press.

Petkova, V. I. and Ehrsson, H. H. 2008. If I were you: Perceptual illusion of body swapping. *PLoS One* 3 (12): e3832. DOI: 10.1371/journal.pone.0003832.

Pettit, P. 1996. *The Common Mind.* Oxford: Oxford University Press.

Pezzulo, G., Barsalou, L. W., Cangelosi, A., Fischer, M. H., McRae, K., and Spivey, M. J. 2011. The mechanics of embodiment: A dialog on embodiment and computational modeling. In A. Borghi and D. Pecher (eds.), *Embodied and Grounded Cognition* (196). Frontiers E-books.

Pickford, M., Senut, B., Gommery, D., and Treil, J. 2002. Bipedalism in *Orrorin tugenensis* revealed by its femora. *Comptes Rendus Palevol* 1 (4): 191–203.

Popper, K. R. 1972. *Objective Knowledge: An Evolutionary Approach.* Oxford: Oxford University Press.

Postle, N., McMahon, K. L., Ashton, R., Meredith, M., and de Zubicaray, G. I. 2008. Action word meaning representations in cytoarchitectonically defined primary and premotor cortex. *Neuroimage* 43 (3): 634–44.

Prinz, J. 2004. *Gut Reactions: A Perceptual Theory of Emotion.* New York: Oxford University Press.

Prinz, J. 2009. Is consciousness embodied? In P. Robbins and M. Aydede (eds.), *Cambridge Handbook of Situated Cognition* (419–37). Cambridge: Cambridge University Press.

Proffitt, D., Bhalla, M., Gossweiler, R., and Midgett, J. 1995. Perceiving geographical slant. *Psychonomic Bulletin and Review* 2 (4): 409–28.

Proffitt, D., Stefanucci, J., Banton, T., and Epstein, W. 2003. The role of effort in perceiving distance. *Psychological Science* 14 (2): 106–12.

Proffitt, D. R. 2009. Affordances matter in geographical slant perception. *Psychonomic Bulletin and Review* 16: 970–2.

Proffitt, D. R. 2013. An embodied approach to perception: By what units are visual perceptions scaled? *Perspectives on Psychological Science* 8 (4): 474–83.

Proust, J. 2003. How voluntary are minimal actions? In S. Maasen, W. Prinz, and G. Roth (eds.), *Voluntary Action: Brains, Minds, and Sociality* (202–19). Oxford: Oxford University Press.

Pulvermuller, F. 2005. Brain mechanisms linking language and action. *Nature Reviews Neuroscience* 6: 576–82.

Pylyshyn, Z. 1999. Is vision continuous with cognition? The case for cognitive impenetrability of visual perception. *Behavioral and Brain Sciences* 22 (3): 341–65.

Quaeghebeur, L., Duncan, S., Gallagher, S., Cole, J., and McNeill, D. 2014. Aproprioception and gesture. In C. Müller, E. Fricke, A. Cienki, S. H. Ladewig, and D. McNeill (eds.), *Handbook on Body–Language–Communication* (2048–61). Berlin: De Gruyter Mouton.

Ramsey, W. 2007. *Representation Reconsidered*. Cambridge: Cambridge University Press.

Rao, R. P. N. and Ballard, D. H. 1999. Predictive coding in the visual cortex: A functional interpretation of some extra-classical receptive-field effects. *Nature Neuroscience* 2 (1): 79–87.

Rassler, B. 2000. Mutual nervous influences between breathing and precision finger movements. *European Journal of Applied Physiology* 81 (6): 479–85.

Rietveld, E. and Kiverstein, J. 2014. A rich landscape of affordances. *Ecological Psychology* 26 (4): 325–52.

Rizzolatti, G., Fogassi, L., and Gallese, V. 2001. Neurophysiological mechanisms underlying the understanding and imitation of action. *Nature Reviews Neuroscience* 2: 661–70.

Robertson, L. C. and Treisman, A. 2010. Consciousness: Disorders. In E. B. Goldstein (ed.), *Encyclopedia of Perception*. New York: Sage.

Rochat, P. 1989. Object manipulation and exploration in 2- to 5-month-old infants. *Developmental Psychology* 25: 871–84.

Rochat, P. 1993. Hand–mouth coordination in the newborn: Morphology, determinants, and early development of a basic act. In G. J. P. Savelsbergh (ed.), *The Development of Coordination in Infancy* (265–88). Amsterdam: North-Holland.

Rochat, P. and Senders, S. J. 1991. Active touch in infancy: Action systems in development. In M. J. S. Weiss and P. R. Zelazo (eds.), *Newborn Attention: Biological Constraints and the Influence of Experience* (412–42). Norwood, NJ: Ablex.

Rock, I. and Harris, C. S. 1967. Vision and touch. *Scientific American* 216 (5): 96–104.

Rockwell, W. T. 2005. *Neither Brain nor Ghost: A Nondualist Alternative to the Mind-Brain Identity Theory*. Cambridge, MA: MIT Press.

Rode, G., Lacour, S., Jacquin-Courtois, S., Pisella, L., Michel, C., Revol, P., Luauté, J., Gallagher, S. Halligan, P., Pélisson, D., and Rossetti, Y. 2015. Long-term sensorimotor and therapeutical effects of a mild regime of prism adaptation in spatial neglect: A double-blind RCT essay. *Annals of Physical and Rehabilitation Medicine* 58 (2): 40–53.

Roepstorff, A. 2008. Things to think with: Words and objects as material symbols. *Philosophical Transactions of the Royal Society of London. Series B, Biological Sciences*, 363 (1499): 2049–54.

Rohde, M., Di Luca, M., Marc, O., and Ernst, M. O. 2011. The rubber hand illusion: Feeling of ownership and proprioceptive drift do not go hand in hand. *PLoS ONE* 6(6): e21659. DOI: 10.1371/journal.pone.0021659.

Roitblat, H. 1982. The meaning of representation in animal memory. *Behavioral and Brain Sciences* 5 (3): 353–72.

Roll, J-P. and Roll, R. 1988. From eye to foot: A proprioceptive chain involved in postural control. In G. Amblard, A. Berthoz, and F. Clarac (eds.), *Posture and Gait: Development, Adaptation, and Modulation* (155–64). Amsterdam: Excerpta Medica.

Rossetti, Y., Jacquin-Courtois, S., Calabria, M., Michel, C., Gallagher, S., Honoré, J., Luauté, J., Farné, A., Pisella, L., and Rode, G. 2015. Testing cognition and rehabilitation in unilateral neglect with wedge prism adaptation: Multiple interplays between sensorimotor adaptation and spatial cognition. In *Clinical Systems Neuroscience* (359–81). Tokyo: Springer Japan.

Rossini, P. M., Martino, G., Narici, L., Pasquarelli, A., Peresson, M., Pizzella, V., Tecchio, F., Torrioli, G., and Romani, G. L. 1994. Short-term brain 'plasticity' in humans: Transient finger representation changes in sensory cortex somatotopy following ischemic anesthesia. *Brain Research* 642 (1–2): 169–77.

Rowlands, M. 2006. *Body Language*. Cambridge, MA: MIT Press.

Rowlands, M. 2010. *The New Science of the Mind*. Cambridge, MA: MIT Press.

Rowlands, M. 2012. Representing without representations. *AVANT* 3 (1): 133–44.

Roy, J-M., Petitot, J., Varela, F., and Pachoud, B. 1999. Introduction. In J. Petitot et al. (eds.), *Naturalizing Phenomenology: Issues in Contemporary Phenomenology and Cognitive Science*. Stanford: Stanford University Press.

Rucińska, Z. 2014. Basic pretending as sensorimotor engagement? In J. M. Bishop and A. O. Martin (eds.), *Contemporary Sensorimotor Theory*, Studies in Applied Philosophy, Epistemology and Rational Ethics, vol. 15: 175–87. New York: Springer.

Rucińska, Z. 2016. What guides pretence? Towards the interactive and the narrative approaches. *Phenomenology and the Cognitive Sciences* 15: 117–33.

Rupert, R. 2004. Challenges to the hypothesis of extended cognition. *Journal of Philosophy* 101 (8): 389–428.

Ryle, G. 1949. *The Concept of Mind*. London: Hutchinson.

Ryle, G. 1971. Phenomenology versus *Concept of Mind*. In G. Ryle, *Critical Essays: Collected Papers I* (187–204). London: Routledge.

Sainsbury, R. M. 2009. *Fiction and Fictionalism*. London: Routledge.

Salice, A., Høffding, S., and Gallagher, S. 2017. Putting plural self-awareness into practice: The phenomenology of expert musicianship. *Topoi*. DOI: 10.1007/s11245-017-9451-2, pp. 1–13.

Sartori, L., Becchio, C., and Castiello, U. 2011. Cues to intention: The role of movement information. *Cognition* 119: 242–52.

Saxe, R. R., Whitfield-Gabrieli, S., Scholz, J., and Pelphrey, K. A. 2009. Brain regions for perceiving and reasoning about other people in school-aged children. *Child Development* 80 (4): 1197–209.

Schacter, D. L., Reiman, E., Curran, T., Yun, L. S., Bandy, D., McDermott, K. B., and Iii, H. L. R. 1996. Neuroanatomical correlates of veridical and illusory recognition memory: Evidence from positron emission tomography. *Neuron* 17 (2): 267–74.

Schmidt, R. A. and Lee, T. D. 1999. *Motor Control and Learning: A Behavioural Emphasis*. Champaign, IL: Human Kinetics.

Schnall, S., Harber, K. D., Stefanucci, J. K., and Proffitt, D. R. 2008. Social support and the perception of geographical slant. *Journal of Experimental Social Psychology* 44 (5): 1246–55.

Scholl, B. J. and Leslie, A. M. 1999. Modularity, development and 'theory of mind'. *Mind and Language* 14 (1): 131–53.

Schultze-Kraft, M., Birman, D., Rusconi, M., Allefeld, C., Görgen, K., Dähne, S., . . . and Haynes, J. D. 2015. The point of no return in vetoing self-initiated movements. *Proceedings of the National Academy of Sciences* 113 (4): 1080–5.

Schurger, A., Mylopoulos, M., and Rosenthal, D. 2015. Neural antecedents of spontaneous voluntary movement: A new perspective. *Trends in Cognitive Sciences* 20 (2): 77–9.

Schurger, A., Sitt, J. D., and Dehaene, S. 2012. An accumulator model for spontaneous neural activity prior to self-initiated movement. *Proceedings of the National Academy of Sciences* 109 (42): E2904–E2913.

Searle, J. 1992. *The Rediscovery of the Mind*. Cambridge, MA: MIT Press.

Searle, J. 1983. *Intentionality: An Essay in the Philosophy of Mind*. Cambridge: Cambridge University Press.

Searle, J. 1984. *Minds, Brains, and Science*. Cambridge, MA: Harvard University Press.

Sebanz, N., Knoblich, G., and Prinz, W. 2003. Representing others' actions: Just like one's own? *Cognition* 88: B11–B21.

Segal, G. 1996. The modularity of theory of mind. In P. Carruthers and P. Smith (eds.), *Theories of Theories of Mind* (141–57). Cambridge: Cambridge University Press.

Setti, A., Borghi, A. M., and Tessari, A. 2009. Moving hands, moving entities. *Brain and Cognition* 70 (3): 253–8.

Shapiro, L. 2011. *Embodied Cognition*. London: Routledge.

Shapiro, L. 2014a. When is cognition embodied? In U. Kriegel (ed.), *Current Controversies in Philosophy of Mind* (73–90). New York and London: Routledge.

Shapiro, L. 2014b. Book review: *Radicalizing Enactivism: Basic Minds without Content*. *Mind* 123 (489): 213–20.

Shapiro, L. A. 2004. *The Mind Incarnate*. Cambridge, MA: MIT Press.

Shapiro, L. A. 2007. The embodied cognition research programme. *Philosophy Compass* 2 (2): 338–46.

Shapiro, L. A. 2009. A review of Frederick Adams and Kenneth Aizawa, *The Bounds of Cognition*. *Phenomenology and the Cognitive Sciences* 8 (2): 267–73.

Sheets-Johnstone, M. 1990. *The Roots of Thinking*. Philadelphia: Temple University Press.

Shotter, J. 2001. Towards a third revolution in psychology: From inner mental representations to dialogically-structured social practices. In D. Bakhurst and S. Shanker (eds.), *Jerome Bruner: Language, Culture, Self* (167–83). London: Sage.

Shuler, M. G. and Bear, M. F. 2006. Reward timing in the primary visual cortex. *Science* 311 (5767): 1606–9.

Siegel, S. 2011. Cognitive penetrability and perceptual justification. *Noûs* 46 (2): 201–22.

Skagestad, P. 1993. Thinking with machines: Intelligence augmentation, evolutionary epistemology, and semiotic. *Journal of Social and Evolutionary Systems* 16 (2): 157–80.

Skagestad, P. 1999. Peirce's inkstand as an external embodiment of mind. *Transactions of the Charles S. Peirce Society* 35 (3): 551–61.

Skoyles, J. R. 2006. Human balance, the evolution of bipedalism and dysequilibrium syndrome. *Medical Hypotheses* 66: 1060–8.

Slotnick, S., Thompson, W., and Kosslyn, S. M. 2005. Visual mental imagery induces retinotopically organized activation of early visual areas. *Cerebral Cortex* 15: 1570–83.

Soon, C. S., Brass, M., Heinze, H. J., and Haynes, J. D. 2008. Unconscious determinants of free decisions in the human brain. *Nature Neuroscience* 11 (5): 543–5.

Sparaci, L. 2008. Embodying gestures: The social orienting model and the study of early gestures in autism. *Phenomenology and the Cognitive Sciences* 7 (2): 203–23.

Sparks, G. G., Pellechia, M., and Irvine, C. 1999. The repressive coping style and fright reactions to mass media. *Communication Research* 26: 176–92.

Stapleton, M. 2013. Steps to a 'properly embodied' cognitive science. *Cognitive Systems Research* 22–3: 1–11.

Steiner, P. 2008. Sciences cognitives, tournant pragmatique et horizons pragmatistes. *Tracés. Revue de sciences humaines* 15: 85–105.

Steiner, P. 2010. Philosophie, technologie et cognition: état des lieux et perspectives. *Intellectica* 53 (54): 7–40.

Sterelny, K. 2007. Social intelligence, human intelligence and niche construction. *Philosophical Transactions of the Royal Society of London*. Series B, Biological Sciences, 362 (1480): 719–30.

Sterelny, K. 2010. Minds—extended or scaffolded. *Phenomenology and the Cognitive Sciences* 9 (4): 465–81.

Straus, E. W. 1966. The upright posture. In E. W. Straus, *Essays in Phenomenology* (164–92). The Hague: Springer.

Strauss, M. S. and Curtis, L. E. 1981. Infant perception of numerosity. *Child Development* 52 (4): 1146–52.

Tamietto, M. 2013. Attentional and sensory unawareness for emotions: Neurofunctional and neuroanatomical systems. Conference presentation. *The Scope and Limits of Direct Perception*. Copenhagen, 13 December.

Thierry, G., Athanasopoulos, P., Wiggett, A., Dering, B., and Kuipers, J.-R. 2009. Unconscious effects of language-specific terminology on preattentive color perception. *Proceedings of the National Academy of Sciences* 106: 4567–70.

Thomas, A. 1997. Kant, McDowell and the theory of consciousness. *European Journal of Philosophy* 5 (3): 283–305.

Thompson, E. 2007. *Mind in Life: Biology, Phenomenology and the Sciences of Mind*. Cambridge, MA: Harvard University Press.

Thompson, E. 2014. The embodied mind: An interview with Evan Thompson. Fall 2014. http://www.tricycle.com/interview/embodied-mind.

Thompson, E. and Stapleton, M. 2009. Making sense of sense-making: Reflections on enactive and extended mind theories. *Topoi* 28: 23–30.

Thompson, E. and Varela, F. 2001. Radical embodiment: Neural dynamics and consciousness. *Trends in Cognitive Sciences* 5 (10): 418–25.

Trevarthen, C. and Hubley, P. 1978. Secondary intersubjectivity: Confidence, confiding and acts of meaning in the first year. In A. Lock (ed.), *Action, Gesture and Symbol: The Emergence of Language* (183–229). London: Academic Press.

Trevarthen, C. B. 1979. Communication and cooperation in early infancy: A description of primary intersubjectivity. In M. Bullowa (ed.), *Before Speech* (321–48). Cambridge, MA: Cambridge University Press.

Tylor, E. B. 1881. *Anthropology: An Introduction to the Study of Man and Civilization*. London: Macmillan.

Uller, C., Jaeger, R., Guidry, G., and Martin, C. 2003. Salamanders (*Plethodon cinereus*) go for more: Rudiments of number in an amphibian. *Animal Cognition* 6: 105–12.

van Gelder, T. 1995. What might cognition be if not computation? *Journal of Philosophy* 91: 345–81.

van Gelder, T. 1999. Wooden iron? Husserlian phenomenology meets cognitive science. In J. Petitot, F. J. Varela, J.-M. Roy, and B. Pachoud (eds.), *Naturalizing Phenomenology: Issues in Contemporary Phenomenology and Cognitive Science* (245–65). Stanford: Stanford University Press.

Vaneechoutte, M. 2014. The origin of articulate language revisited: The potential of a semi-aquatic past of human ancestors to explain the origin of human musicality and articulate language. *Human Evolution* 29 (1–3): 1–33.

Varela, F. J. 1999. The specious present: A neurophenomenology of time consciousness. In J. Petitot, F. J. Varela, B. Pachoud, and J.-M. Roy (eds.), *Naturalizing Phenomenology: Issues in Contemporary Phenomenology and Cognitive Science* (266–314). Stanford: Stanford University Press.

Varela, F. J., Thompson, E., and Rosch, E. 1991. *The Embodied Mind: Cognitive Science and Human Experience*. Cambridge: MIT Press.

Vignemont, de F., Majid, A., Jola, C., and Haggard, P. 2009. Segmenting the body into parts: Evidence from biases in tactile perception. *Quarterly Journal of Experimental Psychology* 62: 500–12.

Vygotsky, L. S. 1986. *Thought and Language*. Cambridge, MA: MIT Press.

Wapner, S. and Werner, H. 1965. An experimental approach to body perception from the organismic developmental point of view. In S. Wapner and H. Werner (eds.), *The Body Percept*. New York: Random House.

Weber, A. and Varela, F. J. 2002. Life after Kant: Natural purposes and the autopoietic foundations of biological individuality. *Phenomenology and the Cognitive Sciences* 1 (2): 97–125.

Wegner, D. 2002. *The Illusion of Conscious Will*. Cambridge, MA: MIT Press.

Welton, D. 2000. Touching hands. *Veritas* 45 (1): 83–102.

Wheeler, M. 1996. From robots to Rothko, in M. Boden (ed.), *The Philosophy of Artificial Life* (209–36). Oxford: Oxford University Press.

Wheeler, M. 2005. *Reconstructing the Cognitive World: The Next Step*. Cambridge, MA: MIT Press.

Willems, R. M., Hagoort, P., and Casasanto, D. 2009. Body-specific representations of action verbs: Neural evidence from right- and left-handers. *Psychological Science* 21 (1): 67–74.

Wilson, M. 2002. Six views of embodied cognition. *Psychonomic Bulletin and Review* 9 (4): 625–36.

Wilson, R. A. 1994. Wide computationalism. *Mind* 103: 351–72.

Witt, J. K., Proffitt, D. R., and Epstein, W. 2005. Tool use affects perceived distance, but only when you intend to use it. *Journal of Experimental Psychology: Human Perception and Performance* 31 (5): 880–8.

Wolpert, D. M., Doya, K., and Kawato, M. 2003. A unifying computational framework for motor control and social interaction. *Philosophical Transactions of the Royal Society of London.* Series B, Biological Sciences 358: 593–602.

Woodruff, G., and Premack, D. 1981. Primative mathematical concepts in the chimpanzee: Proportionality and numerosity. *Nature* 293: 568–70.

Woodward, A. L., Sommerville, J. A., and Guajardo, J. J. 2001. How infants make sense of intentional action. In B. Malle, L. Moses, and D. Baldwin (eds.), *Intentions and Intentionality: Foundations of Social Cognition* (149–69). Cambridge: MIT Press.

Wrangham, R. W. 1980. Bipedal locomotion as a feeding adaptation in Gelada baboons, and its implication for hominid evolution. *Journal of Human Evolution* 9: 329–31.

Xu, Y., Zuo, X., Wang, X., and Han, S. 2009. Do you feel my pain? Racial group membership modulates empathic neural responses. *Journal of Neuroscience* 29 (26): 8525–9.

Yarbus, A. 1967. *Eye Movements and Vision.* New York: Plenum Press.

Young, I. M. 1980. Throwing like a girl: A phenomenology of feminine body comportment motility and spatiality. *Human Studies* 3 (1): 137–56.

Zahavi, D. 2013. Mindedness, mindlessness and first-person authority. In J. K. Schear (ed.), *Mind, Reason, and Being-in-The-World: The McDowell–Dreyfus Debate* (320–40). London: Routledge.

Zajac, F. E. 1993. Muscle coordination of movement: A perspective. *Journal of Biomechanics* 26 (suppl. 1): 109–24.

Zautra, A. J., Fasman, R., Davis, M. C., and Craig, A. D. 2010. The effects of slow breathing on affective responses to pain stimuli: An experimental study. *Pain* 149 (1): 12–18.

Zelano, C., Jiang, H., Zhou, G., Arora, N., Schuele, S., Rosenow, J., and Gottfried, J. A. 2016. Nasal respiration entrains human limbic oscillations and modulates cognitive function. *Journal Neurosci* 36 (49): 12448–67.

Zhu, J. 2003. Reclaiming volition: An alternative interpretation of Libet's experiments. *Journal of Consciousness Studies* 10 (11): 61–77.

Ziemke, T. 2001. Disentangling notions of embodiment. In *Proceedings: Workshop on Developmental Embodied Cognition,* 83–7 (citeseerx.ist.psu.edu/viewdoc/download?doi=10.1.1.5.9097&rep=rep1&type=pdf). Accessed 22 May 2016.

Zlatev, J. 2010. Phenomenology and cognitive linguistics. In S. Gallagher and D. Schmicking (eds.), *Handbook of Phenomenology and Cognitive Science* (415–43). Dordrecht: Springer.

Index